Dummy

Dummy

a memoir

David Patten

Jonquil Press
Berkeley, California

NOTE: *This work is a memoir. It reflects the author's present recollection of his experiences over a period of years. Certain names, locations, and identifying characteristics have been changed, and certain persons described are composites. Dialogue and events have been recreated from memory, and, in some cases, have been compressed to convey the substance of what was said or what occurred.*

Primary Book Editors: Doug Childers & David Smith
Copy Editor: Nancy Carleton, NancyCarleton.com
Front Cover: *the*BookDesigners / www.bookdesigners.com
Book Design & Composition: Dave Blake
Print Management: Dave Blake, david94703@gmail.com

To order additional copies or for bookseller inquiries, please visit dummythebook.com

Library of Congress Cataloging-in-Publication Data

Patten, David, 1954-
Dummy : a memoir / David Patten.
    p. cm.
  ISBN 978-0-9350-7927-2
1. Patten, David, 1954- 2. Autism spectrum disorders —
Patients — United States — Biography. 3. Learning disabled
children — United States — Biography. 4. Learning
disabled — United States — Biography. I. Title.
  RJ506.L4P38 2012
  616.85'8820092 — dc23
  [B]
                                                    2011049006

Printed in the United States of America.
3 5 7 9 8 6 4 2

To my wife, Maria

Contents

Acknowledgments

Books have always represented something bigger than life and entirely inaccessible to me. Because of my learning disabilities, I couldn't have written this book without the dedicated, in-depth support of friends and professionals. For some of them, it was an arduous and time-consuming commitment. To all, I extend my deepest gratitude. Their support, along with the electronic assistance of my software, made something I had thought impossible possible. The story that was my life was clawing at me to get out; now it has become a book, and it takes nothing away that I can't read it without assistance.

First, I want to thank my wife. She has been a deep source of support for me as our life has evolved together over more than twenty-eight years. During the writing of this book she became my most important editor. I valued her opinion and her judgment above all others. She was the most honest and critical, for which I am most thankful.

Next, I want to thank my son and daughter, who have been extremely supportive and who had to learn more about their father's life than any kids, even full-grown kids, should ever have to know. My daughter was the first to encourage me to write, and helped me to organize a beginning storyboard.

Along the way I also worked with many editors, but two stood out: Doug Childers, the very talented published writer who came in as the book was floundering and gave it structure and a new life, and David Smith, a talented writer and dear friend for more than thirty years, whose undying patience and perseverance helped me bring the manuscript to a satisfying end.

I'm also grateful to others who helped with the manuscript over the years involved in its creation, including Dave Blake, Nancy Carleton, Hannah Eckersley, Janet Voss, Jesse King, Sema Arslan, Dan Millman, and Paul, Marilyn, and Ben Hughes. So many people have helped over such a long period that I hope I haven't inadvertently omitted anyone!

Then there were the many friends and acquaintances who were willing to read the early drafts and provide their valued comments. In particular, I want to thank both of my brothers, as well as Laurie Rotecki, Margo Siegenthalar, Marcia Fields, Angelina and Suzanne Saunders, Holly Thurlow, Cara Patten, and Jodi and Dan Dresel. Also, my thanks to Jacqui Schiff and Adi Da, for invaluable lessons learned along the way, and to Adyashanti, for final clarity in the end. Many thanks to all!

I am not bound to win,
but I am bound to be true.
I am not bound to succeed,
but I am bound to live up to what light I have.

—Abraham Lincoln

Prologue

*S*poke at one key on my keyboard, then another. With my mouse I find some old emails I've saved in a special folder labeled "Pieces of Boss's Emails." I'm looking for an email, or a piece of one, where my boss emailed me about the cable company he wants me to use for a job. I'm not supposed to, but I have a personal program on my company computer. It reads aloud to me in my headset when I move the cursor through a document. I try to hide from my coworkers how I do my work. I've found it's better for them to just see the results. I open one email after another, looking for the word *cable*. Scanning, I first look for the letter *c*, and finding *c* I look for *c-a*. *There it is.* I copy and paste it into the email I'm piecing together for this project.

My office phone rings."Hello, IT support, this is David Patten."

It's my boss, Kenji. "David, come to the main conference room."

I've known this call was coming. I've been dreading it ever since my coworker, Kenji, got promoted and became one of my bosses. Things are changing in the company, and things are changing in the telecom industry. My specialty has always been troubleshooting on mainframe computers for large telephone systems, but recently the technology has changed and systems are becoming Internet based and no longer driven by room-sized onsite computers. In my past jobs I'd been able to take my paperwork home, where I had special software to read to me, and with my wife's help on reports, I'd always gotten by. I'd been very successful in the telecom business for twenty-seven years; now I was working in the head office of a major phone provider. Even though I've known this moment was coming, I'm not as prepared as I thought I'd be. I just say, "I'll be right there."

My boss hangs up without another word. I save my work and get up slowly, then head for the conference room. As I open the conference room door I glance around at all the faces. The head of Human Resources is here, and her assistant. They both give me kind but cautious smiles. Kenji isn't in the room, but his boss, Nancy, and her manager, Rod, and his boss, Tony, the director of operations for the western region, are all seated around the conference table. Tony greets me with a somber look and with a movement of his hand shows me my seat. As I look around, nobody will make eye contact with me. Tony begins by saying that the head of HR for the western region is on the speakerphone and will be leading the meeting. I'm handed my yearly review and told that we'll be reviewing it item by item, to make sure I'm clear about my new job description and the expectations for my performance.

I'm silent as the woman on the speakerphone reads out each item. Suddenly I'm on probation, and I'll need to meet the following requirements: I can no longer take work home; all my communications to management and other employees will have to be through email or written documentation; I'm not allowed to get assistance from other people, software, or devices that aren't supplied directly by my manager. I can no longer quote other people's emails, and all communications from me must be without errors. Then there's a list of new responsibilities, each one requiring reports and documentation. None of them is working with equipment.

I'm stunned. Suddenly I feel like I'm seven years old again and being told that I'll have to repeat second grade. Other memories wash over me — worse memories: being trapped in a snow cave by my brother, being institutionalized in a mental hospital after attempting suicide, and more.... I can't believe this is happening. Once again I'm confronted by an irrefutable fact about myself: I'm functionally illiterate. I can barely read or write.

As I listen, I hold my tongue. It never did me any good to get defensive. I'm thinking about my newly promoted boss who used to be a coworker, and about the fact that I've never gotten one complaint about my work, only about the way I do it. Until now all my reviews have been excellent. I've always given them clean, quality work. They'd never known I was using pieces of other people's emails until my boss, not believing I was functionally illiterate as the handicap statement at my hiring had stated, asked me, "If you have trouble reading, how do you write all your emails?" I had to tell him.

I feel like the floor is shifting under my feet. The woman on the phone asks if I have any questions. I begin, "All of you knew what my disabilities were when I was hired. I was hired as a handicapped person. I was told that my skills and certifications were invaluable to this company, and that the company would work with me to accommodate my liabilities. I was told I'd be given the necessary equipment to help me with my reading and writing."

Tony responds by saying, "Your work was excellent for the position you were in, but the job has changed. The job is now primarily IT, not telecom; it's no longer about servicing equipment, and now we need a traceable path of accountability."

It's clear that if they want to get rid of me, they can easily find an excuse, that they can find someone "better qualified" to be on their team, someone who can read and write. With the new job description, they can probably get off the hook for hiring me as handicapped when they replace me.

"This all seems disingenuous," I say. "You've written this specifically so that I won't be able to do the job. You could at least allow me to use the equipment necessary to do what's required."

The speaker on the phone breaks in. "No, we want you to be able to meet all the expectations laid out for you here, and we'll do all we can to support you in that."

When they'd first hired me, they'd provided a software program that would read aloud to me, but it didn't work. I'd asked if I could bring my own program to the office, or take the work home, and they'd said no. I'd done it anyway and hid it from them.

I look right at Tony. "Tony, can you look me in the eye and tell me that you want me to meet these expectations?"

He looks at me and says, "No, I don't."

The HR person on the other end of the line screams, "Yes we do!"

I say to Tony, "Thank you for your honesty."

Then I turn to the phone as if it were a person in the room. "How can you say that you want me to succeed when you won't allow me to use the tools I need?"

All she says is, "Speaking for the company, we want you to succeed."

"But without the tools?"

"Yes."

I feel desperate. I turn to the group. "I can't do this thing you're requiring of me. Can anyone help me find a way to get the job done, or to do part of it from home? I promise I'll get it done right, as I always have, without putting any of you out."

Tony jumps in. "No, it's been decided."

I face Tony again. "I know if you want to get rid of me, you'll find a way. So if you tell me right now that you want to get rid of me, one way or the other, I'll quit right now."

Tony says, "Yes, one way or the other."

My mind becomes a swirl of thoughts, looking for answers, or an argument that will make them understand. But all the thoughts are the same old ones that have never worked before, have never been able to make someone else understand my situation. I don't say anything, and everyone looks at me, waiting for what I'll do or say next. Something's happening to me; my sensory perceptions are becoming distorted. I sit, unable to speak, with my throat choked up. The voice inside my head is saying, *What am I going to do? What's going to happen to me? What good am I?*

The silence in the room is broken by the voice on the phone asking, "David, what do you say?"

I'm in a full-blown panic. I feel totally disoriented. My field of vision becomes fragmented, as if it's breaking apart. The ground of my very existence is crumbling. I'm falling with no net, and no idea where to or how far. My eyes begin to tear up. *What's happening to me? Shit, I'm falling apart in front of everybody. I can't let them see this.*

Finally I say, "What can I do?" Then I hear the words —

with an unexpected crack in my voice — come from my mouth: "What's going to happen to me?"

I realize what I've said and look around the room. I see that the HR woman's and Nancy's eyes are filled with tears. This only makes it worse. I'm losing it. I can't think. Struggling to come back strong, I say, "Then I quit."

— 🤖 —

At age fifty-two, I watched my life, which had been so hard to put together, fall apart. I'd owned my own business. I'd traveled all over the United States as a technical consultant in the telecommunications field. Corporations had flown me in as a highly paid specialist to fix their phone systems when they crashed. I'd made top money by taking over computer systems in crisis and handing them back in perfect shape, saving the customer millions of dollars in lost revenue — and winning my company millions in new contracts. I'd gotten great satisfaction from having an excellent reputation and helping people out in critical situations.

In short, even though I couldn't read, I was great at what I did. I had to be the coolest head in the room when everybody was freaking out.

But now I wasn't the coolest head in the room. I was once again a kid who couldn't do what the world expected of him. A kid who was sent to the hallway and could never keep up with his peers. A kid who couldn't learn to read. Like a tsunami, my old ghosts swept over me. I thought I'd dropped all vestiges of that boy long ago. I wasn't the man I thought I was. The ground I'd stood on so surefootedly all my adult life fell away, and over time I slid into a deep depression.

I was once again being forced to deal with the consequences

of not being able to read and write. The world seemed to have no place for me. I began asking myself all the same questions that I'd asked when I was growing up: *Why is this happening to me? What am I going to do? What value do I have? How will I ever be happy?* Suicidal thoughts from the past began coming back to me: *Why should I keep on living?*

I turned these questions over and over in my mind, tormenting myself. In time, however, I noticed that all my thoughts were repetitive, never really leading to anything new. It seemed to me that there was an unconscious pattern—a story—that I'd been living out, over and over and over. In the beginning, I didn't set out to write a memoir. I thought if I could write down my thoughts, I could discover the repetitive patterns and maybe uncover the meaning underneath—the real me. I soon realized that I couldn't separate the thoughts I'd been thinking from the actions that had occurred in my life. So I found myself beginning to write the story of my life. Ironically, it seemed that my only hope of pulling out of my depression was to write a book—the very thing that seemed most impossible for me to do.

With the aid of my specialized software programs, I began typing one letter at a time, trying my best to sound out the words. The spelling and grammar programs helped convert my mostly unintelligible spelling into words and sentences, and with the speech program reading it back to me, I was able to work with what I'd written.

As I struggled to tell my experiences as truthfully as possible, I realized that no matter how deeply I dug into my past, or how perfect a job I did on the book, I could never capture who, or what, I truly am. The more I examined my patterns of thought, the more I saw that they were just patterns, that there was no "real me" at the bottom of it all — no objective entity that could truly be said to exist that was "me."

What was there, in every moment of my experience, was conscious Awareness, observing it all while being completely untouched by the experience. I couldn't find myself in my story. I was the witness to my story. This witness, this Awareness, didn't care if I could read or not; it was unaffected by it.

Although, on the surface, this seems like no realization at all, it changed me. After that, I began to think that this book might be useful to others. This isn't the conventional story of a hero who triumphs over all obstacles. Instead, it's the story of someone who, in the face of constant rejection and failure, discovers his true Self. My disabilities were extreme, but I know that there are many people who suffer similar problems and who are struggling to find their way in life. Something ordinary people don't understand is that conventional solutions don't work for nonconventional people. I was forced to find a radical solution. I hope my story will offer inspiration to those who are facing extreme hardships in their lives, and serve to let them know that the strength they're looking for is already there — if they just know where to look for it.

The Plan

What is it? There's something on the back of my neck. I've noticed it before, but now it's driving me crazy. I can't stand it another second!

Squirming in my seat, I reached back, pulled the collar of my shirt around, and tilted my head to peer inside it.

Oh, it's the tag.

Glaring at the offending tag, I grabbed it between my thumb and forefinger and ripped it off with a tearing sound. A thundering crash startled me out of my inner world, followed immediately by —

"David!"

I whirled around to find the rubber tip of a crutch a foot away from my face. My second-grade teacher had slammed her crutch on the top of my desk and shrieked my name.

"Pay attention when I'm talking to the class! Next time I'll hit *you* instead of your desk!"

My body vibrated with a freight train of energy from rushing adrenaline. My brain short-circuited. I tried to force myself to look up at her, but it was impossible. I couldn't move my gaze from the dirty rubber tip of her crutch. "You're the laziest student

I've ever tried to teach! You won't look at me, and you never pay attention! I've had it with you! If you don't care enough to try to learn, I can't teach you!"

Her anger overwhelmed me and filled me with hopelessness and shame. "Take your desk and chair," she said sharply, "and slide them to the back of the class between the toys and the windows. Then you can stare into space to your little heart's content. That will be your permanent place from now on." She went back to the wheelchair by her desk and sat down with a sigh, as if I'd worn her out.

The room was silent. I felt a shiver and a sense of release; then I was able to move. I was shaking as I got up to drag my desk to my new location, apologizing to the students who had to move out of my way.

This wasn't the first time Miss Terry had screamed at me in a fit of rage in front of the class. I thought she must be right; I was lazy, I was stupid, I was slow. I tried to pay attention, but I couldn't focus long enough to learn, and I couldn't seem to remember the facts and information that I did hear in class. I wasn't a daydreamer. Things inside and outside just distracted me and absorbed my attention. I was well into second grade, and I still hadn't mastered page one of my first-grade reading book. I'd learn a new word one day, and the next day I would have forgotten it. No matter how hard I tried, my learning never seemed to stick.

Yet it wasn't that simple. In some ways, I seemed to know more than most of my classmates. My mother had taken me to some experts who gave me a series of intelligence tests. I performed in the genius range in abstract thought. But the tests, and the experts, couldn't tell me how to use my intelligence to succeed in school. In general, I was unable to focus my mind or

control my attention. Sometimes I even had trouble controlling my body, just as my eyes gazed on the tip of Miss Terry's
crutch. At times my eyes would lock into a stare that could last
a few seconds, or even minutes. Then I couldn't move my eyes,
or focus or respond, even when my name was called. When this
happened, Miss Terry assumed that I was daydreaming or being
disrespectful and rebellious. It infuriated her.

It was 1961 and no one knew about learning disabilities. Kids
were either smart, average, or stupid. Then there were the lazy
underachievers. Back then, corporal punishment was the norm at
school and at home. It was commonly assumed that laziness could
be spanked or whipped out of you. Another common motiva-
tional method was to demean and humiliate underachievers into
improving their school performance. It hadn't worked with me.

I truly wanted to learn. I was curious about life and even
the subjects in class, but I was separated by a mysterious barrier
I couldn't penetrate, by a weakness of attention I couldn't seem
to overcome. Often, when I tried to find a word for something or
to say a name, I wasn't able to. It was as if the word was an object
behind a crystal-clear waterfall. I could clearly see the word just
behind the waterfall, but when I'd reach for the word through the
water my hand would disappear. The object remained visible on
the other side, but with no hand I couldn't grasp it. It was as if I
knew exactly what I wanted to say, but I couldn't quite grasp how
to say it. I'd try with all my strength to find the words, only to experience profound frustration instead, and with that came anger.

I was told my problem was that I was lazy, so I concluded this
inability to grasp my words must be from laziness. I wondered
if there was a way that I could learn but hadn't yet discovered.
I knew that pain got my immediate attention. I figured they must

be right. Maybe I *needed* spanking and being yelled at. Maybe that *would* *h*elp me learn. But it never worked. I never paid better attention the next time, and my difficulties remained.

All of Miss Terry's yelling, demeaning, and paddling never produced any positive results, yet her lack of success never seemed to discourage her from continuing. She wasn't sure how stupid I was, but she was convinced that I was lazy, and because of that, a disruptive influence on the class.

My new location at the back-right corner of the classroom, behind the shelves of toys, was exile. I wasn't facing the teacher anymore, only the back row of the other students in the class. At first I was excited to be out of her direct view, and there were toys and blocks close by. But I wasn't sure if I was allowed to play with them or not, and I didn't want to get into more trouble.

As the next few days went by, I started to feel separate from the class and realized how alone I was. Miss Terry no longer yelled at me to pay attention. I was out of the way so I was no longer a disturbance to her. She only yelled at me when I bothered the rest of the class by making too much noise or moving around too much in my seat.

Weeks later, I arrived at school one morning to find that Miss Terry had given me an alternate location, this time out in the hall. I now had two desks. At first, she only occasionally sent me to my hallway desk, and for brief periods of time. Then she began to send me there more frequently, and for a longer time. Within a few weeks the hallway had become my primary location, and for the rest of the year I spent most of my days there.

Sitting alone in the hall, I played with my erasers as if they were cars, and with pencils as if they were people. I'd sharpen my pencils shorter and shorter. I was obsessed with the pencil sharpener, with the gears inside, with the sound it made, and with how the shavings uncurled as I twisted the pencils gradually down to nothing. I brought little toys and electrical wire from home to play with. I wound the wire around the leg of my desk in the shape of a gearshift, then pretended to go racing up and down the halls. Often I'd get up from my desk to peek into the classroom through the small window in the door, straining to hear whatever I could. On bad days, when I was sure no one was looking, I'd cry.

I wasn't smart enough to keep up with the other kids, but I was desperate to know what I was missing. They were learning all the important things that they would need to know in order to live on their own someday. The things they did with relative ease, such as reading books, memorizing the multiplication tables, and passing tests, seemed like magic to me. Sometimes, when I was allowed to sit in my classroom desk, I'd find a way to sneak into Miss Terry's trash can. I'd pull out one of my classmate's discarded worksheets to see what they were learning. Later, when I was alone, I'd study it, trying as hard as I could to make sense of it, but I never could. I even carried these wrinkled worksheets around in my pocket, hoping that these pieces of trash would help me in some way. Perhaps, somehow, I'd understand them over time, with the help of someone, maybe a friend. But I never was able to understand, and it hurt. It hurt that I couldn't understand the things my friends understood so easily.

It was a deeply disturbing emotional and even physical pain.

I was an outcast in school, and there was nothing I was measurably good at, yet my neighborhood friends all liked and respected me. We'd start a club, and they'd often want me to be the leader. When we played war games, they'd follow me into battle.

Outside of class, I was their equal. They appreciated me. Many even told me I was their best friend.

— 🤖 —

That year, my older brother, Emerson, took me to the theater to see a science-fiction movie about three astronauts from Earth who land on Mars. While exploring the planet, they encounter hostile aliens and are separated from their spaceship. At the end, the Martians chase the astronauts back to their spaceship. But only two astronauts make it back and manage to board the ship. The third astronaut falls behind and arrives after the doors have closed and the ship is taking off. He knows the Martians are coming for him. The abandoned astronaut cries out to his departing comrades, who look out at him sadly as the ship slowly rises from the surface of the hostile planet: "Don't leave me! Please don't leave me alone!"

As the movie ends, he stands alone on the desolate landscape, waiting heroically for the Martians who are coming to kill him. He could have tried to run back to the cave where they'd been hiding, but instead he decided to confront his enemies and die rather than live in fear.

The movie made a deep impression on me and haunted me. I had nightmares for weeks afterward about the man left behind. I started daydreaming that I was from another planet, and I'd been stranded on Earth — like Superman. Superman must have felt out of place, alone, and misunderstood. Then he found a way to excel. Maybe I could, too. Superman knew he was stronger and smarter than the others. I knew I wasn't Superman, but maybe I had some special powers I didn't yet know about. Maybe one day I'd figure out what they were, and then I could live a happy, normal life like everyone else. But for now I was alone, stuck in a long, dark, empty hallway, day after day.

Looking through the little window separating me from the class, and from my friends, I recalled the two astronauts in the movie looking through the portal at the friend they were leaving behind forever. But my classmates weren't looking through the window at me; I was looking at them. They didn't seem to remember I was there. They were too busy learning all the things I couldn't learn.

I sometimes thought to myself, *I'm the guy in the movie being left behind. And I'm going to be stuck on Mars for the rest of my life.* I loved my friends, and I knew they loved me, but they were going to move on in their lives without me, and I sensed that I'd be left behind for good, alone in a hostile world where I wouldn't be able to survive. I realized then that I hated this world—a world that would let someone fall behind and not reach back for him, that wouldn't even look to see the fear in his eyes. I swore to myself that if I saw that kind of fear in someone else's eyes, I'd do whatever I could to help. I'd never leave someone else behind, especially someone I loved.

The last day of school was warm and sunny. Since Miss Terry wasn't teaching any of the regular curriculum that day, she let me stay in the classroom and participate in all the activities. We were going to be doing fun stuff. It felt like a celebration. I was so happy to be with everyone that I could hardly contain myself.

Before the first bell rang, a group of my closest friends gathered around my desk. We all talked excitedly about how we would spend the summer. We were going to build a fort, and maybe even a tree house. We'd all go swimming together in our community pool. My best friend Toby and I talked about how my parents were going to buy us baby ducks, and how we'd keep them in his backyard pen. We would take care of them together. I told my friends Marsha and Linda that my dad was going to install a rope swing in the giant cottonwood tree in our front yard. I was so excited about our plans, and about being included again now that school was over and summer was here, that I hugged them all. It was a rare gesture for me.

Miss Terry seemed to be on her best behavior, and I did my best not to make her mad. She barely yelled at me the whole day. Finally, she handed out our report cards. Then the final bell rang. I was surprised how quickly the day had passed, and how nothing bad had happened. I quickly opened my report card and saw a row of incompletes. There was a note in red at the bottom of the page. I asked Toby, who was standing next to me, to read it to me.

"Not advancing to third grade," he read.

I was stunned. Devastated. The nightmare I had been living in my fantasy world was coming true. I *was* being left behind. In disbelief, I asked several students around me what the notes on their report cards said. Only mine said "Not advancing." Everyone else was moving forward to the third grade. My mother had already warned me that I might not go on to the third grade, but I didn't exactly know, or perhaps couldn't believe, what that meant.

I left school and ran all the way home to ask her. She was still at work, so I turned on the TV to watch Bugs Bunny. I couldn't focus. Anxiety coursed through my body. I pressed myself into the couch and alternately held my ears and closed my eyes, trying to shut down all my senses. Everything was too much, too intense, too disturbing.

That night when it was time for bed, my mother took me into her bedroom so we could talk in private. I knew this was serious because my brothers and I didn't go into my parents' bedroom very often. My father stayed in the living room. He had great faith in my mother and always relied on her to handle the difficult moments with us. He'd never known his own father and didn't trust himself to deal with such things. My father was a very loving man. We all respected him; when he said something we listened, and when he whistled for us, we knew to drop everything and go to him immediately. But he was detached from most family matters. He handled the physical discipline, when necessary, but otherwise took refuge in his 1950s role as chief breadwinner. I loved my dad and felt his humor and warmth, but my extreme problems were for my mother to handle, not him.

Mom turned on the small light on her dresser. The room was dim. The walls, covered with bookshelves, were in shadows. Through the open sliding door of my father's closet I saw his shoes lined up on the floor, and his familiar flannel shirts, suits, and starched white dress shirts on hangers. I wished he were in here with us now. He always seemed to make things brighter and funnier.

Mom and I sat on my parents' huge bed, and she explained to me that I wouldn't be going on to third grade with the rest of my class; I'd be staying back in second grade for another year. The thought of repeating Miss Terry's class was too much for me. I started crying and yelling, thinking my mother could change things.

"No! No! I have to go to third grade! All of my friends are going!"

I cried while she sat there with me. She seemed sad.

"I'm sorry, honey. I did the best I could to change Miss Terry's mind. There's nothing else I can do."

When I finally calmed down, I asked her, "Why am I the only one flunking?"

She was crying now. I could see that she wanted to comfort me, but there was nothing she could say. She gave a little, artificial smile. "I don't know, David. You're just having trouble learning in school."

"Why am I so stupid? Why can't I be smart like the other kids?"

"You're not stupid. Don't think that. You're very smart. You just have more trouble learning than the other kids."

"Why? What's wrong with me?"

"I don't know. Nothing's wrong with you. You're just having trouble learning."

My questions went on, even after she ran out of answers. Finally, I lay on the bed, exhausted. I wished I had a secret power that could stop the world, make time go backward, and make myself normal like everyone else.

At one point I looked up at her. I caught just a moment of fear in her eyes. That was all it took. It told me she thought I'd never be able to function like a normal person. In that moment I could feel that she was afraid for me, afraid of who I might become, afraid of who I *was*. At that moment, I felt she had completely separated from me emotionally. In a flash I felt the fear move from her body into mine. This fear was now alive in me. I didn't want her to ever be that far away from me again, so I willingly took her burden in, as deep as I could. I took on my mother's fear about me as my own. If she was afraid for me, then I was afraid, too. Only now I felt afraid of who I was. I felt afraid of *myself*. It also gave me the set point for the level of fear that I had to maintain in my approach to life. This fear became my inheritance.

Back in my own bed and alone, I stared into the darkness, unable to sleep or stop my mind. Worst-case scenarios ran through my head. I imagined being in class with younger kids and watching them learn things I still couldn't learn. I imagined flunking second grade again, and being with even younger kids the next time. I imagined Miss Terry being my teacher over and over. Maybe I'd never pass the second grade. My mind was filled with paralyzing thoughts of failure, humiliation, and ever-increasing isolation.

Why me? What did I do? What's wrong with me? What's going to happen to me?

During the last month of that school year, my mother took me out of class every Tuesday and Thursday to see a psychiatrist. Once the visits with the psychiatrist started, she stopped coming into my room at night to comfort me. She'd stopped telling me everything was going to be all right. I didn't know that the psychiatrist had told her not to coddle me, or give me false expectations. Now it seemed like nothing was ever going to be all right again.

Finally, tormented by my thoughts and unable to sleep, I got out of bed. I knew my mother didn't want to talk about this anymore, but I couldn't stop myself. I opened my bedroom door and looked through the family room. I could see her standing at the kitchen sink washing the dishes. I called out to her, "Mom!" and got no response. So I called louder. "Mom!"

Her body froze. Then she turned off the water, and I heard her low sharp voice. "What?"

I could tell she was upset. I tried to hold back my tears, but my voice quavered as I asked her, "What's going to happen to me?"

She still didn't turn around. "I don't know," she said.

"What am I going to do when I'm grown up?"

"I don't know."

"Will I be able to have a job?"

"I don't know," she said, a little louder.

"Can I ever have kids and a family?"

"I don't know!" Her voice was sharp and irritated now.

"Can I ever get married?"

"I — don't — know!" She dropped the pot she'd been scrubbing into the sink with a loud clatter and grabbed the front of the sink with both hands. She stood, staring down at the sink, her body quivering. It looked like she was crying, but she still didn't turn around. Then she spoke in a firm, measured voice, pausing for emphasis throughout, "David, I'm going to say this just *once*. And don't *ever — ask — me — about — this — again!* You may have to be institutionalized when you're eighteen."

I lay awake all that night, churning in anxiety over my future. My family was smart and successful. My dad managed a medical clinic. My mom was a school psychologist. My grandfather and aunts and uncles were all doctors, pharmacists, lawyers, and accountants. But I was different from them. I was never going to learn the things they'd learned. I'd never have a job or a family. Who would marry me? I was going to end up in a mental hospital. That was the way it was. That was what my mother had said, and probably what my whole family believed.

I lay there contemplating my dismal, lonely future, imagining my life in a mental institution. Back then, the "retarded" were put into mental institutions with the insane. I knew my mother didn't think I was insane, so she must have thought I was retarded. I understood from movies and TV shows that mental institutions were dark, dirty places where crazy and retarded people sat silently all day, or walked around mumbling to themselves, or screamed and acted out until men in white coats came and dragged them away. There was nothing to do there but play checkers and walk up and down the halls. I'd heard that once you were sent there, you never got out.

My mother sometimes told us stories about her psychology training at a teaching hospital. One story was about a small, unusual-looking child whom she'd done developmental testing on. After passing the low results on to her instructor, she was given the child's records. The child was older than she was! It wasn't a child at all. I could tell from the way she told the story that it had profoundly affected her. This story came back to me now as I lay in bed. I wondered if my mother thought that I was more like that person in a child's body than I was like a normal person.

I wondered if I could somehow change my fate. Maybe if I worked harder I could get my school lessons through my thick skull. I repeated over and over to myself: *I've got to learn to read. I've got to learn to read. I've got to learn to read!*

The world seemed like such a horrible place. I had no control over my life. I couldn't believe this was happening to me. If what my mother had just told me was true — that I'd be put into a mental institution — then I couldn't trust the people who were taking care of me and who were controlling my life. I couldn't even trust my own mother. She was now preparing me for a life that I wasn't willing to live. I had to find a way out.

— ⚙ —

I often thought of the abandoned astronaut in the movie, and how he'd made a decision when his ship took off and left him behind. Abandoned and alone, without resources in a hostile world, he turned to face the Martians who were coming to kill him. He chose to die rather than hide. By choosing death, he took control of his life and kept his self-respect. The movie had portrayed him, and his decision, in a heroic light. It had inspired me. Now his courageous decision seemed to offer a solution to my dilemma. I also wanted to take control of my life. If I was going to end up in a mental institution with no way out, I had nothing to lose. If I had any hope of changing my fate, I'd have to start living as if my life was at stake. I'd have to be willing to do anything and try anything, and if everything failed, then I could kill myself. But would I be willing to die? To take my own life? The thought of suicide had never occurred to me before.

In a flash it came to me. I knew exactly how I could do it. I had the perfect plan — simple and guaranteed to work. Months earlier I'd attended a father-son program called Indian Guides. In the course of the program, each father gave a presentation to the group. My dad had given a talk about liquid mercury, and he brought a test tube of the magical silver liquid from the medical clinic where he worked. He rolled it around in a bowl and we all thought it was so cool. Then he told us that mercury was a deadly poison. It could make you very sick if you even touched it. If you swallowed it, it would kill you. Death would be painful, violent, and certain. No one could save you.

I imagined swallowing the mercury from my father's test tube and dying. In that moment, I felt incredible relief. I felt more powerful than I'd ever felt before. I felt free! I had no concern for the future. That's when I knew I could commit suicide. Not right away — I'd still try to learn and succeed. But now I had another option. I could end my life anytime I chose. I wouldn't have to go to a mental institution. This gave me a superstrength. It could be my secret superpower, like the one Superman had.

I realized in a way I couldn't have articulated that I wasn't afraid of disappearing or dying, maybe because I couldn't really imagine what death was. What terrified me was living a left-behind, lonely life and having no control over it. Now the possibility of suicide seemed like a magical solution. I suddenly wasn't worried about my future in the same way. Everything had changed.

Still, I had to secure my plan. My bedroom was behind the garage. The rest of the family slept upstairs on the other side of the house. It was after midnight and everyone had gone to sleep, so I got up and snuck out of my room. I went to the basement, where my father had his workshop, and stole the test tube of liquid mercury from the cabinet near his workbench. The tube wasn't full, containing about a half of a mouthful, but I felt confident there was enough to do the job.

I returned to my room and hid the test tube in my sock drawer, which I could easily reach from my bed. When I finally climbed back into my bed and lay down, I felt calmer and was eventually able to fall asleep. When I awoke, I was different in a fundamental way. Death was now within arm's reach. I had control over my life. From now on my life would be a fight to the death, but I'd have the final choice. I could now live with self-respect in my present moment, the way other kids lived, without being smothered by fear of my future. The future remained a dark cloud, but now I had ultimate control. These weren't just thoughts in my head, but feelings, mysterious certainties that gave me relief.

The mercury would wait, hidden in various locations. Over time I improved the plan. I realized that I'd also need sleeping pills. My mother always had some in her medicine cabinet. I could take them first, wait a bit, and when I began to get drowsy, take the mercury before I fell asleep. That way, death might not be as painful. I'd find a way to steal some of her sleeping pills when she was out. I'd never stolen anything before my dad's mercury. But this was life-and-death. From now on, I had to be willing to do anything.

With the mercury safe in my hiding place, I now had another choice besides the inevitable isolation that lay ahead in my future, possibly in the form of commitment to a mental institution. I had a plan. I possessed the power and the means to end my own life. This knowledge proved to be an immense comfort in the hard times to come.

The Co-op

*I*n the mid-1950s, my parents, both progressive idealists, moved into the York Center Community Co-op. This progressive alternative community was located on a one hundred-acre corn field in an unincorporated area near Lombard, Illinois, eighteen miles west of Chicago's Loop. It was founded by members of the Brethren Church, one of three American "peace churches" along with the Quakers and the Mennonites (best known for the Amish). It invited people of all races and religions to live together as a witness for peace and brotherhood.

The earliest families to move into the co-op built their own homes with their own hands. In pioneer barn-raising spirit, they joined together to help one another pour concrete foundations, "raise a roof," and even build a community water and sewer system. The community eventually grew to more than seventy families. We moved there when I was three years old, and my older brother, Emerson, was six. My younger brother, Neil, was born in the co-op the following year.

In addition to members of the Brethren congregation, people came to the co-op from varied backgrounds. They were a motley, controversial group. There were conscientious objectors who had spent World War II in prison; there were Japanese who had been confined to internment camps; there were educated "negroes," as African Americans were then called; and there were labor organizers, civil-rights activists, mixed-marriage couples, and even theologians. They all gathered to live their various faiths and creeds together and create a community of tolerance in very practical ways.

Each family had building rights for one lot (usually about an acre), but the co-op jointly owned the entire property. Each family lived in its own separate household, often with its own garden, but all the families did things together as a community. They held work bees to maintain the community park, the shelterbelt, and the water system. They planted trees for seclusion around the co-op's perimeter. They built the main roads and the water system. Road rights were ceded to the local government, which maintained them as public streets, but everything else, including the water system, remained privately owned by the co-op. Some families got together to shop in bulk in order to cut down on costs. And there were endless committee meetings. Everyone was independent financially, but people tried to help one another out in whatever way they could. The children attended the nearby public schools.

The prevailing spirit of neighborly goodwill and innocence in the early years of our community had a great impact on me. No one locked their doors because we all trusted one another. If we got thirsty playing outside, or got hurt and needed a wound washed and a Band-Aid, we could go into almost any home and be taken care of. The usual social boundaries didn't apply in our hundred acres. I could visit the homes of my friends anytime, walk in without knocking, and feel completely welcome. If no one was there, I could turn on the TV and wait for them to return. The community was my whole world, my whole life. The people in it were my family. The other children were my brothers and sisters. We went through everything together and formed deep bonds.

The outside community was very conservative and regarded our co-op with suspicion, fear, and mistrust. The main issue was that we were racially integrated. We were the classic "there goes the neighborhood" real-estate nightmare multiplied by seventy families. The year before my family moved there, someone burned a cross on our neighbor's front yard, and fired a gunshot into one of the other houses. The racial diversity of the co-op lowered its property value, so our homes were assessed at values less than those in the surrounding communities.

The racial tension and the animosity toward our co-op were relatively passive until the mid-1960s, when the conflict intensified during the Civil Rights Movement, the Vietnam War, and the hippie phenomenon. Many co-op kids were multiracial and therefore a visible target in the local community. Outsiders started coming into the co-op at night to make trouble. On one occasion a Molotov cocktail was thrown at a house; on several other occasions homes and cars were painted with swastikas. It was a frightening time for our community.

One night when I was eight, during my father's turn as co-op president, I awoke to hear angry voices in the entryway. I peeked out my bedroom door and saw several strange men who had pushed their way into the house. I recognized one of them. They were shouting at my parents and calling them communists. My parents were not communists, or even socialists, but simply liberals. My father stood up to them. Raising his voice and his fists, he waded directly into the group and managed to force them back out the door. It was the only time I ever saw him raise a fist to anyone.

The man I recognized that night had joined the co-op as an extreme left-wing fanatic. He later converted to the far-right John Birch Society and plastered his house with signs demanding the impeachment of Justice Earl Warren for his antisegregation rulings. This man and several other John Birch members from outside our community later sued the co-op to try to break it up. The lawsuit went before the U.S. Supreme Court, and our co-op's victory became one of the key rulings that established the legal basis for the housing co-ops and condominiums that later proliferated.

My mother, born in 1916 in Lynn, Massachusetts, was from an old New England family that had come to this country in the 1600s. Raised in an intellectual environment by two well-educated parents, she excelled academically. After graduating from a renowned boarding school in Europe, she was accepted into the University of Illinois, where she studied developmental psychology and became a child psychologist.

My mother had a devastating miscarriage in her late thirties. The doctors warned her that another pregnancy could result in serious risks to her life, but she decided to take her chances anyway. My parents were living on the South Side of Chicago at Ninetieth and Jeffrey at the time my older brother and I were born. Emerson was born in April 1951. I was born three years later at Cook County Hospital after a grueling thirty-six-hour labor. I was a perfectly healthy, handsome eight-pound brown-eyed baby with a full head of jet-black wavy hair. My birthday was May 17, 1954, which was also the date of the *Brown v. Board of Education* victory, when the Supreme Court, led by Chief Justice Warren, ruled unanimously that segregation in public schools was unconstitutional. This coincidence was very important to my mother. She mentioned it every year on my birthday, or whenever my birthday was mentioned.

Back then, mother and baby were kept in the hospital for a few days after the birth. The baby was taken to the nursery at night, and sleeping medications were commonly given to the new mother. The nurse brought me from the nursery to my mother's room every few hours, waking her from her medicated sleep to nurse me. On the second night, the nurse left me with my mother for a feeding but neglected to raise the safety bar on her bed. My mother, heavily medicated, fell asleep and relaxed her grip on me. I fell headfirst three feet to the linoleum-covered cement floor. My cries woke her, and the nurse rushed in and whisked me away to be examined by doctors. X-rays showed that I had a skull injury. My mother wasn't allowed to see me until the next day.

Very early on I became a distressed, "colicky" infant who needed nearly constant attention. My first two years I barely slept. My nervous system was on high alert; my senses were raw and fragile. Sudden lights, sounds, or uninvited touch overwhelmed me, causing me great anxiety and pain. My body would stiffen when I was touched and I'd withdraw into myself. I would cry for hours on end with terrible stomach cramps, and even after I was exhausted I would still be unable to sleep. I had no regular feeding or sleeping schedule. By my second year, doctors were giving me Seconal, a powerful barbiturate that allowed me, and my mother, to sleep for a few hours a night.

My mom noticed that I'd lie immobile for long periods of

time, sometimes for hours, staring passively into space. At times I'd smile at her, but I hardly ever laughed. She said I was a solemn, gentle baby, but I seemed to have no inner drive to explore or to learn.

I was also very sick for the first two years of my life, plagued by severe and mysterious ailments. I believe this health history may have been a significant contributing factor to my problems. My ailments turned out to be the result of severe allergies to grains, eggs, and dairy products. My first allergy symptoms were reactions to my mother's milk after she ate any of those foods. When I was weaned from breast milk to cow's milk, my allergic reactions increased. Finally, when I was two, the doctors discovered the cause of my symptoms and I was weaned from milk onto soy formula, which seemed to relieve my worst agonies.

My mother's degree in developmental psychology ended up having tremendous value. It equipped her to recognize my condition, and to care for me, with all my complex and baffling problems. She was able to observe, understand, and respond effectively to behaviors that would have completely overwhelmed most mothers. I was her round-the-clock case study, the test of her capacity as a developmental psychologist, and as a mother. She observed me tirelessly and took great effort to maintain eye contact with me, even when I was shrieking in pain or withdrawing into myself. Of all the experts I went to throughout my childhood, my mother was the best and most astute. No doctor came as close to discerning the subtle patterns and changing dynamics of my troubling condition as she did. She refused to stop trying to change things for me and continued to believe that she could make a difference.

The challenges my mother faced with me in those first few years were immense. More and more I wouldn't look at anyone or anything. It was becoming harder for her to reach me. She realized that I was drifting toward autism, disconnecting from the outer world of stimuli, sensations, and human connections. She was determined not to let this happen.

She observed that after I was held for a long period of time, being touched didn't seem like such a shock to me. I could tolerate more eye contact, and I wasn't as likely to withdraw into myself. So she began to hold me for longer periods of time, often twenty hours or more, only putting me down briefly to change me. I became her constant companion. She carried me on her shoulder so often that she called me her "little lapel pin." Because I was virtually a full-time job, my parents hired a practical nurse to take care of my brother Emerson. Had my mother not engaged me with such persistent, loving determination, I might have drifted deeper into autism and disappeared forever within myself. Instead, I stayed with the pain in order to maintain a sensory connection with my mother. This hyperconnected awareness was the antithesis of my natural tendencies, as is the case with most other autism spectrum children.* But instead of shutting out awareness of the outside world, I stayed aware of it through the constant connection to my mother. I still had autism spectrum hypersensitivities and was easily overwhelmed, but I'd learned to modulate my nervous system by synchronizing with

---

* All children with autism spectrum disorders (ASDs) demonstrate deficits in 1) social interaction, 2) verbal and nonverbal communication, and 3) repetitive behaviors or interests. In addition, they will often have unusual responses to sensory experiences, such as certain sounds or the way objects look. Each of these symptoms can run the gamut from mild to severe. They present in each individual child differently. For instance, a child may have little trouble learning to read but exhibit extremely poor social interaction. Each child on the autistic spectrum will display communication, social, and behavioral patterns that are individual but fit into the overall diagnosis of ASD. National Institute of Mental Health, http://www.nimh.nih.gov.

my mother's. Later, television began to replace my mother as an anchor for my attention, and as a way to synchronize with the outside world.

Due to my hypersensitivity, I was subject to a degree of pain and stress that most children never experience. Although looking at a face on TV was safe, actually looking into the face of a person who was present could be overwhelming and would provoke extreme anxiety. Feeling emotions through the eyes of other people could start an avalanche of emotions in me that would overwhelm my nervous system. It was something like looking directly into a bright light. Simple sensory input, especially something sudden, could also be overwhelming. Sights and sounds typically set me off, but so could unexpected or unwelcome touch, taste, smell, and emotions. My body would stiffen as intensely painful sensations flooded through me. It was as if my body was screaming.

When feeling somewhat safe in the depths of my inner isolation, I'd crave some limited contact or distraction, as long as it didn't pull me "out there" where I was vulnerable and afraid. At those times I'd be willing to cautiously peek out at the world. It was like opening a thin crack in either my sense of vision or my sense of hearing. I'd look for a sparkle of light, or listen for a safe sound, something I could trust that wouldn't invade me. I craved touch, but only on my terms, when I was ready and able to receive it. The more trust I felt, the more I could open to it, bit by bit, more and more.

My mother eventually realized that science didn't have the answers. Looking to professionals for help, she was told many times that my problems were her fault. Back then it was commonly believed that autism spectrum symptoms and developmental problems like mine were caused by indifferent or cold-hearted mothers. But calling my mother warm and caring would be a vast understatement, and she expressed the full spectrum of her warm and caring nature during my early childhood. Years later, however, the challenge became too much for her. In her desperation and self-doubt, she eventually ignored her intuition and accepted the advice of a prestigious psychiatrist. This would prove to be a serious mistake.

Most people at the time thought the causes of symptoms like mine were psychological, but my mother was convinced that they were neurological, triggered, or at least intensified, by allergies.

Meanwhile, I developed unusual coping strategies. I found that by concentrating very hard on something, I could deaden physical pain and the simmering emotional anxiety that could erupt at any moment. I would obsessively run the lobe of my mother's ear between my first and second fingers as she fed me, or repeatedly wrap my fist tightly around her thumb and pull until I lost my grip. Sometimes I would repeatedly strike my head with the palm of my hand, or bump my head against a wall. Self-inflicted and controlled pain was preferable to pain inflicted by the outside world.

When too much input sent me into a panic, my senses would start to shut down — usually my sight first, then my hearing, then my touch, and so on. I would instinctively compartmentalize my senses. The feeling of this dissociation process was like retreating into a hole where pain couldn't reach me. These coping strategies distracted me from the overwhelming input of my environment, which I couldn't otherwise control. I think this compartmentalizing of my sensory experience made the sensory integration that is necessary for later multisensory learning (such as speech) difficult and aggravated my learning disabilities.

When I was older and I got upset with my mother, I'd go into my room, squeeze myself between my mattress and the wall, and disappear inside of myself. Squeezing myself this way put a consistent pressure on my nerves that helped calm them, but without the irritating demand for attention and emotional connection. It was similar to squeezing a finger when it's injured in order to relieve the pain. I could stay there all day, all night, and into the next day, with no sense of time passing, if only my mother would let me. But she always stayed with me, maintaining contact, not letting me withdraw too deeply. She would talk soothingly to me and run her hand gently through my hair, maintaining that essential thread of physical and emotional connection. Yet the urge in me to dissociate was overwhelming. Her opposition to this impulse and her insistent pull on my attention became immensely irritating to me. Her presence and her touch made me want to crawl out of my skin, but it was her fierce attention and monitoring of my states that kept me from withdrawing into myself and slipping deeper into autism.

At first, I peeked out at the world through the filter of my mother's experience and emotions; as I got older I began to open to my own perceptions of vision and hearing. Many believe that people are more comfortable with one form of sensory input than with another. If they are more responsive to visual input, they tend to learn more visually; others might be more responsive to auditory input, or to tactile input. My understandng is that most people on the autistic spectrum find sight to be more comfortable, and so they think in pictures. Being so connected to my mother, however, I found emotions to be preferable, so I think in narrations of emotions. This is highly unusual, the opposite of how most autistic children respond, because even the existence of other people, let alone the observation of their emotions, can be overwhelming to them. I suspect that's why I have an exceptionally high emotional memory even though I have a much lower-than-average linear memory. As a child, I experienced and remembered events as a florid, emotionally narrated story, but with no memory of faces, names, time, or place, unless they played a part in the emotional context of the event.

I didn't begin using recognizable words until I was four. No one could understand my babbling. I sounded as if I was speaking a language of my own. Finally, my mother cracked the code of my weird jabber. She realized that I was articulating words, but only pronouncing the last parts, omitting the beginning sounds.

Many people, including some experts, suspected I might be "retarded." The mother of one of my friends thought I might be deaf instead. At times it seemed that I might be partially deaf. My mother noticed how I'd watch people's faces intently, trying to figure out what they were saying. When I was five, doctors thought that perhaps I was severely hearing impaired, a defect that would account for my slow learning and my delayed speech. To improve my hearing, they removed my adenoids. I did seem to experience some improvement after six months. I've since learned that false deafness is another symptom associated with being on the autism spectrum.

It's unknown whether or not my fall from the hospital bed caused my learning disabilities. They were not typical of a traumatic brain injury. Nonetheless, my mother always felt profoundly guilty about the accident.

As I grew older, the symptoms of my disabilities increased. My instinctual tendency to shut down or cut off in order to control my sensory input caused problems with sensory integration — that is, with learning. Conventionally, *sensory integration dysfunction* is defined as a neurological disorder causing difficulties with processing information from the five senses. In my experience, it might be more true to say that because of a neurological disorder I both consciously and unconsciously engaged in compartmentalizing my sensory experiences, causing difficulties with processing and integrating information from the senses.

As an infant and as a young child, feeling it necessary to separate and compartmentalize my sensory experiences, I chose what to let into my field of perception. That way I could be on guard against the shock of each sensory input. Too many sounds or sights were very difficult and confusing for me. For example, when someone spoke to me I couldn't accurately choose what to pay attention to. I couldn't put the sounds together in order to understand that the sound (or word) had a relationship with, and could be synchronized to, what I was looking at. Later it proved to be nearly impossible for me to comprehend the subtleties of unspoken social rules, because this required me to recognize people's facial expressions and coordinate those expressions with voice tone or words. This was especially difficult because I was cutting out or ignoring what was most intense. Unfortunately, what is often most intense, like emotions in faces, is also most important in understanding social interactions.*

A turning point came one day when I was four. I'd retreated

---

* This is a critical point, since most communications are through body language, facial expression, and tone of voice rather than through actual words. I believe with a better understanding in this area we will see greater success in helping people with autism spectrum symptoms. I plan on explaining this in more detail and covering ways to work with this in a later book.

to my safe place between the mattress and the wall, to disappear into that hole where I no longer felt, saw, or heard the outside world. I'd been there all morning and into the afternoon. My mother sat in her usual place on the edge of my bed for most of that day, talking to me, stroking my head, keeping me aware of her presence, preventing me from disappearing completely. Yet disappearing was my all-consuming need.

I remember hating her with my whole body for not leaving me alone, not letting me go. I began hitting my head against the wall harder than usual. I had to override the outside input with stronger and stronger responses. My mother tried to stop me, which sent me into panic and hysteria. She finally let me go, and I calmed down. Then she stayed there with me, not touching me or talking to me, but leaving me alone, knowing that was what I wanted. When I finally "came out," it was already dark outside, I hadn't eaten all day, and it was way past dinnertime. My mother was still sitting there on the bed. I became angry again when I saw her, and I yelled, "I hate you! Why can't you just leave me alone?"

She grabbed my shoulders. There were tears in her eyes as she spoke to me. "David! All your life I've known that look in your eyes. When you start to go away, I'm afraid you'll stay wherever it is you go. Maybe I'll never get you back. That's why I can't leave you alone. Do you think you would come back if I didn't fight for you?"

She had told me her secret fear. Then I told her my secret.

"I don't want to be here, but you won't leave me alone."

Her honesty had pulled the words out of me. With tears in her eyes, she leaned toward me and hugged me tightly. I cringed, my whole body tensed in overload reaction. I'd thought she already knew, but she hadn't known my secret at all. I was immediately sorry that I'd told her. Somehow in that exchange, in that connection, the escape door closed inside of me. From that day on, I was aware of the passage of time and never able to disappear into myself in quite the same way.

Faith

*A*t age four I began attending the local nursery school. My teacher's name was Anna Hasegawa. She lived in the co-op, and two of her kids were good friends of mine. All my best friends from the co-op were there.

After entering nursery school I began to come out of myself in a significant way. This was due to my mother's heroic ministrations as well as to the fact that I was now mixing in with a group of kids my own age on a daily basis. I hadn't begun to speak coherently yet, but I was functioning mentally and socially far beyond the predictions of the doctors and experts who had examined me.

I still had autism spectrum tendencies. When I was afraid, angry, or upset, my nerves felt as if they were on fire, my skin got hot, and I'd break into a sweat. If anyone touched me while I was in this state, I'd instinctively strike out in self-defense. But I was now available for relationships. I was emotionally present and able to connect to others in a meaningful way. My keen sense of empathy allowed me to connect deeply with friends and schoolmates, and made me a good friend, with a strongly protective instinct for the weak, vulnerable, and helpless. I also had a strong love for animals and babies.

I befriended one little girl in my nursery-school class who was too frightened to speak. I often took her by the hand, led her into the group, and encouraged her to participate. We became friends, and I often visited her at her house. Her father, the converted John Bircher who later sued the co-op, was an angry and abusive man. Whenever he yelled at her during my visits, I'd go stand between them. After a while, any time he came around I rushed to her side to protect her.

Nursery school connected me with my peers and made me feel like an integral part of our little community. The love and connection of my family and playmates, and my baby brother, who arrived when I was four, absorbed my attention and nurtured me. I barely noticed my learning disabilities since they didn't interfere with these primary relationships.

Because of my learning disabilities and my predilection toward autism spectrum symptoms, I rarely had normal expectations placed on me at home. But I'd always looked normal, and at four years old, other than not being able to speak coherently, I wasn't obviously different from other kids. I was a fully participating member of our group, making my own unique contribution. In nursery school, kindergarten, and grade school, my parents never pushed me to function at the level of my peers. I don't think they knew what to demand or expect of me. They responded to my various difficulties and poor academic performance with compassionate support. As a result of my mother's prolonged struggle to draw me out of my autistic shell, she'd already pressed me far beyond my natural limits.

In those early years my life in the co-op and with my family were idyllic in many ways, with two major exceptions: my learning disabilities, and my older brother, Emerson. Emerson hated me almost from the day I came home from the hospital when he was three years old. With my arrival, he essentially lost his mother. He went from being the center of her attention into a kind of exile that must have been excruciating for him. For the next two years I was rarely out of my mother's arms, and Emerson was rarely in them. Finding himself suddenly handed off to a live-in nurse, and deprived of virtually all attention from and physical contact with our mother, he suffered the anguish of abandonment and the torment of jealousy. I think he was too young to recognize that I was human, which enabled him to take it out on me with a vengeance. And this behavior persisted, even to young adolescence. I saw a coldness in his eyes when he looked at me. I felt that he didn't see me as human, and that he was capable of doing anything to me.

My mother told me that many times my parents found him at my crib, covering my face with a blanket or a pillow. I have memories of waking up suddenly, kicking and thrashing in a panic, unable to breathe — to find Emerson smothering me. He would try to pull me off the changing table by tugging at the feet of my pajamas. He would step on my hands as I crawled on the floor. Feelings of fear and panic associated with Emerson pervaded my childhood. He acted out to get my mother's attention and to express his pain. He broke things, and one time he flushed some of her jewelry down the toilet. He had poor impulse control, and today would probably be diagnosed as hyperactive.

My relationship with my younger brother, Neil, was a loving counterbalance to my troubled relationship with Emerson. I was completely fascinated by Neil from the moment he came home from the hospital. I'd watch him in his crib, and I learned to gently rock him to sleep. I followed my mother around when she held him so I could be near him. When he stopped breast-feeding, I fed him bottles. As a result, we became very attached to each other.

I found Neil easy to be with. Physical contact, emotional contact, and eye contact with him weren't the stressful demand on me that they were with others. From the time he could walk Neil was my little shadow, following me around the house. When he was old enough to go out, I took him with me everywhere. He hated for me to leave him, and at times he would rush out the door after me in his pajamas. I think my relationship with Neil helped me come farther out of my shell, and enabled me to love without being ambivalent or needy.

Emerson hardly seemed to notice Neil, who was now enjoying the lion's share of our mother's attention. I appreciated Neil even for this, because as long as I'd been the central object of our mother's attention, I'd also been the object of Emerson's wrath. Emerson seemed to pick on Neil just to rile me. I was Neil's protector. If I caught Emerson bothering him, I flew into a rage. I kept a watchful eye on both of them, and I was always ready to intervene at a moment's notice. I protected Neil more fiercely than I protected myself.

Our family life revolved around the dining-room table, where we all gathered for dinner every night. My mother had to sit next to Emerson in order to control him. Neil and I sat together on the opposite side of the table. Emerson and I always got into some kind of fight, throwing things at each other or kicking each other under the table. I felt bad for Neil, who watched our battles with fear and helplessness, at times screaming and crying for us to stop.

As Emerson and I got older, our relationship degenerated into ongoing warfare. He taunted and teased me, jabbed me and poked at me with things, threw rocks at me, and once threatened me with a broken milk bottle. He often overpowered me physically and held me down, spitting on me or tickling me until I went into a claustrophobic panic. Though smaller and weaker, I fought back with all my strength, using my fists or whatever object was handy. Sometimes we fought with sticks and even boards with rusty nails.

At times, Emerson's abuse was dangerous. One time he was chopping wood while I watched from the side, safely I thought. He swung the axe wildly in my direction and hit me in the head, slicing my forehead to the bone just above my eyebrow.

On another occasion, he followed me onto the roof of our house, trapped me near the edge, and tried to push me off. I was terrified of being pushed — and terrified to jump. But I knew it would be worse to be pushed than to jump, and I preferred to decide *how* I went off the roof. I turned and jumped fifteen feet to the ground below. I landed hard, bruising both feet but fortunately not breaking any bones.

Emerson finally broke me. He was bigger and older than I was. He could overpower me when he got hold of me and do whatever he pleased. I felt deep shame about this. But through Emerson I learned the secret of dealing with pain and fear. I discovered this ability while being held down and tickled by him, one of his favorite ways of tormenting me. Besides the tickling itself, the feelings of helplessness, panic, and rage were unbearable. On one occasion the feelings became so intense that something shifted; I did something completely different. I relaxed *into* the discomfort and panic, and moved through to the other side, into a remarkable state of calm.

After that I was able to make this shift consistently, often immediately, relaxing and taking slow, deep breaths while focusing intently on the feelings of panic or pain. When the shift happened, I was able to physically relax and remain aware even while Emerson was tickling or hurting me. Some might call this a state of dissociation, but I felt as if I'd entered a stark, present reality, detached from suffering and filled with a calm, surreal clarity. In this state, things seemed to unfold in slow motion, and everything appeared brighter than normal, as if someone had turned on a light. Sometimes I heard a loud rushing noise in my ears.

Finding this calm, clear place inside myself — on the other side of fear, pain, and rage — proved to be an invaluable skill. It allowed me to relax and respond effectively to high-pressure or dangerous situations, and to face painful events and crises with unusual clarity, rather than succumbing to confusion, fear, and overwhelming emotions. On more than one occasion it saved my life.

After a record-breaking snowstorm when I was ten, I dug a long, narrow tunnel into a ten-foot-tall snowdrift that ran the length of our house. Emerson found me inside and collapsed the tunnel behind me, trapping me in pitch-black darkness with my body jammed in tightly packed snow. I couldn't move, let alone turn around. My first reaction was panic. I knew that a couple of feet of thickly packed snow separated me from daylight. I didn't know if I'd be able to dig through it, and I didn't know how much oxygen I had in the confined space I was trapped in.

In that moment I experienced the terror of being buried alive. I tried with all my strength to push my way out but only managed to move the snow an inch or two. I realized that I was only packing it harder and tighter around me. My thoughts raced, and the panic escalated. So I began my well-practiced routine, consciously relaxing into the panic and slowing down my breathing. Within moments, I passed through the fear and entered into the familiar calm, clear place. From there I assessed my situation, got my sense of direction, and figured out a strategy for digging my way out. With no space to put the snow, I carefully distributed and packed each handful of snow around my body, and managed to dig my way through two feet of snow to daylight.

As long as I can remember, the mere sight of Emerson triggered anxiety and fear in me. I was living with an enemy who I believed wanted me dead. If we were sitting in the same room watching TV, I'd feel as threatened as if he were chasing me through the house or physically overpowering me. His mere presence was a threat, and I believed he might really kill me, either through an impulsive act or out of gross carelessness at an opportune moment. Whether his motives were conscious or unconscious, he was the source and symbol of terror during my entire childhood.

Throughout my childhood my parents remained in denial about this side of Emerson. Most of what went on between us happened out of their sight. He would tell them, "It was a mistake. I didn't mean to hurt him." They seemed unwilling to consider that he wanted me to disappear or wished me dead. Yet they were painfully aware that ours was no garden-variety sibling rivalry. Our conflict had such a reputation in the neighborhood that my parents were unable to find babysitters. It reached a point where my parents began to lock Emerson in his room for hours each day. When they let him out, they tried to reassure me that he wouldn't kill me. I felt they didn't take my fears of Emerson seriously, or recognize the threat he posed to me in my own home.

My conflict with Emerson also taught me that it was a short jump from being really scared to being really angry. And I learned to make that shift like flipping a switch. When Emerson was around, I'd feel a rush of fear. If he came near me, I'd flip the switch to anger and hit him in the face. Once he came after me and I pushed him backward down the stairs. Sometimes my own anger frightened me. I didn't know if I had control of it anymore. Yet he continued to push me to that point. It culminated in an incident when I was ten, when I tried to kill him with a screwdriver.

I had been practicing throwing knives and screwdrivers for a couple of years and had gotten very good at it. I had excellent aim, power, and control. By visualizing each throw in my mind and following through with full force, I could hit my target almost every time and bury the blade deep. I could usually tell by the feel of the throw as it left my hand if it would find its mark. That day, Emerson and I had one of our usual fights, and I fended him off with my fists. To get back at me, he went up to Neil and pushed him down on the floor. Neil hit his head very hard on the stone entry and began to wail. I went berserk and ran after Emerson. He took off, running up the stairs. As I reached the bookshelf near the bottom of the stairs, I stopped and grabbed a screwdriver with a six-inch shaft that I kept there on top of some books. It was time to carry out my plan to kill him. I'd hidden screwdrivers in various places around the house — to have weapons ready just in case.

I stood at the bottom of the stairs in a throwing stance, watching Emerson with tunnel vision as he ran up the stairs. I was already visualizing the throw, seeing the screwdriver hit its target — Emerson's right temple. As he reached the landing I took

a deep breath, whipped my arm back, and threw the screwdriver
with deadly force. A thrill of anticipation ran through me as the
screwdriver left my hand. Mesmerized, I watched it fly, blade first
like an arrow — helping it in my mind to hit and penetrate Emerson's temple. But Emerson glanced back and ducked his head.
My heart sank as the screwdriver flew past him, missing his head
by a fraction of an inch, and stuck in the wall behind him with
a thud. Emerson ran down the hall and into his room, shutting
and locking the door behind him. I went upstairs and pulled out
the screwdriver, deeply embedded in the wall.

Holding it in my hand, I relived the thrill I'd felt when
I thought I had him. And I was stunned by the realization that
I had wanted to kill my brother and had almost succeeded.
If he hadn't ducked, the blade would have punctured his skull.
I realized that I'd crossed a line I'd never crossed before, and I
realized something about myself that I hadn't known until that
moment — that I had it in me to deliberately kill someone.
It scared the hell out of me. And I hated Emerson for pushing
me to this point.

Emerson also knew a line had been crossed that changed
things between us. He told my mother I'd thrown a screwdriver
at him and he'd felt it fly past his head. The severity of what I'd
done was brought home to me again by the look in my mother's
eyes. But Emerson was afraid of me after that. He later admitted
to me that until then he hadn't considered me human. He never
picked on me in quite the same way again.

— ⚙ —

First grade marked the onset of my academic troubles. My co-op
classmates and I now attended the local Lombard public school.

Mrs. Brent, my first-grade teacher, began to single me out, criticizing me for not paying attention, and at times slapping my hand with a ruler. I had no idea what I was doing wrong. I wasn't misbehaving. I was doing my best. But there was so much going on inside of me that it was hard to pay attention to what was going on outside of me. Any discomfort or sensation in my body, any noise, or any movement in the environment would draw my attention.

I tended to slip in and out of my own inner world without noticing it. I'd start one of my self-soothing activities without realizing it, softly tapping or clicking my fingers, scratching myself, or wiggling in my seat. I was often, literally, uncomfortable in my own skin. I don't think I disturbed the class, but my teacher noticed my odd behavior and perceived me as a problem and a distraction to the rest of the class. She punished me for things over which I had no control. I didn't understand it, and I felt unfairly picked on. I also began to feel I was different from the other kids: inadequate, and excluded in a way I had never felt before.

None of this seemed to change the way my co-op friends viewed me, but it strongly influenced the perceptions of the other kids who took their cue from Mrs. Brent that something was wrong with me. Most of them began to exclude me from their activities, and some even ignored me when I tried to talk to them. I started feeling bad about myself, and wondered if something was wrong with me. My co-op friends mixed in easily with these Lombard kids, but it was much harder for me. I was behind developmentally and academically, and I lacked the social and communication skills shared by most kids my age. I had also missed many key developmental steppingstones due to chronic illnesses, which compounded the effects of my learning disabilities.

Everything seemed disjointed and random to me. I had problems with sequencing and organizing my thoughts. I had terrible difficulty remembering the days of the week and people's names, including the names of my brothers. I was unable to remember my own address and phone number. I also had difficulty with hand-eye coordination; knowing my right side from my left; understanding directions such as north, south, east, and west; and sensing my location in space, which made me terrible at sports. All this increased my feelings of isolation. I had a frustrating inability to pay attention to anything for very long, and only the reactions of others at my inability to pay attention let me know I had a problem.

That year my developmental state and my learning problems became significant issues. My parents began taking me to experts, who administered a variety of tests. After extensive testing, they decided I was not "retarded" as they'd suspected. Due to the discrepancy between my exceptionally high IQ test results and my exceptional low practical ability results, my parents were told that my problems had to be psychological. In those days, if you were proven to be intelligent but had trouble learning, the contradiction was attributed to psychological factors. My parents intuited that I had neurological and perceptual problems, but under the pressure of the prevailing psychological view, and perhaps with the hope that it would provide a solution, they sent me to see a psychiatrist. I also began to receive private tutoring.

From the end of my first year in second grade all the way through sixth grade, I had daily visits with my private tutor and twice-weekly visits with a psychiatrist. The era of prescribing psychotropic drugs to children with learning or behavioral problems hadn't yet begun. So my sessions with my psychiatrist were traditional talk therapy. I found this embarrassing. My parents and teachers timed these visits to occur when the class was engaged in subjects I was unable to learn. The psychiatrist gave my parents an ultimatum: He would meet with me only if they would do everything he said, even if it went against their instincts. The ground rule was that they weren't allowed to "lie" to me anymore. They could no longer protect me from painful truths. They had to be ruthlessly honest with me. I had to understand the consequences of not being able, or willing, to learn.

— ⚙ —

On a family vacation when I was eight or nine, my grandfather discovered another side of me. He took me off alone for a few hours each day to observe me and test me in his special field of knowledge. My grandfather had taught college-level mathematics. My parents already knew I had a basic aptitude for numbers, but they didn't know to what degree. My grandfather, also a doctor, had heard all the professional theories and diagnoses about my learning disabilities. Now he determined to find out for himself how intelligent I was.

The first day he began to teach me a form of binary code, and how to count in the base-two number system, the basic numerical language used in electronic circuitry and all modern computers today. To my grandfather's amazement, I acquired a working understanding of the basic concepts in our first thirty-minute session. His visible excitement told me that I'd done something remarkable and completely unexpected. Our little game of numbers turned out to be a dramatic event.

After that first lesson, he decided to see how far he could take me. He sat down with me over the next few days. In that time, I was able to transition from base two all the way through to base sixteen, and even add and subtract. My grandfather told my parents that my ability to grasp and utilize the various conceptual ideas of binary-to-hexadecimal code was far beyond my age and grade level, and indicated "genius qualities." He told us that many of his college students had trouble grasping these concepts as quickly as I did. It seemed all the more remarkable given my substandard performance in almost every other area of learning.

I was also excited by my success. Yet to my disappointment, it meant virtually nothing when I returned to class. My newly discovered facility for numbers didn't erase the list of defects and disabilities compiled by the experts who had tested me, nor did it allow me to learn the basic subjects of my grade level, which remained beyond my grasp.

I wanted desperately to meet the expectations of my parents and my teachers. Meeting expectations helped me feel part of the world. I wanted to rise to challenges and succeed. I wanted to learn the same subjects as the other kids and be as competent as they were. I didn't want to be criticized, punished, written off, and left behind. But that's what was increasingly happening to me.

Despite my nonathleticism, clumsy social skills, and poor scholastic performance, I managed to succeed in one unexpected way: fighting. In our semirural school system, there were fights almost daily, primarily to establish pecking-order dominance. I managed to earn the respect of other kids in a few well-chosen confrontations, mostly in response to someone else's aggression. I never sought out a fight for its own sake, or got into a fight with anyone who didn't deserve it. I only fought bullies who were hurting or intimidating me or other weaker kids.

My years of combat with Emerson had made me accustomed to fighting. It had also instilled in me feelings of sympathy for the underdog and outrage toward all bullies. Despite being small and uncoordinated, I had fighting experience most kids didn't have, and a reckless intensity other kids found intimidating. Fear, violence, pain, and blood didn't frighten me. I never lost a fight. Whether I was winning or losing, beating or being beaten, it didn't matter to me; the other kid would eventually quit when I hurt him enough. And I was willing to take on anyone. Yet most of the kids and adults who knew me saw me as a kind and friendly boy — and mostly I was.

My first school fight occurred in my first year of second grade. Another second-grade class from a tough neighborhood had temporarily relocated to our school while their building was being renovated. There were a few bullies among them, and when the toughest kid in the new class started picking on one of my classmates, I stepped in.

He was a heavyset kid, much bigger than I was. I wasn't particularly proficient with my fists, but I'd learned a trick with Emerson: I'd take punches and throw a few myself while I moved in close. Then I'd lunge and grab my opponent in a headlock. Once I got him in a headlock, and I often did, he was mine. I'd simply squeeze until he couldn't breathe. I found that everybody, big or small, gives up when he can't breathe. This was how I won all of my fights through my adolescence.

That first fight was my only fight at school that year. I got the bully in a headlock and squeezed until he gave up. Having defeated the toughest kid from a tough Chicago neighborhood, my reputation was established. I didn't need to fight again. I could intimidate any other bully and get him to back down without coming to blows. That victory, and my sudden status in my class, gave me a kind of self-esteem I'd never felt before. It felt good to be admired for something — anything — and it compensated somewhat for the low self-esteem I experienced due to my learning disabilities.

Failing second grade that year was a turning point, the beginning of a downward spiral that set in motion a completely new course in my life — a course I didn't want to take but was unable to change. Despite my best efforts I continued to fall behind during my second year in the second grade. The other kids, a year younger than I was, were still smarter than I was. With a sinking feeling, I watched them learn, succeed, and leave me behind academically.

At the end of that year I should have been held back again, but the school realized I wasn't going to learn and decided that I couldn't continue repeating second grade forever. Despite the fact that I could barely read or write, I was promoted to third grade. After that, my teachers would pass me along, year after year, through the rest of elementary school. And because I was being passed along, I believed I really was moving forward.

My second year in the second grade was worse than the first. My classmates were acutely aware that I was older, slower to learn, and unable to keep up with them in class. My closest friends were still the co-op kids whom I'd known since nursery school, but they were now a grade ahead of me.

That year I had a terrible nightmare, one that evoked the profound sense of isolation that was simmering in me. In the dream, a kid who seemed like me wandered aimlessly around the school playground. He had a blank look on his face, and a big snakelike worm was wriggling out of a hole in the top of his head. The other kids seemed not to notice him as he wandered zombielike in their midst, yet they maintained a ten-foot circle of space around him at all times.

I'd been seeing my psychiatrist twice a week for nearly a year, but nothing good had come from our sessions. I felt no sense of caring or compassion from him, no sense that he had any interest in me as a person. I felt only a cool, impersonal detachment from him, and a sense of being judged by him. I thought he was an idiot, and I refused to talk to him. He periodically fell asleep during our sessions. I did, too. I'd nap on the couch, or climb into the toy cabinet, close the door, and doze in the dark. My parents didn't know what was happening during our sessions. The psychiatrist made various excuses for my lack of progress. I believe he was the one who had advised my mother to threaten me with the possibility of institutionalization.

I'd noticed my parents' behavior toward me changing under the doctor's supervision. I didn't realize until years later how much they'd been troubled by the new rules that the doctor had laid down as a condition for working with me. I misinterpreted their hesitation and frustration as disapproval and anger at me. I didn't know the anguish my mother felt at having to treat me according to the psychiatrist's ground rules. She'd always followed her instincts with me, often against professional wisdom, but as she helplessly watched me falling increasingly behind, I think she lost faith in her own instincts. Blindly following the advice of a doctor whom she didn't trust placed a subtle wedge between us, and plunged her into a private hell. But I didn't know she'd lost faith in her instincts. I thought she'd lost faith in me.

Fighting My Way to the Bottom

*F*ailing second grade and my mother's warning that I might end up in a mental institution triggered deep feelings of anxiety in me and a sense of urgency about my future. The specters of illiteracy, hopeless disability, and institutionalization haunted me. How would I be able to earn a living and take care of myself when I grew up? Would I be a valued member of society or would I find myself alone and isolated as an adult? What job could I get if I couldn't read or write? If I couldn't even learn the things I needed to pass second grade, how could I learn all the things I needed to know in order to live and function in the world? And then there was the one thing that I wished for, the thing that haunted me more than anything else: Would I ever be able to have a family and provide for them?

Several things had become clear: My mother couldn't protect me; I didn't know how to take care of myself; and I had to learn how to learn. I had to figure out how to manage my own life. I had to become independent and develop life skills.

My fears gave me a powerful motivation to become independent. I began to distance myself from all of my family members except for Neil. I stopped telling my parents that I loved them.

I asked to be sent away to school. I questioned decisions my parents made, needing to make sure they matched my own perceptions. When they added a new ground-floor bedroom on the far side of the house — away from the other bedrooms — I asked if I could move there. They let me. This gave me a literal distance from my family, and the sense of being on my own that I needed.

My mother knew I had to become more independent. She also began to distance herself from me, letting me take risks and learn the consequences of my own decisions. She still provided basic care, but she shifted from her previous way of relating to me and became noticeably detached. At times I interpreted her lack of concern and her noninvolvement in my activities as abandonment and neglect. Yet mostly I appreciated the newfound sense of freedom.

Then, in fifth grade, I stumbled into a possible vocation, one that held the promise of success and the feeling of self-esteem that I desperately needed. I had a terrible sweet tooth and frequently brought candy to school. My classmates often asked me to share it with them, but they wanted me to share more than I could afford, so I offered to buy it for them. After figuring out what they wanted, I started bringing candy with me and charging them extra. So began my career in sales. As more kids found out, they wanted candy delivered to them at school, too. So I started buying candy in larger quantities and selling it to my classmates for a profit.

I bought penny candy, which was big in those days, and nickel packs of gum with five strips. I'd put the gum strips in a bag with the penny candy and let my customers pick two pieces for a nickel, or three pieces if they were good friends. I also bought nickel candy bars and sold them for ten cents. I noticed which items were the most popular and refined my inventory accordingly.

I never understood why kids would buy candy from me when they could buy it on their own, but they seemed to like buying from me and so I did a steady business. Every day before school, during lunch, and at recess a crowd of kids would gather around me. I kept the candy in a book satchel that I rigged with a make-shift alarm. It was my first invention and my first venture into electronics. I wired a battery and buzzer together in my dad's workshop and attached it to the handle. It had to be opened in a very precise way or else the buzzer would go off.

I tried to keep my business low-key, but I never tried to hide what I was doing. My parents and teachers became aware of my candy selling, but they didn't seem to mind as long as it didn't cause problems. I was learning a lot about business through hands-on experience, and before long I had a fairly profitable business going.

Business dramatically increased when I began to manufac-ture and market my own product. I began to dip toothpicks in cinnamon oil and sell cinnamon toothpicks. To advertise, I'd walk around with a cinnamon toothpick stuck between my teeth. And I passed out samples. It worked. My cinnamon toothpicks became very popular, a local fad. I got so busy that I hired my good friend Larry to help me manufacture toothpicks and sell candy and toothpicks at my school. Then I decided to expand my territory. I started hiring kids from other schools, including the local junior high school, to sell my toothpicks. By the end of the year I had a steady business with four salespeople working for me, and we were all making a profit. I was a highly motivated entrepreneur.

For the first time I began to believe in my future. I was learning through experience in a way I'd never learned from schoolbooks and chalkboard scribbling. I had good people skills, marketing savvy, and a knack for sales. I learned to purchase products that people liked, and how much I could mark up the price. I learned how to sell and how to motivate other people to sell for me. I learned financial self-discipline. I didn't spend my profits frivolously, or squander them by eating my products. And I learned how to keep my personal money separate from business money by paying myself a salary.

I saved all my profits except for those I put back into the business. I had a plan. I was saving a nest egg for the future. My goal of achieving independence now seemed realistic. I believed I could become a successful businessman, thereby achieving my bottom-line goal of not ending up in a mental institution. And maybe, just maybe, even have a family.

Academically, nothing changed. I was still lost and struggling, unable to spell many first-grade words. I could spell a few three-letter words, but no four-letter words. I never tried to answer questions in class for fear of public humiliation. When teachers called on me, I made jokes to try to cover up and avoid looking stupid. I was a class clown. But I was making money. I was finally succeeding at something. And it felt great.

At age ten, in 1964, I began going to Circle Pines summer camp near Kalamazoo, Michigan. Circle Pines was designed to provide underprivileged city kids and middle-class kids with a shared summer camp experience at a very low cost. They accomplished this by incorporating hard work into the daily camp activities. We did the usual things such as swimming, hiking, campfires, singing, and storytelling, but we also did real work. For a number of hours each day we dug ditches, cleared brush, hauled stones, and put in roads. We even built a couple of cabins. The camp counselors instructed and supervised us in our work, and we learned practical skills that most kids never learn at camp.

At Circle Pines I met Robert, with whom I shared a small cabin. He would become a good friend. Robert was a year and a half older than I was and lived on the South Side of Chicago. His knack for talking and flirting with girls he'd never met before earned him the camp nickname Casanova. This was a skill I wanted to learn. I'd grown up around girls at the co-op and had never gone through the typical "not liking girls" stage. I felt comfortable with girls. I trusted them and liked talking with the girls I knew. But approaching girls I didn't know and striking up a conversation was different. Robert and I became camp buddies, with this matter of girls being a key focus and topic of conversation between us. One night the topic became a matter of personal exploration.

There were two girls we really liked. We had flirted with them a few times. One night we had a campfire gathering where scary stories were told. Afterward, Robert and I walked back to our cabin. When we got there, to our surprise we found the girls hiding in our sleeping bags. We ended up in the sleeping bags with them and stayed up late, talking with them and holding them throughout the night. This first real experience with a girl left me feeling close and connected.

I had another influential experience at camp — my first personal experience with Eastern cultures. I saw one of the kids in our cabin practicing the mantra "Namyohorengekyo." The tone and repetition intrigued me. He seemed like a very calm and responsible kid with more common sense than most of us. When

I showed interest, he was very willing to show me how to do it. I practiced this twice a day for a number of months, then only periodically after that, but an understanding of its potential value stuck with me.

When summer camp ended, I started taking subway trains into Chicago to visit Robert. Venturing into the city made me aware of my limited possibilities in the sequestered world of the co-op. My mother encouraged these solo excursions. She and my father often drove me to the train station eleven miles from our house.

"I don't want you to grow up being a naïve suburban kid," my mother told me. "I want you to know the world and be able to get around in it."

If my mother thought I ought to know something, or be able to do something, I believed her. I'd try to meet those expectations as if my future depended on it. But there was more to it than that. There was an edge of anxiety and fear that I felt drawn to when I ventured out into the greater world. It wasn't the same anxiety that I felt in my daily life. I'd always felt anxious about going to school, about failing, about being excluded and left behind. But that wasn't the same edge of fear I was drawn to now. There was no excitement and no adventure in school, only shame, humiliation, and the dreadful anticipation of more of the same.

The edge I sought was about risk, danger, and plunging into the unknown world "out there." I had an obsessive need to step beyond my comfort zone, confront my fears, and push beyond them. My future independence required a sense of urgency and drive. I found all of these while traveling the subway trains and venturing into the city of Chicago. I wanted to see if I could make myself do things I was afraid to do, and then repeat them until

I could do them without fear. At first, just going on the trains alone accomplished this. Then it became things like talking to strange girls, even while their parents were sitting next to them. I'd also go up and talk to bums and crazy people on the train. By doing these kinds of things I got good at pushing myself beyond my fears. I was able to go places and do things that other kids I knew wouldn't dare to do.

When I stepped onto the subway I was exploring a new world, and looking for something that was lacking in my familiar world at home. I was looking for other kids like me — kids who were different, who struggled, who didn't fit in. I was looking for a place where I *did* fit in. I was looking for opportunities, challenges, and adventure. I wanted to see how far beyond my edge I could go, to discover what I could or couldn't do, to find out who I could be if I dared.

I discovered that when it came to taking risks, fear wasn't a final barrier. I discovered that the secret to overcoming fear was to repeat what was fearful until it became familiar. I'd take unreasonable risks if I thought I might achieve a meaningful breakthrough, some new level of strength, resilience, or independence.

I also wanted to understand good and evil, and the meaning of life, though I didn't think of it in those words. I was curious and hungry for experience, truth, and knowledge. Were there rules to live by or was it dog-eat-dog? Would I be able to make it on my own out there? For a few hours? For a day? For a lifetime? I wanted to see what kind of people were out there. I wanted to see how they lived and what they did. I wanted to see people who made it, who succeeded. I wanted to see people who failed, who were beaten down and destroyed, who had become what I was afraid I might become. All of these curiosities motivated me. They made me feel alive and aware.

My father subtly encouraged my new adventuring. One time he gave me a rare, uncharacteristic glimpse into his own difficult childhood. He told me how he'd run away from home as a kid and gotten his first job at a local circus. They began teaching him how to be a fire-eater and sword-swallower. He gave me an actual demonstration. First he doused both hands with lighter fluid; then he lit them on fire and let them burn briefly before putting them out. Then he lit a cigarette and put it out on his tongue. He did both without getting burned. After that he got a silver butter knife, held it by the edge of the handle, leaned his head back, and slid the knife down into his throat until it disappeared. He said he could put a sword down into his stomach without getting hurt.

I was the only one he showed these things to. I think he understood how much I was struggling in my life and was trying to tell me that some of us have to do things to survive that others might not understand. He was letting me know that he'd had hard times in his youth, too.

My dyslexia was a recurring problem on public transit. I almost always got lost at some point by getting onto the wrong train, getting off at the wrong stop, or forgetting directions and the names of the stations where I wanted to get off. I couldn't read the signs. I had to ask strangers for directions and help. On my first few trips into the city my mother wrote down my itinerary on a piece of paper, with the names of the stations and the number of stops in between. I couldn't read it myself, but if I got lost or confused I showed the paper to strangers and asked them to read it to me. Someone would usually let me know how many stops to my station, or, if I'd already passed it, how to get back on the right train.

But asking for help didn't always work. When people told me how many stops to my station, sometimes I'd lose count. If they named the stop, sometimes I'd forget the name by the time the train arrived in that station. Every trip was, to some degree, a disorienting ordeal that triggered anxiety and confusion as well as excitement. A couple of times I rode around lost for hours, getting off at the wrong stops and onto the wrong trains, ending up at the end of the line on the North Side of Chicago. My mother had to drive all the way out to the Skokie Station to get me.

Yet my excursions were also about simple fun, hanging out with friends and meeting girls. Robert lived near the end of the subway line on the South Side of Chicago. We'd leave our houses around the same time, catch a train, and meet somewhere in the middle, usually at the White Sox Baseball Park. Our primary goal was to flirt with girls our age, who were usually with their parents. When we saw girls we liked, we'd try to talk with them. Sometimes we'd serenade them with absurd love songs we made up. Robert would take out his recorder — a miniature flute he always had with him — and play a melody while I sang the words. If that went over well, we'd start little conversations and try to get to know them. We never expected anything beyond fun conversation. Most of the parents saw that we were harmless kids doing silly stuff to get the girls' attention. They were often amused, and the girls usually liked the attention. For lunch we'd buy hot dogs, which I often paid for since Robert was poor.

We took the trains everywhere, exploring as much of the city as we could in the hours before I had to return home. I was always getting lost when I was alone, but Robert and I got lost together a few times, too, and got mugged more than once. The first time we got mugged was when we got off at the wrong stop, out near the Midway Airport. It wasn't a good neighborhood for two young white boys to be traveling alone in. It was the territory of the infamous Blackstone Rangers, the largest youth gang in America back in the 1960s, the predecessor of the Bloods and Crips.

As we stood up on the elevated platform with the train pulling away, we saw six black kids running up the stairway toward us. When they jumped the turnstile and headed straight at us, I knew they weren't running to catch a train. I always carried a pocketknife in case of trouble, but I wasn't about to pull it on a gang of six kids who were bigger and several years older than we were unless I was sure that my life was in danger. They ran up and grabbed us, demanding our money. I gave them what little money I had, except for what was in my shoe, which wasn't much. One of them took a ring I was wearing. When Robert resisted, he got slugged hard on the side of his head near his left eye, which swelled in a huge lump. Later he was able to rest his recorder on the lump and his left ear without it falling off. When I told my mother about getting ripped off, she said in a matter-of-fact voice, "Well, you've got to be more careful than that."

In my sixth-grade year, instead of going outside during recess I went to a special-ed class for mentally "retarded" kids. I wasn't sent there because they thought I was "retarded." I'd volunteered to help them as a kind of assistant. I don't know exactly why I did it, other than wanting to help kids who I imagined were struggling more than I was. I felt a little funny about being associated with "retarded" kids. Having a learning disability was difficult enough; I didn't want people thinking I might be "retarded" too. Yet, I found caring for these kids each day to be truly fulfilling. I learned to love them, and I kept in touch with some of them for years after.

I was still doing my candy-and-cinnamon-toothpick business, but toward the end of that year my business came to a sudden end. The principal of the junior high that I would be attending the following year had learned of several boys selling cinnamon toothpicks in his school. When he talked to them, he found out they all worked for me. He already knew who I was because he knew my mother very well. She was the psychologist for our school district and was often called in to help him deal with troubled kids in his school.

This principal called one evening just before dinner. My mother answered the phone, and they spoke briefly. Then she called me over, handed me the phone with her hand covering the mouthpiece, and whispered with a scowl, "Why is the principal of Jackson Junior High calling you?"

I had no idea. I shrugged with a puzzled look and took the phone. "Hello?"

"Hello, David, this is Principal Schultz of Jackson Junior High." His voice was stern. "Are you selling cinnamon toothpicks to students in my school?"

He was clearly unhappy about it.

"Um…yeah."

"Well, David, you'd better stop immediately. And I don't mean just in my school. I mean stop altogether. If you don't, you won't be allowed to attend my school next year. Students aren't supposed to conduct business of any kind on school property — in *any* school."

"Okay, I'll stop."

"Good. I'll speak to your mother now."

That was it. My youthful business career was over, temporarily. Deeply disappointed, I handed the phone back to my mother and went to my room. Once again, it seemed that the world was cutting off any possibility for me to succeed.

— ❧ —

The next year, when I started seventh grade, all my disabilities were suddenly magnified. It was 1967. For years I'd been passed along from grade to grade, despite my failure to learn the basics in each grade. I knew I was way behind, but because I'd been passed along I maintained the fantasy that in the eyes of my classmates I really wasn't hopelessly far behind everyone else. I knew I wasn't a very good student, but, hey, I was passing, right?

Now, in junior high, the rules suddenly changed. No more would I be passed undeservedly up the ladder. Now I was expected to learn — or flunk. Years behind my peers academically, I was put into the remedial classes for the "slow" kids. But even there I was unable to keep up.

Until now, the kids I'd identified with and hung out with were the good kids, the normal kids, even the smart kids. Many of them were my longtime friends. Yet a subtle parting of our ways had begun after I fell a grade behind them. They were always a year ahead of me now, learning things I'd probably never learn, moving confidently toward normal, conventional, probably successful lives. I looked at them and saw smart kids, good students, who were learning with ease. They would graduate, go to college, get well-paying jobs. They would have families, and enjoy lives of effortless freedom and fulfillment.

I felt detached from the kids in my class now, since they were younger than I was and had their own bonds together. Now I was in a special remedial class and falling behind everyone there as well. It was suddenly obvious to me how far behind I really was academically, and how *stupid* I really was. When I'd try to read, I'd slowly sound out the words, but I couldn't understand what I'd read. The anxiety I felt from being exposed as a dummy in front of all of my friends was overwhelming. I dreaded the loss of their respect, and perhaps their friendship. My future suddenly seemed threatened again, and more in doubt than ever. My chronic insomnia kicked in bigtime, and a sense of doom followed me everywhere I went.

In my English class we had spelling bees. The teacher, out of some misguided attempt to help me, would save the simplest words for me. She would say, "Okay, David, *candy*."

I tried to spell *candy*, sounding out the word in my mind, and searching for the letters that matched the sound: *k...n... d....* When I said the letters together out loud, they sounded like *kandy*.

The laughter from the other students let me know that I hadn't even come close. This would have been bad in early grade school, but I was in eighth grade! I sat in my seat, flushed with embarrassment, acting as if I'd blown it off on purpose. The more this happened, the more I could feel the other kids pulling away. I was becoming more and more isolated.

Sixth grade had marked the end of my personal tutoring, so I was no longer being pulled out of class. I was now exposed to all the material that the others were learning. And I was exposed in front of the class for not knowing the most basic things that they'd all learned years before. *And it was a remedial class!* It was painful and humiliating. Now, every day at school was more frightening and anxiety provoking than any danger I'd encountered in Chicago — getting lost on the trains, getting searched by police, and even getting mugged by Blackstone Rangers. I was separated again, exiled on Mars and threatened by hostile aliens.

Most kids and adults viewed the remedial classes as a warehouse for the "problem kids" who couldn't fit in or function in a normal class. Many of them truly *were* the worst kids — bullies, punks, and thieves. They were often psychologically disturbed and emotionally damaged, not just unable to function academically but socially, too. I looked at some of these kids and saw eventual prison or early death. Yet, as messed up as many of these kids were, they were all way ahead of me academically. I wasn't even close to their level.

I had severe learning disabilities, not severe psychological or emotional problems. I knew I wasn't like them, yet the school system now seemed to see no distinction between them and me. I'd been placed on the same track with them. I feared that I might end up just like them, or worse. And that was unacceptable to me. I fought against it every way I could, and in this class of bullies and troubled kids that meant physical fights as well.

At first I tried reaching out to some of them, even the meanest and worst among them. A few became my friends, but to those who interpreted my overtures of friendship as weakness, I became an object of ridicule. First they gave me a hard time. Then they started to pick on me. And when I put a stop to that by fighting back, they began to ignore me. I began to feel angry and mean myself. Even there I was the alien, the outsider, the misfit.

Eventually I came up with a personal code: I'd be nice to the nice kids, a son of a bitch to the bullies, and a protector of the picked on. I'd developed my own moral code. Never did I steal or purposely do harm to others. I appointed myself class sheriff. My skill and fury in fighting, my willingness to escalate the level of violence, and my lack of fear came in handy. More than once I made a bully whom I'd beaten apologize to his victim as I stood quietly a few feet away. I hoped their shame would stop them. It didn't always.

I never picked fights out of meanness; I only fought to stop a bully in progress. I got along with most of the kids most of the time. Yet students and teachers noticed that I got into fights with the troublemakers. That fueled the perception of me as a troublemaker, too. And that perception began to grow.

The Trip

*M*y mother was always taking me to the newest cutting-edge specialist for testing and to try out the newest theory or program. When I was twelve, I began to experience episodes I didn't understand but knew were part of what one specialist had diagnosed as a "neurosensory processing disorder." Almost daily I instinctively shut down or withdrew internally. I experienced a kind of tunnel vision, with a dulling of tactile, visual, and audio perception. When it was very severe, the shutting down occurred with a *chuh-chunk* feeling or sound.

In the seventh grade the episodes worsened. A few times I shut myself in my room and didn't come out for two or three days. But near the end of that difficult year, grace entered my life. As I was riding my bike one day, I saw a co-op friend named Jane standing in her front yard and talking with a girl I'd never seen before. Jane was black, and the other girl was white. This would have been an unusual sight in most neighborhoods, but not in our co-op.

I stopped to say hi to Jane, and to meet her friend, Janet. Janet immediately impressed me. She was beautiful, with long, vibrant red hair and a radiant smile. The three of us talked for several minutes, and then I continued on my way. The next day Jane told me that Janet liked me, and offered me Janet's phone number. I called Janet, and we had a long conversation. Thus began a close friendship that would become my first real relationship.

I couldn't understand why Janet was interested in me. She was a popular girl with a lot of friends. She was smart, beautiful, and confident, and could have had any guy she wanted. She was also two years older and three grades ahead of me. She attended high school.

Janet was involved in the theater department at her school. She helped build and paint the sets for the school plays. As our friendship grew, I started helping her prepare the sets for the shows. That's how I began hanging out with her crowd. Janet's world was very different from mine. Her friends, mostly jocks and students involved in the school theater, came from families ranging from conservative to reactionary to racist. The theater kids tended to be good students with school spirit who didn't drink or get in trouble. The jocks drank, fought, and got into some trouble.

Janet, however, wasn't conventional. She hungered for something deeper than the conservative world of her parents, and I was a symbol of that new world. I was a nice kid with long hair from an antiwar liberal family living in an interracial community. Janet liked me for who I was. I was a good talker and a good listener. We could talk about everything — school, music, politics, sex, our feelings and problems, our hopes and fears. She said that I made her feel comfortable and that she could tell me anything. She said I really understood her and she always felt good being around me.

I felt safe enough with Janet to tell her everything about myself, knowing she would understand and keep it confidential.

She always listened without judgment. She seemed to understand my inner conflicts, and she never felt the need to give me advice or answers, which I appreciated. I told her about my learning disabilities, my inability to read, and my conflict with Emerson, which had by now mostly subsided. I shared my fears about my future, and even about my suicide option. But there was something I didn't tell her, something that I couldn't verbalize anyway. I wanted the intimacy of a wife and family in my future more than anything, but if I wasn't going to be able to provide for them, then I could never respect myself—and if I couldn't respect myself, then I couldn't live with myself.

I'd only shared my secret plan about suicide with two kids in my school, after I heard them talking about wanting to commit suicide one day. I quickly realized that telling them was a mistake. They saw suicide as a cool idea. I didn't get how feeling doomed to an unhappy life, and planning to die, was cool. I'd have given anything to be normal, to have a life that worked and to have hope for a decent future.

My suicide plan made Janet sad. She really cared about me. From time to time she checked in with me and asked how I was doing, but mostly we talked about her life and I listened, cared, and offered suggestions. Talking to others about their struggles distracted me from my own troubles, and helped me feel less isolated.

Janet's extremely conservative father was intolerant of her seeing a longhaired kid with learning disabilities who lived in the liberal, racially mixed co-op. He would ground her for weeks at a time for seeing me.

Deep down I worried that our relationship wouldn't last, that our worlds were so different we would eventually separate and go in different directions. Yet I was okay with whatever happened, since I believed I wouldn't live very long anyway. My suicide plan gave me a kind of detachment in relationships, and an indifference to common concerns that occupied most other kids. It also gave me a sense of freedom, especially with my friends. It allowed me to open up emotionally, to be present and loving in ways that most of my peers seemed to avoid. It also caused problems.

One evening after dinner, my mother told me that she'd heard I was planning to commit suicide. To make things worse for both of us, she'd heard it from my school principal. The two students I had foolishly discussed suicide with had told our social studies teacher about their plan to commit suicide, and in that conversation they told the teacher I was also planning to kill myself.

This wasn't completely unexpected news to my mother, though the source of it came as a shock. My parents knew what a struggle my life had always been, and they'd seen signs of it worsening in the previous year. I'd told my mother more than once that I didn't want to be alive and that I blamed her and Dad for bringing me into the world. When I realized how much this hurt her, I'd stopped saying it.

Up to that point she didn't know I might be seriously planning to kill myself. When she asked me, I confessed that I'd been thinking about it a lot. I didn't tell her about the mercury I'd stashed away. I told her how much pressure I felt at school, how depressed I was about not being able to learn like the other kids, and how much I hated the remedial class. I talked about my insomnia, and how bleak my future looked. After that, nearly every night at dinner she anxiously asked me how I was doing.

I knew my parents loved me. We had always been closer than most teenagers and parents. They'd tried to give me more freedom, always respecting my privacy and never pressing me for information. My mother had continued to tell me that she loved me; now she told me she would do anything she could for me and would make sure I got whatever help I needed. But she couldn't explain to me how I was ever going to have a future worth living. She took me to see my old psychiatrist and also another therapist, but nothing these experts said deflected my drift toward suicide.

When word of my suicide plans got around school and the co-op, some of the adults tried to help. Mostly they asked me questions that seemed pointless, and said things that didn't help, such as "You don't even know what life is yet" and "You're too young to know what you're doing" and, even worse, "Childhood is the best time of life!" If that were true, I *really* didn't have much to look forward to. It only made suicide seem that much more appealing.

My social studies teacher was genuinely concerned about me and often asked me how I was doing. Several times she suggested I talk to a priest she knew in a church near the school. Feeling desperate, and partly to please her, I finally accepted her offer.

The teacher spoke to the priest about me in advance, and scheduled an appointment for me to see him after school one day. I'd already talked to many psychiatrists, psychologists, doctors, and various other experts; I didn't expect anything different to come from a conversation with a priest.

As soon as I entered the church, my perspective changed. I gazed around at the brilliantly colored stained-glass windows that portrayed scenes from the Bible. Overhead was a large dome and a giant arched ceiling. The atmosphere was eerie, with a palpable presence — as if ghosts or spirits inhabited the place. It stirred a flood of unexpected feelings in me. There was something powerful here that I didn't understand.

I had no formal religious upbringing, and I was uncomfortable with religious formalities. My mother was born into Christianity and didn't go to church, and my father, who was Jewish, didn't go to temple. No religion was practiced or promoted in my home. My only exposure to formal religion was a few scattered visits to churches and synagogues when I was much younger.

I didn't know where to look for the priest, so I just stood there waiting, absorbed in the atmosphere. A couple of minutes passed, and then I heard a voice say, "David, is that you?"

I whirled around to see a tall man dressed in black standing behind me. He had wavy black hair and wore a white collar. The white collar caught my gaze first, and then my eyes fastened on his face. It was a tough face to read: thin, serious but pleasant, and without much expression. He was younger than I'd thought he'd be. I nodded, indicating that I was David.

"Come with me," he said.

I followed him into a small office at the back of the church. We sat down in comfortable chairs, facing each other a few feet apart. He started with basic chitchat. I barely responded. I wasn't good at small talk; it made me uncomfortable and seemed meaningless to me. Then he asked why I'd come.

"My teacher told me to come," I said.

"What's going on? Is there anything I might be able to help you with?" he asked.

I was starting to feel really uncomfortable, as if I were wasting my time. Then it occurred to me that I didn't want to be there any longer than I had to, so I might as well get right to it.

"I don't want to live in my life the way it is," I began. "I have no control over anything in it. Everything seems unfair and pointless, like it's all about winning meaningless games or survival of the fittest. I don't have the skills to succeed or to survive."

I went on to tell him that I thought the world was messed up — the Vietnam War, the nuclear threat, and superficial self-motivated people running everything. It seemed to me that being a good person was a luxury for people who fit in, and that some of the so-called bad people were just good people caught in a bad situation. I told him that I was unwilling to live without self-respect. I was unwilling to be, as I saw it, one of the desperate who had to fight over the scraps left behind by the more fortunate, being judged by people who didn't know anything about desperation — as if they would do something different if they were truly desperate — as if being judgmental could keep them safe. It was easier to judge than to think.

"I don't want to be part of it," I told him. "How come when I can see through all the bullshit, I'm the stupid one? I've had to fight my whole life, but I keep falling farther behind. I don't think I have what it takes to get ahead. My brother does. He's all about himself and what he can get for himself. When I was little, I used to think I'd rather be dead than become like him. I'm tired. I'm past tired. If I have to keep fighting just to survive, then it isn't worth it. I'd rather be dead."

He listened attentively until I was finished. Then he sat quietly for a minute, looking thoughtful. Finally he started talking.

He told me I was struggling on two parallel paths in search of happiness and meaning. One was an external path in the world involving things like learning to read, becoming more functional, having relationships, finding an occupation, and being of service to the world. He said he could see my dilemma and didn't know if a practical path would ever work out for me. That path wasn't his specialty. I felt a sense of trust hearing this. I saw he really wanted to help me. I could see he was sincere.

I'd learned that people don't understand your situation, your peculiar angst, by explaining it to them. People only understand your suffering through their own lives and their own experience. I can tell when other people know suffering and have let it touch them because they are not quick to judge, and this was very important to me. This priest seemed to understand suffering in a real way. He clearly understood me. So I hoped he would have a real answer, even if it was that there's no answer.

His specialty, he told me, was the second path. This path was more important — the only path to true happiness — and it was inside of me. He called it an "existential search." He said that he'd never had to talk to someone my age about this path before. He told me it was God's gift of pain and struggle that forced someone to look beneath the surface of life, and that many people never have to ask themselves these deeper questions. He said the answers to existential questions were personal and spiritual. It was his job to help people find these answers, but ultimately it would be up to me.

Then he summarized what I'd told him. He put it in a nutshell, in a way that clarified for me my own thoughts and feelings about myself and about my predicament. So far his words made more sense to me than anything the therapists and psychologists had told me. What he was saying was hitting the mark. God's gift of pain and struggle, the existential search, the only path to true happiness — he was on to something.

I sat up straight and asked, "What's the answer? How do I find it?"

He looked at me for a moment, and said, "It's both simple

and hard. You must realize that you're fundamentally a sinner, and you must accept Jesus Christ as your savior."

My heart sank when I heard that. I thought, *You can't be serious.* "What do you mean I'm fundamentally a sinner?" I asked.

"We're all sinners," he said, "and we must believe in Jesus, who offers salvation."

It sounded too simple. I wished it were that simple and that I could believe it, but I couldn't. Maybe I was missing something. I still wanted to understand what he meant. Trying to be respectful, I asked him, "So what do I do? How do I believe in something that I don't believe in?"

"Only those who believe in Jesus can be saved. Pray for God's grace and forgiveness. Let's pray. I'll pray with you."

He leaned forward in his chair, put his hands together, closed his eyes, and began to pray in a low, soft voice. It was hard for me to follow him. My mind was racing: *Is believing in Jesus really the answer? How can I believe in something that doesn't seem true or make any sense to me? Can something I don't believe in, that doesn't make sense to me, actually be the solution to my problems?*

I believed that Jesus was a transcendent being, but I also knew that people did horrible things in the name of Jesus. And according to this priest, Christians would be saved, while good, kind, honest people — Jews, Buddhists, and anyone else who didn't believe in Jesus — would be damned to hell. It didn't make sense. Wasn't the kind of person I was, and what was in my heart, more important than whatever I believed about Jesus? I couldn't believe in the solution this priest was offering me — that the answer to all my problems was simply to ask for forgiveness and believe in Jesus. I believed he was sincere, but I wondered if he had just told me something he thought would give me hope. Maybe he didn't really have an answer at all.

The priest finished his prayer, and it was over. Nothing had changed that I could feel. I thanked him, got up, and walked out of the room the same person I was when I walked in. The same person with the same problems. In the following days I thought a lot about what he'd said. So many of his words seemed right to me, but I still couldn't believe that God would damn to hell everyone who didn't believe in Jesus. The world was messed up enough without believing that. I didn't think people were fundamentally bad or evil or deserved to go to hell. It seemed that we were all just trying to live and survive in any way we could. Somehow all the insanity of the world came out of that.

Of all the people I spoke to, Janet gave me the best advice. One day, after I'd been discussing the possibility of suicide, she said, "Promise me you won't decide while you're unhappy. You can't do something like this when you're unhappy." This made sense to me. I decided to give her idea every chance, and agreed not to kill myself when I was feeling depressed or hopeless.

But nothing changed. The daily pressures and stresses of school, of chronic insomnia, of failure and humiliation, of living in a world of indifference, cruelty, and abuse, of feeling defective, invisible, and stupid, of being an outsider — it all made me feel increasingly pessimistic and depressed. I felt myself slipping deeper into myself, and disconnecting further from life. My parents watched me anxiously.

— ⚉ —

Martin Luther King Jr. had been killed the year before my conversation with the priest, on April 4, 1968. I admired King's strength in being a pacifist, but I also remembered something he once said: "He who passively accepts evil is as much involved as he who helps to perpetrate it."

Not long after my conversation with the priest, a series of incidents occurred in school that changed things for me. It started when I walked into the boys' bathroom and found a punk from my remedial class pushing a smaller kid up against the wall. He was saying, "Eat it or I'll smash your face in!"

The smaller kid, cowering in front of the punk, began eating a stick of chalk. In that moment I felt rage rising within me, toward everyone, toward the whole rotten system I felt trapped in. I'd been bullied by Emerson and others in the past. I'd been ignored and ridiculed for years. I'd watched kids and adults do mean things to each other for no reason, or sometimes even for sport. Maybe there was something fundamentally wrong with people, with human nature. If there was, I couldn't do anything to change it, but I could make this punk pay right now for what he was doing.

I went right over and shoved him hard. He lost his balance and crashed into the steam heater. His head bleeding, he took off running. But I wasn't finished; I needed to teach the other kid a lesson as well. I glared at him with a look that was mixed with feelings of fear for his safety and contempt for his lack of backbone.

"Are you so scared of getting hit that you'll eat chalk?" I asked him. "Why don't you get pissed off and hit him back? Why don't you stand up for yourself?" Then I said, "Is this really so bad?" and gave him a hard slap upside his head. In that moment, it seemed to me that the kids who get bullied, who don't at least try to fight back, were part of the problem. At least fighting back gave you dignity. Even if you lost and got hurt, at least you had your pride, and it didn't eat you up with regret later on. Nobody should eat chalk. From my experience it was the passivity that haunted you later; it was debilitating and shaming.

Later that day as I walked down the hall between classes, I saw the punk I'd shoved against the heater in the bathroom. As we passed each other, he struck me in the ribs with his books, knocking the wind out of me. I wanted to hit him, but I couldn't breathe. I tried to grab his collar, but the pain was so intense I had to let him go. I bent over, gasping, and put my hands on my thighs. I didn't know until later that he had a piece of wood from shop class stuck in his books, and it had broken three of my ribs.

During my next class the principal called me into his office. As soon as I walked in, I could tell he was angry. He'd heard about the bullying incident in the bathroom. The kid I'd protected and then slapped must have told him about it. Due to the excruciating pain in my ribs, I was having trouble breathing and couldn't stand up straight. He thought I was slouching disrespectfully. At one point he got so mad that he started yelling in my face and poking me in the chest with his finger, just above my injured ribs. Instinctively I shoved him back. It was a defensive reflex, but it made him furious. He came rushing at me, and I panicked. I punched him in the face, which shocked him and scared me. He told me I was kicked out of school for two weeks. But I didn't care anymore. I'd had enough.

Two weeks later, the day before I returned to school, I went to a gathering at a co-op house. For some of the older, more socially aware kids in the surrounding area, the co-op had become a refuge from racism and intolerance. I'd been hanging out with this expanded crowd. Most of them were a few years older than I was. We sat around and played music and talked about the social and political issues of the day and our struggles in life. It was all very personal. Someone had some weed that night, and we smoked several joints. Drugs were just starting to creep into our scene at that time, but none of us were regular users. I'd smoked weed for the first time at Circle Pines camp when I was twelve. I didn't feel stoned then, just happier than usual. I concluded at the time that weed could help me be happy. I didn't try it again until I was fourteen, but now, since I'd smoked weed a few times already, I had a certain status in the group. I felt a quiet pride in my chest at being accepted into a group of older kids that I'd always admired.

The high that I experienced that night was different than I'd felt previously. I felt waves of euphoria washing over me. I felt incredibly happy, for no apparent reason. I hadn't felt this happy in a very long time. All evening I was smiling and laughing joyously.

I got home late, still feeling fantastic. Everyone in the house had already gone to bed. At some point I went into the bathroom and looked into the mirror. My face looked pasty and a little bit weird. Yet I looked happy! As I looked at myself in the mirror, I recalled my promise to Janet not to make a decision about suicide from an unhappy place. It occurred to me that I might never feel this happy again, that this might be the best place to decide if I really wanted to live or die. So I looked at my reflection, into my own eyes, and asked myself, "Do you still want to commit suicide?"

I thought about it for a moment, and I realized that I really did want out of here. I didn't want to live my shitty life. I didn't want to return to the hell that school had become for me. Although I didn't want to go through the ordeal of dying, it seemed better than the future I saw for myself. It would be so much easier to end it now, to disappear and be done with it once and for all. Just thinking about it brought a profound sense of relief, a peace of mind. So I answered myself in the mirror, "Shit, yeah."

I meant it. I felt an assuredness, a confidence in my decision. I wasn't being reactive. I wasn't feeling sadness or self-pity. I wasn't trying to hurt anyone. It just felt right. I was tired of the struggle, and my future looked hopeless. I had waited seven years; now I was ready to go. Janet was right. I was glad I'd waited for this moment. It was time. Everything had fallen into place. Strangely, one of the happiest moments of my life was the moment that I chose to end it.

I went back to my room, looking forward to my death. I wasn't looking forward to what I had to *do* in order to die, however. I went to the central air intake duct next to my room and reached into the inside corner. That's where I kept the glass tube of mercury. I had long ago moved it from my sock drawer, to a series of hiding places.

Over the years I'd had a recurring fear that my parents would find the mercury and take it away from me. This thought always triggered anxiety in me. I'd think, *Maybe I should take it right away?* Then I'd take it from its hiding place and swirl it around in the tube, just to look at it and make sure it was still there. I had to remind myself that I had a plan, and make it real again. Each time I held the tube of mercury, I felt a sobering chill; I was holding my death in my own hands. It made me feel alive, and somehow powerful. I had my own superpower — just like Superman.

Before I took the mercury, I needed the final ingredient: Valium. I walked softly across the house to the bathroom and to my parents' medicine cabinet. There was a cardboard container stacked with rows of small drawers; each drawer was labeled in pencil. I scanned the rows of drawers for the one that started with the letter *V.* There weren't any! For a moment I thought that I might have to do it without the Valium. Then I looked at some bottles off to the side and studied the labels carefully. I found one that started with the letters *V...a ...l....* I had to sound it out in my head a few times. This had to be it. I opened the bottle and poured all but a few of the tablets into my hand. There must have been forty or fifty, probably enough to kill me, but, if not, at least enough to put me out so that I wouldn't feel the pain from the mercury poisoning.

I snuck back to my room and closed the door. As I held the tube of mercury, I felt again the sense of power and a thrill of anticipation. At long last, the moment had come. This was the most important, the most real, thing I'd ever do. I removed the rubber stopper and poured some of the mercury into my cupped hand. I gently rolled the heavy, quivering silver liquid from side to side. I couldn't take my eyes off it. It was cold and heavy as lead. I knew just holding it in my hand could make me sick. That didn't matter now. Holding my guaranteed death in the palm of my hand, I felt again the sense of power and control I'd felt when I first made the decision to kill myself seven years before.

Carefully, I put the mercury back into the glass tube and swirled it around in the bottom. It was alive. It was my friend. Its promise to me was godlike. Once I swallowed it, everything would change. My problems would be over. I would leave the Earth. All I needed now was the courage to act.

Before committing the act, I had to think it through one last time. I had to be certain in what I did. My actions would have real consequences. I wanted to make sure that I understood all the implications, that this was what I really wanted to do. I didn't want to act now and then in the next moment be full of regrets — when it was too late.

I paused to reflect for several moments. Finally I was sure. I was ready. First I swallowed a handful of Valium with water. I waited a few minutes; then I picked up the test tube, swirling the mercury one more time. I felt a momentary sadness over the imminent loss of my family and friends. But the sense of anticipation, knowing I was about to be liberated from my life, quickly returned.

I lifted the tube to my mouth, tipped it back, and emptied it. I felt a momentary shock as the cold, liquid metal rolled across my tongue and slipped down my throat as if of its own volition, as if it knew where it wanted to go and was fulfilling its predestined purpose. I'd always imagined holding it in my mouth and savoring it before swallowing, but there was no need to swallow, no effort required; gravity did the trick. I felt the cool, heavy mercury slide all the way down to the bottom of my stomach. I swayed from side to side and it rolled around in my belly, the way it had in the test tube.

It was done. I looked around my bedroom for what I thought would be the last time — at the desk lamp and the bookshelves, at my stereo and the records I loved. Then, to make it all real, I said out loud to myself, "I'm dead. It's just a matter of time." I was already feeling woozy from the effects of the Valium. I hoped I'd timed this right. I braced for the possibly violent, painful death to come.

Man, I thought. *What a fucking trip!*

Devil Eyes

*F*riday, April 6, 1969.

I'm lying on my back. I'm weak, and my body feels unbelievably heavy. I smell antiseptic odors and hear the sounds of people bustling about, their indistinguishable mumblings, the constant beeping of electronic machines, and other sounds I can't make out.

I can't open my eyes; my eyelids feel heavier than lead. I can't lift my head. I feel something like a seat belt strapped across my forehead. My wrists are also strapped down at my sides. I feel another strap across my chest. My ankles are strapped down, too. I barely manage to open my eyes. The light is harsh, and my vision is blurry. A pattern of small holes on a white surface comes into focus. I'm looking at the white ceiling tiles above me, and fluorescent lights.

I strain my neck, force my shoulders into the bed, and manage to raise my head just enough to make out my surroundings. I'm in a small curtained enclosure. Through the opening I see a parade of nurses moving around, scurrying back and forth. A couple of them are busy behind a tall desk in the area directly in front of me. I try to take it all in before my head falls back to the bed. I'm achy and exhausted; my mind's in a fog. I don't know where I am or how I got here. I lie still, trying to make sense of what's going on. Then it hits me.

I'm in a hospital. Oh shit! I'm alive. It didn't work. What happened?

I experience a profound sinking feeling. Now I have to go back to my life and deal with the same crap, the same people, every minute of every day. I struggle to get up again. *Why am I strapped down?* I try pulling on one strap at a time, to see how strong they are. First I try to bend one leg, then the other, then my arms, then my chest, then my head again. Each time I pull or push I feel sharp pains around the straps. Now I push through the pain against my wrist straps with all the strength I have, trying to force myself into a sitting position. As I strain to get free, I feel an intense pressure in my eyes, as if they're about to burst. Frustrated and desperate, I begin flailing in slow motion, pulling weakly on all the straps in turn.

A nurse arrives at my bedside. She is tall, thin, black, forty-ish, with a fluffy Afro. Her face has a worn look but with a kind expression, as if she's seen tough times but has managed not to become jaded or judgmental. I like her immediately. She puts her hand gently on my chest to reassure me.

"It's okay, honey; just lie there," she says. "You should feel more like yourself in a little while, once the Valium you took finally wears off. You're going to be okay. Do you understand?"

I nod slowly, as much as the head restraint will allow.

"How old are you, hon?"

"Fourteen," I mumble hoarsely.

"Do you know what city we're in?"

I think about it for a second. "Chicago?"

"That's right. You're in the ICU at Cook County Hospital. They brought you in late last night. Are you ready to have a couple of visitors?" I close my eyes without responding. "Your mother will be right back. She's very worried about you. She went to pick up a change of clothes for you." I shrug my shoulders. "There's also a beautiful redheaded girl here to see you." She emphasizes the word *beautiful,* maybe to see if this will help cheer me up. "She says she's your girlfriend. She's under visiting age and not in your immediate family, but she seems to really care about you. She begged us to let her visit you. If you'd like, we can make an exception in her case."

I look up at her and pull against the wrist straps, a request for her to remove them. I wince as I feel the hot sting of wrist burns. I'm beginning to feel pain all over my body, in my muscles, and even in my bones. I wonder if it's mercury damage. *How can I still be alive?*

"Okay," she says. "But I need you to promise that if I take off your restraints, you won't cause me any problems." I nod, but her expression hardens, and she speaks in a stern voice. "Are you sure? You put up quite a fight earlier in the ambulance. You pulled out one of your ankle restraints, and you pulled out of your wrist restraints twice and tore out the IV lines and the tubes they were using to pump your stomach. You also injured one of the officers who was with you. He had to go to the emergency room. I *really* need you to promise me. You need to say it."

"I promise," I say. It hurts to talk. My throat is raw and sore, and my voice sounds gravelly.

She pauses for a moment; then her face relaxes and her voice returns to a more nurturing tone. "All right. I just wanted to make sure." She unbuckles the strap across my forehead, then the straps holding down my ankles. Next she removes the strap across my chest. She pauses, still a little uncertain, then says, "You be good now, okay?" I nod, and she removes the straps holding down my wrists. "Okay, there you go."

What a relief to have those straps off! I start to move my arms and legs. My whole body feels sore and stiff. As I rub my wrist, the nurse pours me a small cup of water from a pitcher on a small table next to my bed and hands it to me. I drink it all. The cool water temporarily soothes my throat.

"How long am I going to be here?"

"We're not sure. I'll get someone to change your sheets. Your mother should be back any minute."

Two nurses in light blue pinstriped uniforms come in to change the sheets, damp from my wet clothes after I pulled out the IV. When I start to get up, the first of the two nurses, who looks about nineteen and is kind of cute, smiles and says, "Stay there. Don't get up; you're still too groggy."

Usually I'd have enjoyed the attention, but I figure her smile is a smile of pity. I'm embarrassed to have a pretty girl close to my age see me like this. I'm finally coming out of the fog. The nurses finish changing the sheets. As they turn to leave, the second nurse says, "Your mother should be back any minute. She's been here for hours."

But I'm not ready to see her. How could I be ready? Last night I thought I'd never have to face her, or anybody else, ever again. I know I've hurt her. There's nothing I can say or do to take away her pain. This is going to be hard. However bad things were before, I've made a worse mess of them now. I feel trapped and more hopeless than ever. Everything I do just makes things worse.

Now my mother walks into the room in a hurry. She looks

exhausted, but there's no emotion on her face. Her clothes look rumpled. She's carrying something in a paper bag. She hands it to the nurse, then walks over and starts to stuff her knitting into her knitting bag. She must have been sitting there, knitting, for hours while she waited for me to wake up. She avoids looking at me, quickly scanning the room with a very cool expression. Things are even worse than I thought. I have a terrible feeling that she wants nothing to do with me. She purses her lips and says, in a dull monotone, "How are you doing, David?"

I don't know what to say, so I say nothing. She looks at me for a moment, but I avoid her gaze.

"David, I asked you a question."

"I don't know," I reply. It occurs to me that she's the staff psychologist for my school district. This has to be a professional blow for her as well as a personal one.

I stare down at the bed sheets, feeling like shit. I don't want to deal with this right now. I can't look at her. I wonder if I'll ever want to make eye contact with her again. I just want this to end. She finishes packing her bag and starts to leave.

"Janet is here to see you," she says. "I'll tell her you can see her now."

She turns and leaves through the curtains, without our having made any eye contact. I'm curious to know what's in the bag. The friendly nurse walks in, and I ask her.

"A change of clothes," she says.

That's right; the other nurse already told me. I'm still groggy. I close my eyes and wonder how this all went so horribly wrong. After years of planning, how did I botch this up? Now I'm alive, and things are worse than ever. My one big chance, and I blew it.

I know I can't try again. I couldn't do that to my mother, not again. I didn't manage to kill myself, but I've killed something in her. Nothing will ever be the same between us. I didn't mean to hurt her; I just wanted to stop the pain. I feel betrayed and abandoned by the mercury, my most trusted friend. All these years I'd depended on it. It had been with me for most of my life. It was a part of me. Knowing it was there made life easier to bear. Then, at the crucial moment, it let me down. I feel more alone than ever before.

Janet walks into the room, looking beautiful as always. Neither one of us knows what to say. She gives me a big smile, and blushes a little. I can tell she's feeling self-conscious and is covering up.

"Hi, David," she says.

"Hi, Janet. You look great."

She reaches my bedside and catches a better look at me. Her smile fades. Now she looks scared.

"Your eyes — they look creepy. I mean, *really* creepy."

"What do you mean?"

"The whites of your eyes are totally red. They look like they're bleeding."

"Bleeding?"

"They're bloody. Do they hurt?" She leans down for a closer look. I almost think she's going to try to touch one of them. "They make you look evil. Like the devil."

She pulls away from me with a funny look. Now I want a mirror so I can see what I look like. *I look like the devil?* Janet is a devout Christian. I wonder if my suicide attempt and my devil eyes will change the way she feels about me.

"They don't feel different," I say.

"Really?"

"Yeah, I'm fine. I'm sorry you had to be involved. Thanks for coming. It's good to see you."

"They're only letting me see you for a minute."

"I know."

"What's going to happen now?"

"I don't know. I had no idea it would go like this. I thought I'd be gone."

"Well, you know, I'm glad you're here." She sounds concerned. "I mean…you know how I feel about this." She bends down, kisses me gently on the lips, and says, "I love you."

"Me, too," I reply lamely.

"I'd better go."

She walks to the exit and turns to give me a little wave; then she's gone.

As soon as she's out of sight I call to a passing nurse for a mirror. She brings me one, and I take a good look at my eyes. There's no white left in them; they're completely red. Janet was right. I do look scary. What was going to happen now? Everyone in my family will probably react differently. Mom is already distancing herself from me emotionally. I hope I haven't messed things up too bad with Dad. Neil is only ten. This must be hitting him hard. I don't think he'll be able to understand something like this, and I can't explain it to him. I'll have to try and make it up to him somehow. Emerson will probably have some goddamn opinion. Now Mom comes back and stands at the foot of my bed. She looks tired, but determined.

"David, you need to get dressed and get ready to go. I've got Neil with me. He's waiting alone in the car."

"I can just leave?"

"Yes, but we need to hurry."

She goes outside to wait. The Valium from last night has mostly worn off. There must have been a lot left in my system, even after they pumped my stomach. I'm a little wobbly, but I feel stronger now. I get up and walk a few steps next to the bed. The friendly nurse comes back and hands me the paper bag with my clothes. Then she asks in a whisper, "Why did you do it?"

It. I realize people don't want to say the word *suicide* to someone who's just attempted it. "You have a wonderful family, and a gorgeous girlfriend."

Her tone is almost chiding. I don't know what to tell her, so I just say, "I don't know."

It's complicated. There's no one reason. It's nobody's fault. My parents are wonderful people who did their best. All my life I've watched them agonize over how to help me; now everything is so difficult and complicated I can't untangle it. I can't fix it. I can't sort it out. Suicide seemed like such a simple solution.

Maybe I was born into the wrong family? Both my parents' families are well-educated overachievers: doctors, pharmacists, and lawyers. Our house is full of books. Every bit of wall space is lined with tall bookshelves — in the rooms, the halls, even the closets. There are even bookshelves in my room. Those books have both fascinated and tormented me all my life.

I take off my dirty clothes and put on the clean ones, then stuff my dirty T-shirt and jeans into the bag. I step through the curtains, where my mother is waiting.

"Okay," I say.

I follow her down the hallway to the elevators. She's walking fast. Outside the hospital, we slow down and walk to the car. Neil is waiting patiently in the front seat. He seems small and vulnerable. He just looks at me, bewildered, as I climb into the back. Then he turns his head to peek at me over the front seat. It's like he's trying to figure out if the brother he's always known and loved is still here. He can't take his eyes off of my eyes. I must look like I've come back from the dead.

"Are they okay?" he asks.

"I think so," I tell him.

"Your brother is okay," Mom says curtly. "During the struggle last night he broke blood vessels around the whites of his eyes. He'll look normal in a couple of weeks."

Mom has always talked to us like we're adults, but it's a little funny to hear her talk to Neil that way about this. On the drive, Neil never takes his eyes off me. Every so often he asks me a question, and each time Mom breaks in to answer, as if I'm not to talk to him directly. I stare at the back of my mother's head as she drives. Her shoulders are stiff. She looks like she's barely holding it together. I've permanently broken her trust. It never occurred to me that I might live and have to face her like this.

I stare out the window at the trees going by. My mind is full of questions I don't dare to ask: *Why aren't I dead? How did they find me?* My memories of last night after swallowing the mercury are hazy. I go over it in my mind, and flashes come to me. I remember lying down with the Valium coming on. I have vague images of police coming into my bedroom, and me flying into a rage. The last thing I recall was getting up from my bed and rushing at them, shouting, "What the fuck are you doing here? I'm going to kill you!"

I wanted them out of my room. They weren't supposed to be there. A week before, I'd taken the train into Chicago to attend a peace rally; when the police started clubbing the demonstrators, it turned into a riot. I got caught in the crowd and clubbed in the side of my head. When the police entered my room, it must have triggered all my rage.

The nurse said I put a cop in the emergency room. I hope he's okay. After all, he was trying to help me. But I can't ask my mom if he's okay. I can't ask her anything about last night — how she found me, why the mercury didn't work.... I'll probably find out later, one way or another.

Now she makes an unexpected turn onto the Dan Ryan Expressway. This isn't the way home.

"Where are we going?" I ask, a bit alarmed.

"I'm taking you to another hospital," she says matter-of-factly.

Her body is stiff, and her eyes are glued to the road. I bolt forward in the seat.

"What hospital?"

"Lake Forest."

My stomach sinks. Lake Forest is a mental hospital.

"Why are you taking me there?"

I try to keep my voice calm, to control the rising panic. Is she done with me? She'd warned me in second grade that I might end up here. Was this it? I can't blame her. I know her life would be so much easier without me. But I don't want to go.

"When someone has done what you've done, you have to be evaluated in a psychiatric hospital." Her voice is calm and flat; she's trying to be patient with me. "Besides, you injured a police officer last night. He said he wouldn't press charges if we had you committed for evaluation."

"For how long?"

"I'm not sure. This is a very good private hospital. I have a psychiatrist friend who has hospital privileges there, which means he can work with you as an inpatient. I'm working with him to get you out in two weeks, depending on how you do. Do you understand?"

"Not exactly." I slump back in the seat.

"Okay, the less trouble you are, the sooner you'll get out. So it's really up to you. If you have to be hospitalized for more than thirty days, our insurance may not cover the costs, which means you'll have to transfer to a public facility. I promise, none of us want that. I worked very hard to get you into this hospital, where I know someone. They'll be watching you closely. So, David, it's important that you…"

I tune her out, lost in my paranoid thoughts. *What if she isn't telling me everything? What if she's wrong about how long I'm going to be locked up? Who knows what will happen once I'm in. One slip, and I could be held there indefinitely. Maybe in a few years I'll be calling it home. I'd rather be dead.*

"What if I don't want to go there?" I ask.

"David, I'm not going to get into a fight with you if you refuse to go right now." She spoke fiercely, cutting to the point like cold steel. "But one way or another, you're going to end up in a hospital. You're very lucky I was able to get you a bed here; there's a waiting list. If you don't go in here now, under your own power, you'll be sent somewhere else later. You might end up somewhere much worse. This is an expensive private hospital. Your best chance is to go in here now if you want to get out anytime soon."

I can't detect any empathy in her voice or manner. None at all. She's never spoken to me like this before, or acted like she had to protect Neil from me. She's not just mad; it's more like she's written me off. It feels as if she's circling the wagons to protect the family, but I'm on the outside.

"Okay," I say.

I owe her at least that much. I've caused enough problems already. I think she still loves me, but I'm not sure she likes me anymore. Maybe I'm two different people to her now: the son she's always known and loved, and the boy sitting in the back seat who tried to kill her son. Right now, she's speaking to the killer.

My mother and I lost something then. Something we never got back after that.

The Mental Hospital

*m*om turned off the freeway. We drove through a housing development of new homes with newly mowed lawns and small trees in front. We passed several strip malls and eventually made a left turn into the hospital parking lot.

The structure looked like any nondescript two-story office building. I remembered seeing movies and TV shows where mental hospitals were usually old, Gothic-looking brick buildings with green lawns and sterile rooms, and hallways where insane patients sat catatonic, wandered about like aimless zombies, talked and gestured wildly to themselves or imaginary people, or erupted in random fits of violence. Men in white uniforms kept strict order and subdued unruly patients, tied them up in straitjackets, and carried them off to padded rooms, or immobilized them with powerful drugs and administered shock treatments, or, worse, lobotomies.

Man, I really fucked this whole thing up!

My mind was full of questions I dared not ask my mother: *What will happen now? In the next hour? The next day? The next week? How long will they keep me here? What kind of people will I meet? Will I have to return to my old life when I get out?*

What about school? What about clothes and toiletries?

My mother pulled into the emergency ambulance bay at the back entrance to the hospital. Before she'd even turned off the ignition, two large male orderlies in white uniforms appeared and stationed themselves on either side of our car. Both had crewcut hair and looked like soldiers. This wasn't a movie. My fears were fast becoming reality. A woman in regular-dress clothes stood in the entrance.

"Is that David?" she called out.

My mother didn't respond, didn't look up, didn't move at all. She just sat facing forward with her hands on the wheel and her head bowed. Then I realized she was crying silently. All the fight drained from my body.

"Is that David?" the woman called out again, a little louder.

Now the men made their move. One, a big guy with a small chin, stepped in to block the car door opposite from me, in case I decided to use it as an escape hatch. The other guy, slightly smaller, opened my door and stood in the gap, waiting for me to get out. They clearly had this choreographed with military precision. Neither spoke, yet their bearing and impassive faces issued a clear warning: Don't make trouble.

I got out, and in a flash the bigger man was around the car and I was standing in between them. They didn't need to lay a hand on me; I went peacefully. As we passed through the entrance to the hospital, a nurse joined the rear of our parade. I turned my head to look back at her and saw a metallic object in her right hand. It was a large old-fashioned stainless steel syringe with metal loops for finger grips — emergency backup in case I got out of control. I would see a lot more of that shiny syringe.

As they walked me through the building I tried to guess which room I might be put in, which window I might be looking out of. I wondered what kind of people would be on my ward. Were there any patients like me who couldn't read? How many locked doors would there be between my room and freedom? I wondered how many were doomed to spend their lives here, and how many had come for a temporary stay that became permanent.

As we approached a metal door with large hinges, the nurse stepped to the front, unlocked the door, and then opened it. Suddenly I didn't want to go in. When that door closed behind us, I'd be locked in. I tried to turn around and look back, but firm hands grabbed me high under each arm and lifted me off the floor. I squirmed and resisted, but all that moved were my legs. The two orderlies carried me inside, and I heard a loud *chuh-chunk* as the metal door closed and locked behind us. Then they lowered me to the ground and we continued walking through the seemingly endless hallways.

I was paying close attention to everything. The doors were painted a 1950s avocado green, and the linoleum floor was dark and worn. I paid attention to every turn in the hallways and every door, trying to memorize the path we were taking, noting specific details of how it would look going in the opposite direction. We continued down a hallway and went through another locked door. The nurse opened it with a key, then closed it behind us, and it locked automatically with the same disturbing *chuh-chunk* sound. Then we walked up a dim stairwell and went through another locked door. *Chuh-chunk.* Then down another hallway and through another locked door. *Chuh-chunk.* By now I'd given up trying to memorize the route. I'd never be able to remember my way out.

We arrived at a large main room with a nurse's station in the middle and two hallways extending off each end. Nurses moved

busily around, and patients milled randomly about. The two orderlies let go of my arms as we passed through the nurses' station, following the nurse with the syringe. We walked down one
of the hallways and finally arrived at my room. It was a surprisingly bright second-story room. But as I looked around I thought,
You fucking idiot. I hated myself; I'd failed in everything I ever
did. Now the biggest fuckup of my life has gotten me put in this
place — the last place in the world I'd ever wanted to be.

Two thick glass windows embedded with chicken wire faced
a parking lot and the suburban view beyond. Two single beds
rested against the wall in opposite corners. Following us into the
room was my roommate, a lanky guy about eighteen with long
blond hair. His name was Philip. He was strikingly handsome and
seemed completely normal to me. I wondered why he was here.

I was taken to the main common room, because we were not
allowed in the bedroom during waking hours unless we were
supervised. After finding a seat on a couch, I contemplated the
events of the last twenty-four hours. Finally I was able to relax
and accept my situation.

That night I lay awake for hours, unable to fall asleep. Something had changed in me. I had faced my death. I had acted to
end my own life. I had believed it was all over and accepted it.
I had crossed another line. I could feel it. I knew the difference
between life and death. I could choose to live or I could choose
to die. It was up to me. All I had to do was decide, and then act.

The fear of being hopelessly trapped, which had been with
me for years, was gone. I had a calm feeling of confidence.
But I still needed to get out of there. The fear of ending up in
a mental institution was still with me. Whatever I wanted to do
about my life, I couldn't do it from in here.

Instinctively, I began to think again about how I might kill myself when I got out. I began to plan my suicide in the far-off future. I picked the age of twenty-seven, thirteen years in the future. If I didn't get my life together by then, it was pretty much over anyway. That would give me time to separate from everyone close to me, so they wouldn't be as affected. I'd make it look like an accident, something like swerving off a cliff. But that was risky: I might survive the attempt and be crippled. Still, I had thirteen years to figure something out.

Having resolved the problem, at least theoretically, gave me a sense of relief and a feeling of control over my life again, but it also reminded me of just how badly I'd hurt the people I cared about. I returned to the question of whether my life even belonged to me. I wondered if I owed it to them to stay alive, even if I wanted to die. Would I have to live a life that I didn't want to live just to keep from hurting the people who love me? Was the purpose of my life to sacrifice myself by staying alive in a personal hell for their sake? Was my life even my own?

Lying there calmly, locked in a room at the end of a series of hallways, behind a series of bolted doors in a mental hospital, I began to wonder: *What is the purpose of my life? Of any life? Who am I? What am I? What in the hell is existence anyway?*

At that moment I realized I didn't know. And even though some people pretend to know, nobody knows. It's a mystery, a complete mystery. I began to feel a shift in my awareness. The fierce anger that had lived inside me for years just vanished. I felt a pleasant sensation of energy begin to radiate throughout my body. I had no idea who I was. I'd lost all control and, along with it, my desperate identification with my mind and its tortured thoughts. The constant chatter of my mind that I'd always thought of as "me" subsided, and I fell back into an awareness of a peaceful silence. My hopes and desires for the future had been based on ideas — thoughts — that seemed to promise my only hope for survival. These hopes had been a result of my fears. My biggest fear from the age of seven was that I'd be institutionalized. Now I'd realized my worst fear, yet I was left with a simple, grateful enjoyment of being, and a loving desire to serve. I had no hope for the future, and yet I felt a most unexpected sense of relief. Giving up hope wasn't a sad thing, or a loss of anything. It was a relief. Hope was a burden that kept me living in the future, struggling for control, fighting against situations beyond my control, trying to escape the painful sense of myself. But there was no escape until I gave up and let go.

A feeling of profound contentment and peace washed over me. I felt as if I was seeing things clearly for the first time in my life. Life suddenly seemed simple. I was still locked in the same room. I still had the same learning disabilities and the same human problems. I still had no skills to deal with my life and my future. The world was still the same crazy place where all the usual crap would continue. But now none of this bothered me. I no longer minded any of it. I was completely okay with things exactly as they were. I felt happy, free, contented. I felt as if I had come home. It occurred to me that I was in a mental hospital, and maybe I'd gone crazy, but even this thought didn't disturb my sense of peace. At last, I was able to fall asleep.

This experience was important to me. It was the first time in my life I felt truly happy — the first experience of ecstatic happiness that wasn't dependent on circumstance, or ideas of how I thought life could be worth living. Before this I'd had no idea there was this kind of happiness. For most of my life after this,

I searched for how to regain the ecstatic happiness I felt in that experience. This kind of happiness could make life worth living.

The next morning, Philip, my roommate, didn't get up with the wake-up call. When a nurse came in to find him still lying in bed, he threw a cup of water at her. To me, it seemed like an annoying but harmless prank. But the nurse ran out and returned moments later with the metal syringe and two large orderlies. They grabbed Philip and held him down as he struggled and screamed, "No! I don't want to go! No! I'm sorry!"

It was too late. The nurse shot him up with whatever was in the syringe, and the orderlies dragged him out of bed, out of the room, and down the hall. Philip's belongings remained in my room. I asked the orderly if he'd be back, and where they'd taken him. He said he didn't know when Philip would be back and told me he was in "isolation" now. Later I learned that this meant a padded room. I never saw Philip again. But now I had a private room.

— ⚙ —

I could barely make out the garbled message over the intercom, calling me to the nurses' station. Maybe I'd finally find out what was going on. I'd been here a week now, and I still hadn't met with the doctor, still hadn't been evaluated, and still hadn't been given any information about my situation. I'd had no communication from the outside world since my arrival, and no nurse or attendant I'd spoken to had any idea what was going to happen to me.

When I got to the station, the nurse told me to go into the room just off the common room and wait for the psychiatrist. It was a small room. Two chairs faced each other in the middle, and two bad paintings of flowers, probably done in art therapy by a patient, hung on the walls. I sat down in a straight-back chair with a cloth covering. I assumed that the plush, high-back chair was the doctor's.

Over the course of the week, the calm, clear awareness that had come over me the first night had slowly dissipated. But the fear and rage hadn't returned. My past and future started to have meaning for me again. My mood and state of mind were once again dependent on my circumstances — which didn't look good.

I knew the psychiatrist was going to ask me about my suicide attempt. I had to be very careful how I explained it to him, and I needed to assure him that I didn't plan any future attempts. I had to be 100 percent convincing rather than 100 percent honest. You couldn't be honest in a place like this, not if you hoped to get out.

A woman's long, shrill scream suddenly interrupted my thoughts. It sounded like she was in pain. I knew all the scream-ers in this ward, and this wasn't one of them. A few minutes later the psychiatrist, Dr. Lahe, came into the room. He introduced himself, shook my hand, and sat down opposite me in the other chair. Dr. Lahe was the person who'd helped my mother get me into the hospital. They'd been fellow students and friends back in medical school. He had a rough complexion, like a blue-collar worker, but a friendly face and smile. He wore a black suit with his jacket unbuttoned, and a white dress shirt with an open col-lar and no tie. His shirt wasn't completely tucked in all the way around. I liked him right away.

"Okay, David; I don't have much time, but I'd like to get a quick history."

"Who was screaming?" I asked him. He shrugged, indicat-ing he didn't know, then opened the file on his lap and started shuffling through the papers, which I assumed were about me.

"What do you want to know?" I asked.

"Well,"— he looked up at me —"have you ever seen a psychiatrist before?"

"Yeah. I saw one twice a week from the end of my first year of second grade until sixth grade."

"Do you know what for?" He pulled a sheet from my file.

"Sort of. They gave me an IQ test because I was flunking second grade. My mom said I got a really high score in abstract thinking. But I got a really low score in linear thinking. She didn't tell me how low. They said such a big variation in IQ was very rare, and I must have psychological problems."

Dr. Lahe jotted a few notes as I spoke.

"You seem to know a lot about this," he said. "Do you recall what the test involved?"

"I've had tests of all kinds since I can remember. I think those were tests with cards and blocks — the little red and white ones. I was supposed to duplicate the patterns they showed me on the cards." I was feeling more relaxed, but also a bit impatient. "When am I going to get out of here?"

"Well, that's the question, isn't it?" he responded. "That depends on how you do here in the hospital, and how forthright you are with me now."

I nodded. I figured I needed to tell him just enough to persuade him I was being honest, but not too much to get me into more trouble than I was already in.

"How am I doing so far?" I asked him.

"I don't know. You'd know better than me. How is it going?"

"It seems like things are going well. I feel okay. I haven't made any trouble. I just want to get out of here."

"Let's finish with your history." He opened his notebook

to a fresh page. "What led up to your suicide attempt?"

"My whole life." It sounded like an exaggeration, but it wasn't.

"Why don't you start with what led up to your being kicked out of school. Tell me whatever you think is important."

I told Dr. Lahe how seeing the punk in the bathroom making the kid eat chalk had filled me with rage, how the kid's fear and submissiveness had tipped me over the edge, and how I'd shoved the punk against the heater and slapped the kid upside his head. I told him how the punk had broken my ribs in the hall, how the principal had poked me there and it hurt so bad I couldn't breathe, and how I'd punched him and gotten kicked out of school for two weeks. Then I told Dr. Lahe some of the things I'd told the priest in the church — about my fears of never having a normal life or being able to take care of myself, about how the world seemed messed up and I couldn't change it, about how I was so tired and frustrated and that I didn't want to play its games.

I talked for several minutes. Dr. Lahe listened attentively and seemed to be interested in what I was saying. When I was finished, I looked at him to see if I was making sense, if he understood what I was saying. He reached down into his briefcase and pulled out a cardboard pack of small cigars. Then he looked at me thoughtfully, extracting a cellophane-wrapped cigar from the pack.

"So you think things are hopeless?" he asked.

"Yeah, for me. Don't you?"

A series of three shrill screams sounded again outside the room. It was the same woman shouting, "No! No! No!" Dr. Lahe seemed a little annoyed as he carefully unwrapped his cigar.

"It doesn't matter what I believe," he said.

Now it seemed to me that he was being rude. I felt irritated.

"If you were honest with yourself, you'd see how hopeless my life is," I said.

I immediately regretted my words. I might have gone too far. I didn't want to sound depressed or suicidal. I wanted to see if he could help me, but I didn't want to have to stay here for long.

Dr. Lahe lit the cigar, took a long drag, leaned back, and exhaled the smoke toward the ceiling in a fast-moving stream that gathered into a large cloud above my head. Then he looked at me expectantly, waiting for me to continue. He held up his cigar and asked, "Is this a problem?"

I shrugged. "I guess not." It wasn't true—I hated tobacco smoke. My face must have given me away.

"Do you smoke?" he asked.

"No."

"Your brother told your mother you smoke marijuana." I shrugged again. "So you just don't smoke cigarettes?"

"Never even tried one. The smell of them makes me sick. I've never tried coffee either. And I don't like alcohol." He tipped his head to the side as if he was thinking, and waited for me to continue. "When I go back to school it's going to be worse than ever," I said. Dr. Lahe silently puffed on his cigar, watching me, listening with interest. "Everyone else gets to have a normal life," I continued.

"So how does that make you feel?"

"I feel like I'm being punished. Sometimes I wish I was too stupid to understand my situation."

"Your mother told me you have learning disabilities— difficulty in reading, things like that. Do you think that means you can't have a normal life?"

"It has so far," I said. Suddenly I felt a lump in my throat and tears welling up in my eyes. I didn't want to do that here.

"What is your worst fear?" he asked.

"That I'll end up here, permanently. That's what my mom told me when I was seven — when they still kept 'retarded' people in these places."

"Is that when you started thinking about suicide?"

"Yeah. That's when I got the mercury ready. Suicide's been in the back of my mind ever since. I still can't figure out why it didn't work. It's supposed to be poison, and it seemed like I took a lot."

"There are different kinds of mercury," Dr. Lahe said. "Liquid mercury is too dense to dissolve in the bloodstream. If they hadn't pumped your stomach, it would've passed right through you."

"Oh…"

All of those years of planning to kill myself, hiding the mercury in various places, and it wasn't even dangerous. I felt like an idiot.

"Do you think you'll ever try something like this again?"

"No fucking way," I lied. "I don't see any advantage to it. It just hurts the people I care about. I didn't realize what it would do to them."

As stupid as it sounded, it was actually the truth. He seemed to accept it.

"Well, David, our time's up," he said. "I have to see another patient now. We'll talk again soon."

"Sure."

I got up and headed for the door. On my way out I heard the lady scream again. The sound was coming from the other side of the door to the left of the common meeting room. I soon learned that it was the ward with the padded isolation rooms. That's where Philip was. That was the place no one wanted to go.

Is This It?

I sat on the couch in the recreation room with the other regulars. My mind was in chaos, and I was grateful for the company and the noise constantly blaring from the TV. The medication they made me take each day didn't seem to do much. I didn't know what they were giving me, and the staff wouldn't tell me. Meanwhile, the slow passing of time wore away the profound clarity and peace of mind I'd felt my first night.

I wished I could get high, but that wasn't an option. I wished they were giving me uppers or downers, but they weren't. I tried to trade my meds for some of the other patient's meds, but they apparently knew what it was I was taking and no one wanted any of it.

The worst part was being kept in the dark about what would happen to me and not knowing when, or if, I would ever get out. Except for the pills they gave me each day, and the brief visit with Dr. Lahe, I'd received no treatment of any kind. My experience was one of nonstop boredom, with rare moments of over-the-top excitement when someone acted out unexpectedly and got dragged away by the staff.

Other than Philip, whom I hadn't seen since the first day,

there were no other teens on my ward; it was mostly the zombie and shock-treatment types. But in art therapy class, which I went to for an hour or two every week, I did see two older teens from other wards. I initially tried to hang out with these two druggies, thinking they'd be more sane and cooler than the other patients. After all, we'd have something in common. I quickly discovered we had almost nothing in common. They had no social or political awareness, and no interest in meaningful conversation. The big thrill they shared in common was sniffing lighter fluid in the music room.

With nothing to do, I spent much of my time playing with a deck of cards. Teaching myself to shuffle was my only accomplishment. I found mindless shuffling to be soothing. Philip never returned. I assumed he was still in solitary confinement in the padded cell. At least I had a room all to myself. A few of the patients were fine to hang out with, but most of them really were too crazy for me to relate to. I knew I was screwed up, but I wasn't insane, at least not the way they were. It wasn't easy to tell those who were in to get clean and sober from drugs or alcohol, and those who were in because they were simply crazy. Some patients seemed perfectly sane for days at a time, then went suddenly and completely nuts. It seemed to occur in cycles. Everyone there was unpredictable, and they were all definitely interesting.

Rosie, a woman in her early thirties, looked like a normal housewife, but she'd been sent there for violently attacking her husband. She seemed sorry for whatever she'd done to him. I never found out exactly what it was, but I got the impression that it was very serious. I couldn't understand why her husband would let her attack him. I figured he must be a weak guy. Rosie didn't look that strong.

Things picked up for me when Sheryl, a cute girl who was a little older than I was, transferred into my ward. She had been in a while and knew the ropes. She seemed nice, and we flirted a bit. One afternoon she invited me to sneak off with her. I followed her through the halls and into an out-of-the-way bathroom. She climbed into the bathtub, lay down on a towel she'd already spread out, and invited me to join her. We stopped just short of having sex. We fooled around a little more over the next few days. I wished I hadn't. When I told her that I might be leaving, she started following me everywhere and constantly watching me. It made me very nervous. I was afraid she'd tell someone that we had fooled around and I wouldn't be released.

Sheryl was more messed up than I realized. I didn't judge her for having psychological problems. After all, I was in the same mental institution for attempted suicide. But I was now in a big dilemma about girls. After my suicide attempt, I knew I couldn't be with normal, sweet, untroubled girls like Janet anymore. Janet loved me, but she also thought I was going to hell because I didn't believe in Jesus. It broke my heart. That people would hold onto dogmatic beliefs based on fear, even more than what they felt in their heart to be true about someone, was the epitome of my dilemma. There was nobody in my life who was willing to fully accept the fact that I didn't have the skills to live in their world. They thought they were helping me by denying my reality and offering me false hopes.

My decision to commit suicide was my way of acknowledging that I'd rather die than become the person I'd have to be in order to survive in the world I was being forced to live in. The paradox was that in order to survive, I'd have to become a person no one would like. I'd have to live on the fringes of society and engage in illegal activities. I'd become a criminal out of sheer necessity. I wondered how far I would have to go. And what hurt more was that the people who wanted me to be alive would see this person I'd become as resulting from my choice instead of theirs. My hope for becoming a person that I liked had died when I attempted suicide. Now, if I were ever going to have a girlfriend, it would have to be someone who was as damaged as I was. Of course, I couldn't tell any of this to Dr. Lahe.

— ⚘ —

I was still waiting for my second visit with Dr. Lahe to find out what was going on. I'd had no contact with him after our first session. I had no idea what his assessment of me was, or when I might be able to go home. I thought maybe I'd blown it by being so candid with him. Finally, two weeks into my stay, I was called in to see him again. I knew I had to be more careful about what I said this time. He started the session by talking about my relationship with Emerson.

"I understand from your mother that you and your older brother don't get along at all," he said. "In fact, she said your fights get pretty awful."

"Yeah, we don't get along," I said. I was trying to play my cards close to my chest, but I'd never been good at that. Soon I was telling him everything about Emerson and me. I even told him how I'd almost killed Emerson when I threw the screwdriver at his head.

"That scared me," I said when I finished telling the story.

Dr. Lahe looked at me calmly, smoking one of his little cigars.

"You mean almost killing your brother?" he asked.

"Yeah, I can't believe how hard I threw it. It felt like I'd crossed a line and I could never go back."

"Everyone can be pushed too far, David. It's good that it scared you. It tells me you're not a sociopath."

It was a huge relief to hear that. That was my secret fear.

"It's weird," I said. "I hate Emerson and I'm afraid of him, but I envy him, too. He knows all about music, books, TV shows — everything. He's really smart. He understands the world and how it works in ways I never will."

"So, you admire him?"

"I guess, in a way. But it's mixed. I hate people like Emerson who are all about themselves and hurt other people, but I envy them because they can fit in and pass tests and get ahead in life. They're one of the reasons I wanted to check out...you know, permanently. But now Emerson admires me."

"How is that?" Dr. Lahe's interest perked up.

"He told me that until a few years ago he didn't think of me as human. But now I can tell he thinks I'm cool, since he found out I smoked dope and have had more experience with girls than he has. Suddenly he treats me almost...I don't know...with respect."

"So what are you going to do when you go back to school?"

Back to school? It sounded as if I might be getting out of here after all. Dr. Lahe hadn't mentioned Sheryl, so he probably didn't know about her and me. I just hoped he didn't find out before they let me out.

"I don't know. I'm not going to do any better academically. I've tried as hard as I can, and I still never learn. I guess I've got to get tougher. I'll probably have to survive in the streets."

"Do you think being tough is helping you or hindering you?"

"I don't know. Probably both. If you're not tough, you get taken advantage of. You've got to be able to take care of yourself.

But some people start thinking you're a troublemaker. Like my principal. But I'm not a troublemaker." Dr. Lahe puffed thoughtfully on his cigar. I could tell he was listening. I decided to ask the main question on my mind. "When do you think I'll get out of here?"

"Do you still want to commit suicide?"

"No."

"Good, because you're going home now. I just wanted to talk to you once more, to get a sense of how you were doing. I think you're ready. Your father is waiting out front. The staff has already packed your things. Good luck, David."

Dr. Lahe sat up straight and tamped his cigar out in the ashtray on the table. The session was over. I was in shock. I was glad to be getting out, but I didn't feel especially prepared to go back into the world. I didn't feel as if I'd gotten any help while I was in the hospital. The two sessions with Doctor Lahe were it. Basically, I'd been warehoused for two weeks. But one thing I did get was absolute confirmation that I'd never let myself set foot in a place like that again.

As I left the little office, I saw my dad standing by the nurses' station chatting with the nurses. He was wearing his work suit. He was handsome, about five feet seven, with jet-black hair. Over the years he'd gotten a bit of a belly. Now, with freedom so close, I suddenly felt desperate to get out of there. I went up to my father. He turned and looked at me with a serious expression on his face, but he was truly happy to see me. I was so happy to see him.

"Hi, Dad."

He held up a bag and said, "Hi, David. I'm taking you home."

A white-uniformed orderly led us silently through the labyrinth of hallways and locked doors to the exit. I stepped out into the sunlight.

I had not seen or talked to my Dad since "I did what I did." He had a special way of undermining the discomfort in almost any situation. The whole time in the hospital, I worried about what it would be like when I saw him. Would he be angry, disappointed, hurt? Was he tired of me and my problems, done with me? Had he written me off as a hopeless case? I didn't know. As we walked silently to the car, the tension was palpable. We got into the car and both opened our windows. Dad was looking out, straight ahead, at the sunny suburban landscape.

"Wow," he said, "what a beautiful day." He sat for a moment, not moving; then he turned to me. "How are you doing?"

"I don't know. Okay, I guess."

His simple warmth was reassuring. It was just like him. After I woke up in the hospital, it seemed everything had changed. Mom treated me like I wasn't me anymore. But I hadn't seen Dad yet, and I didn't know if he would still be the same. But he was.

"I'm glad to have you back and coming home." He paused, and said, "Your mother and I want to help you, but we don't know how. We need your help, David. You're going to have to tell us what you need."

I think I was in shock. The idea of having to face everyone after what I'd done and all the trouble I'd caused felt overwhelming. Other than that, I didn't really know what I was feeling.

"Okay, I'll try." I paused. "I'm sorry. "

Turning back to start the car, he said, in the way I loved about him, "That looks like a fun place, but how about we do all we can to keep you out of there?"

It was good to get out and go home. I felt shaky at first, and very disoriented. It was partly the adjustment of leaving the hospital, and it was partly noticing that my family and friends were now watching me to see how I was doing, and also that I was watching them watching me. I could see that attempting suicide had changed things, in me and in the people around me.

After I got out of the mental hospital, no one knew how to act around me. They seemed both cautious and unusually attentive, as if they wanted to help but were afraid to set me off. I didn't want to deal with anyone. I spent most of my time alone in my room listening to music, or hanging out with my old friends after they got out of school.

I felt stuck. I knew I had no future, and that realization felt like a cloud hanging over my head. But for now I wasn't in school and nothing was required of me. This was a huge relief. I started living in the moment with no plans or consideration for the future. I wanted to see if I could be happy right now, the way I'd felt that first night in the hospital. If I could just do that, then I'd see if that could become something more. This was a newfound freedom after spending years fighting against a world that seemed reluctant to accept me and make room for me.

I felt very uneasy about the prospect of returning to school and a life without my closest friend, liquid mercury. I didn't know how the other kids would react to me. I was afraid they'd look down on me as a pathetic loser, or avoid me out of awkwardness, pity, or fear. Home tutoring seemed the simplest solution; that was what the school recommended. My parents didn't want me to be under any pressure; they just wanted me to be safe and to be happy.

I didn't want to go back and face my peers. I was ashamed of my failed suicide attempt. How pathetic to screw up your own suicide! But I knew I had to go back. I couldn't hide out at home like a coward, even though my mother and the school had already worked out the home-schooling option for me.

Part of it was personal pride. Part of it was morbid curiosity. I had to find out what people thought of me, what they were saying about me. If I didn't go back, people would think I was just a loser, a crazy kid who'd tried to kill himself and was put in a mental institution. I was afraid I might begin to think that myself. But another, more compelling part was a desire to face my fears. Facing my fears, including the fear of intense pain, had been a compulsion of mine for my whole life. I remembered how at eleven I'd slid into a pane of glass, cutting my thigh to the bone. I was bleeding profusely, and the pain began to overwhelm me. I'd looked at my leg, and the muscle in the front of my thigh had severed and pulled back like a rubber band, revealing the bone underneath. Despite the intense pain and fear, I couldn't stop staring at the bone. I'd reached in, grabbed it, and shook it, as if I could conquer the pain that way. Now I had to deal with this even worse pain, that of returning to the circumstance that drove me to suicide. I told my mother I wanted to go back to school.

When I finally went back, I acted as if nothing had happened, as if I didn't have a care in the world. But word had gotten out. Everyone knew I'd done drugs, tried to kill myself, and been put in a mental institution. Kids turned to stare at me when I walked through the hallway. My fears of being shunned, ignored, or pitied turned out quite the opposite: They now thought I was cool. I was a topic of gossip. The fact that I'd been struggling at the bottom of the remedial class didn't matter. Suddenly I had a reputation.

Everything about me now fit my new image. I was a co-op kid; that made me a radical. I was a fighter; that made me tough. I had long hair; that made me a "freak." I was the only known drug user; that made me an outlaw. My lack of social skills now seemed forgotten. I got invited to parties I wouldn't have been invited to before. Even being in the remedial class imparted a strange antihero mystique.

More surprising, I was suddenly a girl magnet. Girls who had never even looked at me now came up and talked to me, flirted with me, and wanted to be with me. They even came to my front door to meet me. Hanging out with me granted a kind of rebel status because I was supposedly a desperate and dangerous character. It bothered me, but I liked the attention. Even kids from other schools had heard about me. One night at a friend's house, I was introduced to a high school kid I'd never met. He gave me a look and said, "Oh, you're David Patten?" He was impressed. That happened several times. I got a kick out of it, but it made me distrust people. If I hadn't tried to kill myself, they wouldn't have been interested in me, or have wanted to hang out with me. Who I really was didn't actually matter to them. I was the druggy, dangerous suicide kid. I didn't get the glamour of it. To highlight the absurdity, one kid who'd been declaring he was going to commit suicide now resented me, as if I'd stolen his thunder. The social scene at school and my dubious hero status got old fast. Soon I decided I'd rather be home tutored after all. My mother contacted the school and made the arrangements. No doubt the school principal was relieved.

After I got out of the hospital I felt more isolated than ever. But I became more decisive and self-directed; I felt a new sense of urgency and energy. I wasn't in a constant rage anymore, but I was still mad at the world and its intolerance of me, so I wanted to find intolerance and fight it wherever I could. I wanted to do new things, to experience more. I wanted to get stoned more. I wanted to hang out with people who talked about important things, who were more political and passionate about what really mattered in life. I was already politically aware as a result of being raised in the co-op. And it was 1969. The Vietnam War had united my generation in opposition to war. The Civil Rights Movement had exposed the brutal oppression of millions of American citizens of color, and given us a model of courageous rebellion against hypocrisy and injustice. Rock music, weed, LSD, and the assassinations of the Kennedys and Martin Luther King Jr. were disillusioning and radicalizing, and had redefined the values of my generation.

Since I was being home tutored and I was no longer in school, I let my hair grow almost down to the middle of my back. Even the high school kids in the city had a dress code, so I was one of the only kids I knew who had such long hair and could dress the way I wanted to. I think this might be part of what allowed me to get into nightclubs even high school seniors couldn't get in.

I was still riding the trains into the city to see Robert and my Chicago circle of friends. They didn't know about my suicide attempt, so I didn't have to deal with weird reactions from them. I'd cooled my contact with Janet since getting out. We were still friends, but she was no longer my girlfriend and we rarely talked. I couldn't be with good girls like Janet anymore who had suburban expectations and believed that I was going to hell.

I continued to hang out with the old crowd. Some of them were the ones I'd gotten high with the night I took the mercury.

Most of them were three or four years older than I was. They'd known me for most of my life, and they accepted me for who I was. Some of them had been Emerson's friends, but Emerson had gone off to college in Ann Arbor.

Despite the age difference, I was accepted as part of the group. I was still smaller than average, but my hair was long and I seemed confident and older than my age. We hung out, talked about music and politics, and got drunk and stoned together. Getting high was our ritual and an important part of our friendship. We did a lot of weed, acid, and mescaline together. We'd stay up all night talking about life, the war, and politics — and how we thought the world should be. We were rejecting the world around us, and embracing a new world with different values that included drugs, music, and altered perceptions.

Many of my peers and friends were open, curious, and thoughtful people who never did drugs. There was never any peer pressure in my crowd to do them. Yet for many, drugs seemed to make it easier to connect at deeper levels. Some who got stoned became more open and real, and felt that their minds really had opened and their awareness really did expand in some remarkable way. Of course, the positive effect tended to fade in those who used drugs frequently and over time. It was replaced by other phenomena: a dulling of awareness, a sapping of motivation, and a disintegration of their personalities.

Drugs were still hard to come by in the suburbs. Since I was able to get drugs through my Chicago connections, I became the main drug supplier for my crowd. This also gave me a kind of status. I'd take the train into Chicago, score some weed, acid, or mescaline, and take the train home again. Sometimes friends would drive me to the South Side to score.

My transition from drug user to drug dealer began the same way my candy business had begun in the fourth grade: as favors to friends. Word gradually spread that I was a reliable source of quality weed. More people started coming to me and begging me to score for them. I did it reluctantly at first, mostly as favors. Then I thought since I was taking a risk, I might as well make a profit. Soon I was doing a brisk and profitable business. It was the cinnamon-toothpick model all over again. At fifteen I was buying two kilos a month, about five pounds. By age seventeen I would be buying twenty-five-pounds at a time.

I was smoking a lot of weed and enjoying the company of my friends, but the joyous high I'd experienced on the night of my attempted suicide was a one-time deal. Now getting high was merely a temporary relief from unhappiness, a distraction from my fucked-up life and my fucked-up mind. I knew I was killing time, but what else was I going to do? I knew that when the high faded, I was the same anxious, pessimistic, unhappy person I had always been. In the end, it was just a habit that became a way of life, and finally a trap that would take me years to get out of. I would learn the hard way that habits are deceptively easy to start, and before you know it they become a way of life. Meanwhile, my future looked as bleak as ever.

Central Y

*M*y parents started giving me a monthly living allowance when I was fifteen. A living allowance was a family tradition with us kids, although they started my brothers when they were fourteen. The idea was for us to learn responsibility with money by buying our own clothes, school supplies, and other basic necessities. If we ran out of money before the end of the month, we got to experience the consequences of poor money management.

I did buy school supplies and other necessities, but I didn't buy new clothes. New clothes felt uncomfortable, so I wore my old clothes until they no longer fit or they fell apart. Any money I had left over at the end of the month I put in my safe for the future; with clothes being the primary expense, I ended up with a lot of money left over. Ironically, my parents decided that I wasn't ready for the responsibility, and my living allowance stopped. I didn't know that I'd soon be making more money than they would ever give me.

I still noticed the impact of my suicide attempt on my relationship with my parents. My mother was very concerned about me and my education, but now she was reserved with me.

The joking relationship with my dad came back, but it wasn't the same as before. My academic difficulties in school persisted. I'd decided to take the school district up on its offer to pay for private tutoring. They didn't want me back in school any more than I wanted to be there. So they hired a woman to come in and work with me for a few hours a day, five days a week. She covered the required material and quizzed me orally. There was no reading. After several months of tutoring, I passed the eighth grade.

I received my eighth-grade diploma in the mail that summer, and I immediately enrolled in summer school at Chicago's Central YMCA High School to get an early start on my freshman year. Central Y was a continuation school located in the financial district in the Chicago Loop. We thought it might be a better fit for me than a regular school. It was designed to teach students the basics in order to complete a twelfth-grade education. Classes ran year-round, and if you attended the full schedule you could graduate in three years instead of four. That was my new plan.

I had to make it to and from Central Y each day on my own via the North Western train system. I took the morning train in, went to classes, and took the train home at the end of the day. I knew the days of the week and most of the months of the year, just not always in order, and not always in real time. This caused me a few logistical problems.

Central Y was partially funded by a federal government project, part of a concerted effort by the feds to deal with an overwhelming and growing gang problem. It was designed to help gang kids and other troubled youth get their high school diplomas, get back on track, and gain a foothold in the "legitimate" world. Many of the students had done time in jail or juvenile hall. Some were on probation. A lot of the kids came straight out of Charlietown, the infamous juvenile detention center in St. Charles, Illinois.

The local Chicago community was proud of Central Y for the educational opportunity it offered underprivileged, marginalized kids. It was a noble idea, a last-chance school for kids who couldn't fit in, or who were too dangerous to put in the normal public school system. This mix of underprivileged juvenile delinquents, criminal misfits, drug addicts, and undiagnosed learning-disabled or psychologically borderline kids made Central Y an unpredictable and risky venture. Some took full advantage of the opportunity. Many didn't. The odds were against them, and the predictable failures far outnumbered the worthwhile successes.

Most of the students were from poor, crime-ridden neighborhoods, and from broken or extremely dysfunctional families marred by alcoholism, addiction, abuse, or neglect. A large percentage of the student body was made up of gang members from different tribes or factions. Unspoken rules and protocols governed interactions between the groups, and racial tension was at the core of it all. It was the era of the Black Panthers, the Nation of Islam, the Black Power movement, and the Watts race riots in Los Angeles. Between classes, the halls of Central Y were a sea of bright colors, long leather coats, bulging Afros, pimp hats, and black berets bobbing to a strut-and-bounce walk.

One classroom was on the first floor, and the rest were on the tenth and eleventh floors. The cafeteria was on the fourth floor. The YMCA owned the building and rented out four floors to the school. The rest was YMCA and YMCA office space, so there were a lot of "suits" in the building.

On one of my first days at school, a white kid sitting next to me in class said he only used the main elevators and warned me to avoid the back stairways and back elevators. From the way he said it, I think he'd gotten mugged there. I soon found out that the front stairs were rarely used, and that the hallways, and even the classrooms, could be dangerous, too.

There was an unspoken rule that whites could only occupy the school cafeteria from noon to twelve thirty. After that we had to clear out. The rest of the time it was blacks only. By the time we got our sandwiches and drinks it was often a quarter past twelve or later, so we rarely even went. We would bring our lunch or buy food and eat outside in the street. In the winter we ate in the underground maze of tunnels, basements, and stairwells that exists beneath the city of Chicago.

Prominent in most major cities at that time was the escalation of well-organized youth gangs like the Blackstone Rangers from Chicago's South Side. The Blackstone Rangers comprised Central Y's largest group. In their prime, the Blackstone Rangers were the largest gang in the United States and estimated to be ten times larger than the Chicago police force. They were a major problem for the city of Chicago, and a large part of the student population of Central Y. The gangs were a source of stress and fear for kids like me who were not gang affiliated and were therefore unprotected. These nonaffiliated kids included loners and long-haired counterculture rebels like myself who called themselves "freaks" and liked to listen to music and get high, and tended to be politically radical.

Another force on the local scene was the Black Coalition. The coalition wasn't another gang; it was a student group formed to address race issues in school. Then there were the syndicate kids with their short, greased-back hair and black leather jackets. They were also not to be messed with. Many were full-fledged criminals, more eager to graduate into the Chicago Italian syndicate than to get a high school diploma. One of these top "connected" kids was the son of a major syndicate figure from the North Side of Chicago. His father had hired a personal bodyguard, an enormous Blackstone Ranger called Chappy, who escorted him everywhere and sat beside him during classes. Chappy was a fierce-looking giant in his late teens, about six feet ten, and weighed several hundred pounds. I never figured out how, given the racial tension, a Blackstone Ranger had ended up as a bodyguard to a white syndicate kid. The grapevine said there was some kind of political arrangement between the two groups.

These mutual understandings between the black and white gangs kept a measured peace between them, allowing them to engage in their various criminal enterprises — drug dealing, burglary, fencing, robbery — without going to war with one another. Chicago's defining characteristic — in politics and crime — was a tightly run, strictly enforced hierarchical organization. That was apparent even at Central Y, where the major Chicago syndicates mentored their protégés. Central Y was at the very bottom of the public school system in terms of education, but it was a graduate school for future criminals and gang leaders. I knew there was no place lower I could go. I figured that if I was going to survive, this was the world I was going to have to survive in.

Most Central Y students were older than the average high school age, with the majority being between seventeen and twenty, and a fraction in their mid- to late twenties and early thirties. The older students tended to be more serious about getting high school diplomas. Some of the white kids were from working-class immigrant families, including second- and third-generation Russian, Polish, and Irish kids. I was shocked to learn that some of my new schoolmates lived in areas of the city, like Polack Hill, that were so poor their houses had no indoor plumbing.

There were also a number of foreign students who had come to America to find a better life. One guy I got to know was a political refugee from Guatemala who had come to the U.S. through Amnesty International. Almost thirty, he'd been imprisoned and tortured by the Guatemalan government for alleged communist activities, which meant anything from political dissent to being in the wrong place at the wrong time. He had ugly scars on his face from being tortured. He told me how government death squads had tortured and "disappeared" thousands of citizens, mostly peasants and laborers, and how the urban poor lived in tin-and-cardboard houses.

Being young, white, short, Jewish, and suburban made me a natural target for a host of unsavory characters at Central Y. Since there were only a handful of whites in the school, I had no natural allies, and so I did everything I could to fit in and look tough. This was a very different world from the co-op and the community I'd been raised in, but it was preferable to the school situation I'd left behind. At regular schools the most popular kids seemed to be the best liars and manipulators, and my inability to lie without my face giving me away had been a major liability. The level of social deception and manipulation in the suburban public schools was over my head. How someone could be your friend one day and not the next, without anything being said, was incomprehensible to me. I used to spend all day Sunday dreading school on Monday, even throwing up from the anticipation of going to school the next day.

At Central Y my lack of sophisticated social skills didn't present the same problem. It was more honest than that. I didn't have to like the other students, and they didn't have to like me. They were more real, and their problems were more real, especially compared to the problems of the suburban kids in regular schools. When someone said they were going to kill you, they meant it. There was nothing to decipher or decode. In confrontational situations, my bluntness and tendency to say what I thought without the normal filters made me seem tough.

As dangerous as it was at Central Y, I actually felt less threatened than I had at regular school. I no longer experienced the dread-filled Sunday nights, and when I walked down the halls on Monday I could breathe without feeling tightness in my chest. I'd learned that fearful people have a hard time anywhere. It was always said that it was because they showed their weakness and therefore became easy prey. I wasn't so sure. Fearful people can't be trusted, and you can't predict their behavior. When people are in a threatening situation, they are extremely wary about whom they can trust and whom they can't. Fearful people might do anything; they might stab you in the back or rat you out. They are cowards and that's the reason they are targeted. I may have been scared, but I was so literal I was predictable. I'm not saying that the ability to bluff or to be a good liar wouldn't have been a help, but since people could read me, they also could see that when I stood up to a threat, I meant what I said. It was a skill I could thank Emerson for.

Central Y hired plainclothes armed security guards. They were off-duty police officers, moonlighting members of "King Richard" Daley's infamous Blue Knights. They patrolled the halls with guns in holsters and handcuffs dangling from their belts. They were intimidating and tough. The safeties on their guns were always off, and we could tell they trusted no one but one another. Given the environment and the era, you couldn't blame them.

These were tense, politically polarized times. Antiwar protests had been going on for several years, and Chicago was a hotbed of political dissent. The riots at the Chicago Democratic Convention in August 1968 were a recent and vivid memory. Mayor Daley, notoriously authoritarian and intolerant of dissent, ruled the city with an iron hand. The hair-trigger Chicago police, quick to use their clubs and draw their guns, also had a fondness for tear gas, or "Chicago cologne," and the air was frequently thick with it.

The infamous Chicago Seven trial was a current event, and daily protests were held outside the courthouse where the Chicago Seven were being tried. It wasn't far from Central Y, and a number of us freaks went there on our lunch break to watch the protests. After the announcement that American war casualties had exceeded thirty thousand, Mayor Daley put twelve thousand police officers on twelve-hour shifts to deal with the increased protests.

I attended many antiwar protests in those years, and saw many riots. I put up posters announcing marches and initiated chants during the marches. On several occasions I ran with tear-gassed crowds from the cops, and twice I was caught and clubbed along with some others. I hated the police and the brutality they represented just as I hated the Vietnam War and all it stood for.

I also attended meetings of the Students for a Democratic Society, otherwise known as SDS, and participated in their non-violent protests. But I stopped going after the Weathermen came on the scene and started disrupting meetings and actively provoking police to the point of violence at peace demonstrations. I hated the Weathermen's tactics and violent philosophy. I'd been in many school fights, but politically I was a pacifist. The Weather Underground actively promoted violence, even against peaceful protesters, to achieve their aims. Like others in my politically aware circle of friends, I felt they were turning the public against the antiwar movement by linking it to violence and anarchy.

— ⚛ —

I didn't have to go to political protests to find violence and anarchy. At Central Y, anything could happen anytime and anyplace. You were only safe within sight of one of the armed security guards. Even the "suits" that worked on the other floors were occasionally mugged by Central Y students.

It would take me a while to learn the rules at Central Y. I'd grown up in an interracial community where there was no racial tension and virtually no crime, and where, with a few exceptions, everyone trusted one another and got along together. But none of that had any value here. The only things that prepared me for this new environment were my fighting skills and feral instincts, my experiences riding the trains into Chicago, and my familiarity with drugs.

Until now, the extent of my drug dealing was buying ounces of weed as favors for friends. Now I was surrounded by people with major drug and organized crime connections. Sensing opportunity, I quickly found my way to the dealers. I only bought from those that I thought could be friends. This strategy took discipline, and limited my contacts and opportunities, but it kept me from getting busted or ripped off. At the end of the first week of that summer semester, I scored two thousand Dexedrine tabs —"mother's little helpers"— standard housewife-prescription speed that wasn't considered addictive at the time.

One Friday afternoon I was heading from the tenth floor to my next class on the eleventh floor. I took the stairway. I always carried a switchblade in a long, thin pocket that a friend had sewn into the right knee of my pants. If I fully bent my knee, the tip popped up for easy access. I also carried a leather pouch with six 35 mm rolls of film on my belt. I carried no camera, but I did have a darkroom at home and I liked taking pictures. But that's not why I carried the film rolls. I'd devised a foolproof method for stashing dope in empty film rolls. I cut the tails off the rolls of film before developing the negatives and taped them inside the empty rolls so they jutted out. It made them look like rolls of fresh film. I kept ten to twenty hits of speed in each roll in my pouch. More than once while hanging out with friends on the South Side, cops would suddenly drive up and approach us. We knew the routine: They would shove us up against the wall and search us. They searched me, and my pouch, but never checked the fake film rolls.

Now, rounding the halfway curve between the tenth and eleventh floors, I looked up and saw three black guys waiting on the upper landing. They were looking right at me, as if they were waiting for me. I immediately stopped. I knew right away I was in trouble. The guy in front wore a loud yellow button-up shirt. The guy standing next to him had a thick gold chain around his neck.

They started down the stairs toward me, and I turned and ran, taking two steps at a time. Just before I reached the tenth-floor landing, the door opened and two more black guys with conked hair came through the door. They also looked at me and started walking toward me. I backed up a few steps and stopped holding on to the banister so I could see both ways. Just then, Yellow

Shirt and Gold Chain came rushing down around the stairways with the third guy right behind them.

Gold Chain reached me first and grabbed my arm in a firm grip. He was a tall, sullen-faced guy a few years older than I was. He looked really familiar. Then I recognized him. He was in my first-period English Lit class. We'd never even exchanged a glance until now. But he clearly knew who I was. Now Yellow Shirt arrived and stood in front of me. He was also several years older and several inches taller than I was. He leaned down and got right in my face.

"What d'ya got?" he demanded, almost casually.

"What do you mean?" I tried to look puzzled.

His cold eyes fixed me with unnerving intensity. Without warning, he palmed me hard in the chest, knocking me back against the banister.

"Don't fuck with me," Yellow Shirt said in the same mono-tone voice. "We know you've been selling."

"Selling what?" I asked stupidly.

They knew what I had because I'd been selling it in school all week. I felt completely stupid, and scared as hell. I was caught off-guard and stalling weakly. There was something freaky about Yellow Shirt, with his cold eyes and unnatural calm. I knew he saw right through me. He was no punk. Most punks had to overcome some level of fear, some inner hesitation, before acting. They had to muster the intensity. Yellow Shirt had a sociopath's calmness. He didn't need to muster anything; he was already there. He was the kind of guy who could slip a knife in you and walk away with no change of expression. He scared the hell out of me.

I stood there looking up at Yellow Shirt, completely tongue-tied. He just stared at me, as if he were giving me one last chance to come clean. The conked-hair guys hovered a couple of steps below, watching. Then they came up and stood beside Yellow Shirt. One of them reached in, pulled on my film pouch, and said, "What's in here?"

"Just film," I said.

I opened the pouch, exposing the dummy film rolls. One of the conked-hairs grabbed at the pouch and said, "Let me see that, asshole."

I pushed his hand away and managed to close the pouch. Now his friend reached in and tried to grab the pouch. This time Yellow Shirt angrily knocked away his hand, growling, "That's my shit!"

"Hey! Hey!" Gold Chain shouted a warning at the two guys, who apparently weren't with them at all. The conked-hair team was working freelance. Apparently I was the focus of a scavenger hunt. It was almost comical, except for the fix I was in, and Gold Chain's painful two-fisted grip on my arm. The third guy stood behind Gold Chain, out of my line of sight.

Gold Chain and the two conked hairs seemed agitated. Yellow Shirt just stood there like the calm in the center of the storm. Then, with a firm sweep of his arm, he shoved the two intruders away from me. He didn't even glance over at them; his eyes were still fixed on me.

"Give me the dope," he said.

I didn't respond. I wasn't going to give them my dope. And saying nothing seemed better than saying something stupid again that might piss him off worse. I was hoping the chaos of the situation would work to my benefit. Maybe the conked hairs would do something stupid, like provoke him. I almost hoped they'd reach in for me again. But they didn't. They were like jackals, hungrily eyeing the lion's kill, unwilling to attack but refusing to leave.

"I'm done talking," snarled Yellow Shirt. "Give us what you've got."

Now his voice was really threatening. I had about fifty hits of speed in my film rolls. Not a lot to lose, but I absolutely didn't want to give it to them. If I caved in now, word would spread, and my reputation as an easy mark would be set. It would be open season on me. Instinctively, I glanced back over my shoulder and looked down the long stairwell, ten floors to the bottom. I wasn't going to give them my dope. I looked back at Yellow Shirt and kept my mouth shut. He nodded slightly.

"Have it your way."

Now the third guy with Yellow Shirt and Gold Chain came out of the background and grabbed one of my legs. Suddenly my legs were high in the air, my left shoulder blade was resting on the banister, and I felt myself sliding backward as if I were going down a chute. I grabbed hold of the banister and clung to it with a death grip. Then one of the conked-hair freelancers reached in, grabbed my other leg, and tilted me further back.

I felt myself sliding over backward as they lifted my legs higher. In a panic, I clung to the banister with both hands and started kicking violently, aiming at their heads. If it weren't for Gold Chain's grip on my shoulder, I'd have gone over. I landed a couple of kicks at the conked hair holding my leg, and he let go and backed away. My head and shoulder were now over the edge, and the third guy still had my other leg. I looked down the center shaft and saw the banister spiraling below, ten floors to the bottom. I couldn't believe they were going to throw me over for a few pills. But giving them my dope, even under these circumstances, was still not an option.

"Let go of me, you assholes!" I kept shouting at the top of my lungs. "Let me fucking go!"

Gold Chain, still gripping my arm, was now forcing me over the banister while the third guy kept trying to hold my kicking legs still and lift them higher. Yellow Shirt had stepped back and stood calmly watching. By now they all seemed to prefer throwing me down the stairwell to scoring my stash. I managed to land a couple more kicks, but the force of each kick made it harder for me to keep my grip on the banister. Finally, the third guy dropped my leg. I now had both feet on the stairs again. They were all really pissed off now, cursing at me in a fury, as if I should have just let them throw me over. Then the third guy and a conked hair grabbed my legs again, lifted them up, and tried one more time to shove me over the railing. I grabbed the banister again, but my grip weakened. Yellow Shirt stepped back in and leaned into me, trying to pry my hands off the banister. I knew I was about to go over. Then I saw his neck right next to me.

"Wait a minute!" I screamed. "I'll give it to you, all right? You can have it!"

They paused, still holding my legs, and I saw my chance. I let go of the banister, grabbed Yellow Shirt in a headlock and squeezed his neck as hard as I could. I was now more pissed off than scared. I wanted to fight. If I was going over the railing, I was taking Yellow Shirt with me. It was the last thing any of them expected, but what did I have to lose? I was planning to kill myself later on anyway; at least this way I'd be doing some good, ridding the world of a sociopath on my way out.

I squeezed Yellow Shirt's neck in the crook of my right elbow, gripping my wrist with my other hand. Our heads were pressed together, my ear to the back of his head. I had him in a vise grip;

he struggled furiously but couldn't get away. He tried to pummel me with his fists, but at such close range he couldn't do much damage. Gold Chain was hitting me in the ribs and shoulder, but I was rushing on adrenaline and felt no pain. I was kicking like a wild man and yelling right next to Yellow Shirt's ear, "You're coming with me, asshole! You're coming with me!"

Suddenly they put my legs back down. Yellow Shirt was leaning against me, breathing hard in my ear. Then I noticed that no one was grabbing me or hitting me. Even Yellow Shirt had stopped fighting. I wasn't sure why. Were they tired? Had they decided I was telling the truth? Had the fact that I was willing to die changed the equation? I decided to let go of Yellow Shirt's neck and see what happened. I couldn't hold on forever. When I let him go, to my surprise he backed away. Then they all went down the steps and disappeared through the tenth-floor doorway.

I sat down on the stairs, breathing hard, and tried to calm down. An unbelievable amount of adrenaline was still flooding through me. I was relieved, exhilarated, puzzled, and scared as hell all at the same time. *Fuck this!* I thought. *I'm gonna quit. I'm not cut out for this place.*

But I didn't quit. I went home for the weekend and decided to go back and face them on Monday morning. It was partly out of pride — I didn't want them to think they'd beaten me and scared me off — but ultimately it was practical. Going to Central Y, as dangerous as it was, seemed like my best chance to get a high school diploma. My parents had told me that if I quit school they would kick me out of the house. In a way, the challenge of Central Y appealed to me. I figured if I could adapt and survive there, I could do it just about anywhere. I saw it as a boot camp, where I could toughen up and hone my street smarts. Central Y was definitely a place where I could learn how the world I'd have to live in really worked.

Fear gripped me as soon as I entered the building on Monday morning. I knew I'd be seeing Gold Chain in my English Lit class. At some point, I'd probably run into Yellow Shirt and the conked-hair guys in the halls. I figured I'd either proven myself to them and they'd leave me alone, or I'd totally pissed them off and they'd be looking for me. But I knew I had to deal with Gold Chain first.

When I walked into class I saw him sitting down at a long table in the back of the room, in one of the cheap metal folding chairs. I played it cool, and so did he. We both saw each other, but neither of us acknowledged the other. I grabbed an empty folding chair, put it next to him, a little too close, and sat down. The tension between us was electric. Neither of us looked over. After a few moments I leaned back, casually, still staring straight ahead. Then I glanced over at him.

"Hey, what's up?" I said.

He seemed confused and on the spot, as if he didn't know what to make of me. A guy he'd tried to rip off and kill a few days ago was sitting next to him making small talk, as if nothing had happened. He tried to ignore me, but I wasn't going away. A passive truce, just pretending nothing had happened, wasn't good enough for me. I had to know if I needed to constantly watch my back. I had to make direct contact with him, and get him to acknowledge me. I figured if you know someone, and they know you, it makes it a little harder for them to rip you off, stick a knife in you, throw you over a stairwell, or whatever.

"Looks like this class has a lot of reading," I said to Gold Chain. "I fucking hate reading." He stared sullenly ahead, still trying to ignore me. I could tell he was flustered. "Do you like writing reports and stuff?" I continued.

Now he sort of glanced over and grunted, "No."

A monosyllabic reply was progress. I kept going. "Me neither. This class is going to be a pain in the ass, huh?"

"Yeah, I guess."

Wow, he was warming up. Then to my surprise, he volunteered more.

"Have you taken any math classes with Graham?"

"Yeah, I have algebra with him."

"Is it a pretty tough class?" he asked.

"Not too bad," I said.

He paused, as if he was thinking of what to say next. *What do you know?* I thought. *We're having an actual conversation.*

"But he gives a lot of homework, huh?"

"Yeah," I said, "that's a drag." Then, in a friendly way, I said, "Hey, I'm David. What's your name?"

I knew I'd never remember his name if he told me. It didn't matter. I didn't plan on becoming best friends; I just wanted to get off his hit list. He grunted and said lamely, "I don't know."

I let that one hang in the air. His reluctance was understandable. He'd tried to rip me off and could have killed me; he didn't want me to know who he was. Maybe I was trying to get something on him. Maybe *I* was the potential psycho now. Fucking with his head would make it less appealing for him to rip me off in the future. Next time they'd rip off somebody else who was less of a pain in the ass. I was definitely putting him on the spot. I just sat there, waiting, keeping the pressure on. I figured he'd either get angry or give in. Then something shifted. Maybe he figured I could find out anyway since we were in the same class, or maybe he just felt stupid telling me he didn't know what his own name was.

"Benny," he said, or something like it, because I forgot it even before class ended. I knew then he wouldn't try to rip me off again. But it seemed I could still push him further. "Cool," I said. Then I looked directly at him, making sure to use his name. "So, Benny, you and your buddies jumped me a few days ago. What the fuck was that about?"

Of course I knew perfectly well what it was about. They'd made no secret about the fact that they wanted my dope. But now we'd had an amiable chat, and I was cashing in on our new-acquaintance status. He looked at the floor for a moment, then answered sullenly, "I don't know."

Wow, he actually seemed somewhat embarrassed, as if he knew he'd done something wrong. At least he wasn't a psychopath.

"Did I do something to you?"

"Nah."

"Okay." I paused, feeling the need for a little more reassurance. "Are you going to try and rip me off again?" I asked, just sounding curious.

"Nah."

"Cool." I paused: mission accomplished. I'd shifted the balance of power. He looked up slightly in my direction, and I decided to change the subject. "Hey, man, do you know where I can get some good weed?"

"No, not really," he said.

I already had some weed, but I wanted to lighten the moment — give it that "no hard feelings" touch. "I know about some stuff coming in — in a few days, if you're interested."

"I don't know. I may have some by then," he said.

"Well, let me know if you need some. I'll see what I can do."

"Sure," he said.

Of course none of what we said meant anything. I wasn't tough enough to stop him from hurting me if he wanted to, but I was a pain in the ass and an unknown quantity, and perhaps all of that was enough for them to leave me alone. Like the joke about the lion: You don't have to run faster than a lion, just faster than the other guy. In this case it was about being more of a pain in the ass to rip off than others.

I shifted my attention to Mr. Brown, our teacher, standing in front of the mostly uninterested class and talking about *Catcher in the Rye*, our first reading assignment. Benny leaned down and rustled in his backpack. A second later he sat up and handed me a paper cup with about half of a shot of gold liquid in the bottom. I took a sniff; it was whiskey. He lightly bumped his cup against mine and we both drank.

At the end of class, Benny and I nodded to each other on the way out. We weren't exactly friends after that, but we had a "How's it going?" relationship in class, and a nodding relationship in the halls. He never bothered me again. Neither did Yellow Shirt or the other guys, who studiously ignored me whenever we passed each other in the halls.

At the end of the summer session I wasn't that happy at Central Y. It was dangerous, and I wasn't learning much. My mother looked around for other options and found an experimental high school located on the second floor of an old monastery, five miles from my house. It only had about forty students. Dr. Lahe's daughter and some of my old friends were enrolled there. It wasn't a remedial or continuation school, but, because it was smaller, teachers were able to work more closely with students than in a public school. The school also encouraged greater student input, so the curriculum would better reflect their needs and interests and stimulate more active participation. The school wasn't yet accredited, but it was working toward accreditation and seemed sure to get it.

I started in the fall, but I encountered the same problems there as elsewhere. I couldn't keep up with the rest of the class, and the teachers didn't know how to deal with my learning disabilities. Grades were not based on conventional tests but on an independently written report. Due to my severe dyslexia, no written test could accurately reflect my knowledge level or actual grasp of the material. I tried to persuade them to grade me on my actual grasp of the material and not on my skewed test scores, but the school was inflexible and unwilling to make any exceptions. I dropped out after a few weeks, immensely frustrated. I later learned that after electing the school's prom king and queen that year, the students held an informal tongue-in-cheek vote for other school titles. Though I was no longer attending, I was still voted "least likely to survive."

I still had to go to school somewhere if I wanted to get a high school diploma. That's how I found myself back at Central Y.

Chappy

I noticed right away that some things had changed for this new school year at Central Y. The blacks had always had their own social politics to deal with—pressure to join a gang and which gang they were in, or not in. Now there were a lot more whites than before. It seemed that the school had become cool to many of the whites in the public schools. Here they had more choices; more interesting, edgy classes; and more freedom. Central Y had become "the place to go to school." With more whites came new cliques; with that came social pressure in the white population to be cool. I didn't feel cool nor did I want to be. The school was safer for whites now, but not for me. More people knew my business now, and some of these kids talked too much.

I continued dealing, very carefully, keeping an eye out for trouble. I never carried more product than I could afford to lose. I didn't get myself into vulnerable situations with people I didn't trust, and I always tried to be as discreet as possible. Business picked up week by week.

My buying connections were longhaired freaks with major drug contacts. They weren't affiliated with any gang, and they scored the best marijuana and psychedelics. When they were dry, I was dry — and nearly everyone else was, too. Shipments of various drugs came in randomly, and, as everything depended on smuggling, there was always an element of unpredictability.

The big Chicago syndicates weren't trafficking in pot and psychedelics at the time. If they had been, the syndicate gangs at Central Y would have been dealing them. Their operations were mostly vice, burglary, and car theft. That would change in a few years when recreational drugs went mainstream and became hugely profitable.

I came to know a few Blackstone Rangers and a couple of Superfly characters who were dealers. They mostly dealt cocaine and heroin, drugs I stayed away from. More and more people began coming to me for speed, acid, mescaline, and pot. I was making more money than my parents had ever given me for living expenses. As with my candy-and-toothpick business, I didn't consume my inventory. I paid myself a little and stashed away a chunk of profits for a nest egg; the rest I put back into the business.

A few months after the stairwell incident, I was sitting in Mr. Brown's English class when the classroom door opened and Chappy walked in. The entire class stared at him as he entered the room, and no one, including Mr. Brown, said a word. Chappy looked around the room, and his eyes locked onto me. Then he walked over to my chair and stood looking down at me from his great height.

"You need to come with me." He sounded firm, but not threatening.

I couldn't think of any reason for him to come get me; we'd never exchanged a single word. Maybe his boss, the Near North Side syndicate leader, had sent him to get me. I didn't get the sense that I was in trouble, and I had no reason to think I was.

But I was definitely nervous.

The room went absolutely silent. Chappy was in charge at the moment, and he clearly wasn't a guy you said no to. I got up and followed him to the door. Being a gentleman, he opened it and let me go first.

I stepped into the hall and stopped in my tracks. There were about fifty black students milling around, and their faces were all turned in my direction. I heard angry, indecipherable murmuring. They were glaring at me, and I had no idea why.

Chappy grabbed me by the shirt collar with his meaty hand and dragged me like a rag doll, shoving me against the wall. Holding me firmly by the collar with one hand, he put his other hand on my chest and glared down at me. His eyes looked crazy; they were slightly red. His breath stank from a mixture of alcohol and halitosis. Now he was one angry motherfucker.

The elevators were to my left, but there was no way I could reach them through the crowd; the back exit leading to the alley was in the other direction, but I was blocked that way, too. Chappy turned and looked around the hall. Suddenly, it went deathly quiet. It seemed as if he were going to give a speech. I gazed into the angry crowd, way past nervous and approaching full-blown panic.

What the hell did I do? I wondered. *Where's a fucking cop when you need him?*

"I want you to meet the Black Coalition," said Chappy in a deep bass voice, swinging his right palm away from my chest in a sweeping gesture as if introducing me to the crowd.

The angry murmuring started up again, and the crowd surged slightly forward. Chappy kept his grip on my collar. He turned to me again, and his crazed, bloodshot eyes stared into mine. "I'm going to kill you, you little white piece of shit!" he announced in a loud, convincing snarl.

A chill traveled down my spine and all the way to my toes. *Oh shit! This is going to hurt*, I thought. *What did I do?*

I was a lightweight compared to these guys who were glaring at me. I didn't know them, and I'd never done anything to them. It made no sense.

"Do him!" someone called out.

Others chimed in with equally encouraging words. Chappy turned to look at the crowd, loosening his grip on my shirt, and I seized the moment. I ducked down, twisted away, and jammed my shoulder into the heavy door of Mr. Brown's classroom. It opened, and I slipped through the gap and into the room.

I darted between the tables to the far side of the room. Students jumped up from their desks and ran. Black Coalition members swarmed through the door and into the room. Chappy stopped just inside the door and looked around, fixing his eyes on me. Mr. Brown was out of his chair and heading for the door.

It was pandemonium, with scuffling feet and the clatter and scrape of chairs and tables that were overturned and crashing to the floor. I watched with a sinking feeling as Mr. Brown forced his way through the crowded doorway, followed by seven or eight students. I guess he was actually a hero leading his students to safety, but I felt completely abandoned.

I looked around for Chappy, who was no longer standing near the door. Glancing behind me, I saw him wading through a maze of fleeing students and overturned desks and chairs. The twenty or so students still in the room were migrating toward the far wall. If Chappy was going to kill me, he'd have to do it in front of witnesses. And he'd have to catch me first.

I managed to evade him by running into a tangle of chairs and tables. The Black Coalition guys were now hovering in a crowd along the wall by the door. They didn't know what to do. Being in a brightly lit classroom full of frightened students was different than gathering in a dimly lit hallway.

Then the pandemonium subsided, and an unnatural calm fell over the room. It was as if everyone had come to their senses. I had my eye on Chappy, fifteen feet away, separated from me by a table and some chairs. He had one eye on me, and he was arguing with several coalition members. He wanted to grab me and take me out, but they now realized that being in the class-room wasn't a good idea.

At that point, two school security cops burst into the room with their guns drawn. They glanced around, quickly assessing the situation. One of them shouted "Nobody move!" I zeroed in on them with some anxiety. These were real off-duty cops. If they searched me and found my dope, I could be sent to Charlietown until I was eighteen, and maybe jail after that. With my attention on them, I didn't notice Chappy backing away from the cops in my direction. Then he was standing near me. Suddenly he lunged and swung his thick fist at my head. I dodged, and he struck the wooden curtain behind me that divided the room in half, splintering a section.

Hearing Chappy's fist crash into the wood, the cops instantly pointed their guns at him. One cop yelled at Chappy to freeze, and the other yelled at me to back away. I did, greatly relieved and looking like the short, scared white kid that I was. Soon the cops had quarantined the coalition members against the wall and began ushering the rest of us out of the room. As soon as I was out of the room, I left school and caught the train home.

I thought I was never going back to Central Y. For the second time in less than six months, someone had tried to kill me; but by the time I got home, I'd changed my mind again. I still hoped to get a diploma. And I had nowhere else to go and no other plan.

I returned the next morning, just after the first class had started so the halls would be empty. Instead of going to class, I went around and checked various classrooms for friends who I thought might know what had been behind the Chappy incident. After a few conversations, the story came together. The whole thing turned out to be a misunderstanding based on a junkie's lie.

The morning Chappy came to get me, a girl named Violet had nodded out on heroin in class. The teacher knew she was on something and took her to the principal. When the principal asked her what she'd taken and where she got it, she said a short white guy with long curly hair cornered her in the elevator and shot her up with heroin. I was the only guy in school who fit the description.

Violet had described me to avoid getting in trouble for using. When they took her to the hospital, the doctor found multiple track marks on her arm and she admitted shooting herself up. By then word had already spread that I'd shot up Violet, and Chappy was already coming after me. Chappy found out the truth when the security cops took him to the office to question him. When they told him about Violet's lie, Chappy wasn't happy. He looked like a fool in front of everybody.

In a way, the incident ended up a plus. Not that anyone felt bad about it; mostly they thought it was funny. Many of the Black Coalition members now recognized me in the halls, and occasionally nodded in a familiar, good-humored way. One survival skill that helped me the most was being able to joke about something, even when nothing about it seemed funny to me. I found myself bantering with them in the hallways. I'd joke, "Yeah, he's lucky he didn't catch me. I woulda kicked his ass."

In the hall one day I passed the guy who was the head of the Blackstone Rangers at Central Y. He called to his friend, "Watch out for my buddy Patten here; this motherfucker thinks he can fly." I figured that was about the banister. I'd had no idea that he knew who I was.

It helped that I didn't talk to the cops about Chappy. I was earning some respect at Central Y, maybe not so much for being a tough guy, but for being a reliable guy who fought back, minded his own business, kept his mouth shut, and wouldn't give up his dope. Now some notable people acknowledged me as I walked through the halls. At any rate, I was no longer the suburban white kid. I had a minor reputation, but a reputation nonetheless.

Being known by this crowd was a plus for my dealing. My drug contacts expanded, and new Blackstone Ranger contacts opened up, including a couple of Superfly guys who otherwise never would have had anything to do with someone so young. All this improved my rep and my self-esteem.

— ⚇ —

In the end, I learned more in the halls at Central Y— about gang protocol, criminal mentality, and feral survival strategies — than from any of the subjects in my classes. It's similar to what you hear people say about prison: It doesn't rehabilitate you; it makes you a better criminal. If it wasn't for my learning disabilities, I might have left with a high school diploma. Instead,

I became a survivor and a better dealer with better connections. That unexpected education would prove useful to me in the next few years. It even proved useful to others, including my logic teacher, Mr. Scofield.

One day I walked into my logic class, and Mr. Scofield wasn't there. At twenty minutes past, he still hadn't showed up and students started leaving. I stared out the window, bored. At half past, only one other guy and I remained. I was about to leave when Mr. Scofield walked into the room.

I had a decent relationship with most of my teachers. I wasn't passing their classes, but I was polite and well behaved. A few of them knew I struggled with learning disabilities and could tell I really was trying to learn and do well. Most of them were not very good teachers. No one wanted to teach in this underpaid, high-stress war zone. You didn't end up teaching here without a reason. If you were here, it meant you couldn't get a job anywhere else. And I mean anywhere else. Some of the teachers had been fired from other schools; some were just bad teachers who didn't seem to care about their students; and one or two were actually senile.

But Mr. Scofield wasn't one of those teachers. He was an antiwar pacifist. He admitted that he had become a teacher to avoid being drafted to Vietnam. However, he really did care about his subject and his students. He tried hard to do a good job. He was a decent guy, and I could tell he liked me.

"Hey, Mr. Scofield." I grinned as he came in. "Party last night?"

He looked grim. "No. Someone broke into my apartment yesterday. They trashed it and took everything. I just finished cleaning up the mess they left behind."

"What did they take?" asked the other student.

"Everything electronic — my stereo system, my typewriter, even my crappy alarm clock. Anything that looked like it might be worth something is gone. The police said I probably won't get it back."

I felt bad for him. Then it occurred to me that the burglary had to be the work of a syndicate guy I knew. One thing I'd learned at Central Y was that the Chicago criminal scene was disciplined and well organized. The major syndicate gangs controlled what went down in Chicago proper and oversaw the junior syndicate gangs. Every guy in every gang, juniors and majors, had a modus operandi and a designated territory, and they never operated outside their area. You couldn't do a burglary or fence stolen goods in Chicago if you weren't connected. If you did, you'd be infringing on someone else's territory, which would be a mistake. By now I knew about the different gangs and the territories they operated in. It made me think....

There were two syndicate gangs in our school. One gang specialized in stolen cars, especially Corvettes, and operated in Chicago proper. The other gang specialized in residential break-ins and stolen home electronics. They operated exclusively on the Near North Side and were the likely suspects.

"Where do you live, Mr. Scofield?" I asked.

He looked at me suspiciously. "Why do you need to know that?"

"I have an idea. I might be able to help you."

He looked at me warily. Finally he said, "Rogers Park."

"Near North Side. Let me go check something out with a friend."

He nodded. "Sure."

He didn't have anything to lose; he'd already lost his stuff, and the cops had said they couldn't help him. I didn't have any clout with the Near North Side syndicate, but a friend of mine, Rick, was in the gang. They usually hung out on the eleventh floor. I left class and headed upstairs looking for Rick. It didn't take me long to find him. I told him I needed to talk with him, and we walked over to the back stairwell.

"What's up?" he asked.

"You know Mr. Scofield — he teaches logic class?"

"Yeah. I'm not in his class."

"That's okay. Someone ripped off his apartment yesterday. He lives in Rogers Park. That's your guys' territory, right?"

"Oh, I think I see where you're going with this."

"Yeah. Scofield's a decent guy. I'm trying to help him out. What do you think?"

"I don't know. Wait here. Let me check something out."

Rick went back to his buddies. He came back a couple of minutes later wearing a poker face. Then he gave me a little grin.

"I'll need his address," he said.

I could tell he was pleased that he might be able to help me out. He was basically a good guy; we were friends, and he wanted to show me that he could make things happen.

"That's great, man! I'll go get it."

"Can't make any promises," he said as I was leaving, "but I'll see what I can do."

I ran down the back stairs to the classroom. Mr. Scofield was standing at a table talking with the other student. He looked up as I came over. He could see I needed to talk to him.

"So?" he asked.

"Hey, Mr. Scofield, I need your address."

He gave me an incredulous look. "I just got ripped off. Why should I give you my address?"

"I'm trying to help you get your stuff back. They're checking to see if they can get it back, but they need your address to figure it out. They already took everything anyway, right?"

"I suppose you're right."

He took a piece of paper from his satchel and wrote down his address. I took the paper and ran up the stairs back to the eleventh floor. Rick was back talking to his buddies. I went up and handed him the paper.

"Here it is."

The guys eyed me with interest. They knew who I was and were interested in helping me recover the stolen goods for my teacher. Rick handed the address to the main guy. He looked at it, then looked up at me, gave a little nod, and shrugged as if to say "We'll see."

I nodded and left, heading to my next class. But now I began to feel apprehensive about the whole thing. I hadn't really thought it through. I was just trying to help Mr. Scofield get his stuff back, but in reality I was asking the Near North Side syndicate for a favor. Now I began to worry about what I might owe them in return.

The next day Mr. Scofield greeted me as I walked into the classroom with a cheerful nod and a smile. Had he gotten his stuff back already? I sat down at a corner table, alone. He finished talking to the class, gave a reading assignment, and came over to me.

"Thanks, David," he said quietly.

"What happened?"

"When I got home last night all my stuff was piled up at my front door."

"Really? Oh, man, that's fantastic!" I was surprised it had happened so fast.

"Yeah. Please thank your friend for me. Tell him and whoever helped him they can sign up for any of my classes and they'll get an A. They don't even have to show up. That goes for you, too, David."

I passed Mr. Scofield's offer on to Rick. He was impressed with me. I'd fulfilled my quid pro quo for the North Side syndicate and was on its radar. I wasn't "connected," but we had a connection. Some of them now acknowledged me in the halls. Curious, I asked Rick if Mr. Scofield's stuff had been safe left outside his door in the hall.

"David, you don't get it!" he said. "That's our territory. I guarantee no one would dare to take it. It was as safe there as if it was in his apartment."

A few days later I introduced Rick and one of his syndicate guys to Mr. Scofield, who made good on his offer of a guaranteed A in his class. I didn't take Mr. Scofield up on his offer. I had my own moral compass. Besides, I needed to actually learn as much as I could to be able to function in the real world.

It finally became clear to me that I wasn't going to make it at Central Y, or at any other school. It was always the same story: I couldn't pass my classes because I couldn't pass written tests. My only successes were in survival and drug dealing. It wasn't what I wanted, but it was what I was given. I had a knack for it, and that seemed to be where my future lay.

When I look back on that time, the strangest part is how I managed to live a double life and keep my two worlds separate. At the end of every school day, I took the train home and had dinner with my parents and Neil. Then I hung out with my friends in our usual way — laughing, getting high, and talking. I'd tell them what happened sometimes, but I couldn't explain what I had to go through each day or what it was like to be a short, white, suburban, learning-disabled kid in a mostly black, inner-city, gang-infested continuation school. My family and friends never saw the darker side of me that came out when the shit hit the fan. They never saw the tough attitude and persona I had to cultivate in order to survive dealing drugs at Central Y. Or maybe I just wanted to believe they didn't see that other part of me. The only person I could really talk to about these things, and who seemed to understand them — and me — was my new friend, Donna.

Guarding the Fountain

One cold Chicago night I went out with Bob and Annie, two good friends from the crowd I now hung out with. They were both eighteen, three years older than I was. We drove around the city in Bob's Volkswagen bug, smoking a joint and trying to decide where to go for the evening. Bob wanted to go to Lolly's, a downtown Chicago nightclub, to listen to one of the blues bands that played there. You had to be twenty-one to get in and I was only fifteen, but I had a fake ID and I looked older with my long, frizzy hair and wispy mustache.

When I wanted to meet girls my own age, I periodically went to the Coffee House, a local teenage hangout in a church basement. That's where we finally decided to go that night. Bob parked the car in a strategic spot in the church parking lot — for a quick getaway if necessary. Things had changed a lot in the short time since I'd first started smoking pot. There were more people doing drugs, and more narcs. I'd scored some dope that afternoon and was holding two ounces of hash cut with black-tar heroin. Narcs now infiltrated various scenes where drugs were bought, sold, and consumed. Selling to someone you didn't know was risky. I had friends who got busted with an ounce of weed and were doing time in federal prison. There were also guys around who would rip you off if they could.

I never sold drugs at the Coffee House. It wasn't a drug crowd. It had an interesting mix of trendy kids with hippie ambitions and little political awareness; suburban kids in bell-bottoms with pop taste in music who tried to act cool and talk about dope; "good" kids, usually church members, who stayed in the front of the room and refilled the punch bowl and plates of stale cookies; the more interesting oddball crowd that hung out in the back of the room where it was darker; and the random punks who would show up and make trouble. Jocks and greasers never came; it wasn't their scene. I usually ran into some of my old friends from my public-school days there. And there were always pretty girls. That was the main reason I came.

Bob and Annie stopped to smoke a cigarette out front before going in. I never smoked, so I went inside to get out of the cold. I stood at the top of the steps overlooking the large basement room, checking out the scene, seeing who was there and what was happening.

The folding table at the bottom of the stairs was lined with the usual plates of cookies and rows of little Dixie cups filled with bright red punch. Nearly a hundred teenagers milled around the main room amid rows of folding tables and scattered folding chairs. They gathered in various cliques, laughing and talking. Steppenwolf blared out of loudspeakers.

As I scanned the room, a girl caught my eye. I'd never seen her before. Tall and thin, she stood alone next to the drinking fountain, her feet touching together and her arms folded behind her back. She wore an embroidered peasant-style shirt and bell-bottom jeans. Her long brown hair hung down in front of her face, and two big brown eyes with dark circles under them peered out through the strands. From the dark circles and her thin frame, I pegged her as a speed freak. She looked like a lost little girl, but something about her was definitely cute.

I knew I had to talk to her, so I headed for the drinking fountain. As I got closer, I saw that she was really pretty. I reached the fountain. Standing right next to her, I leaned down to take a drink, and I heard a feathery voice say, "Please..."

I lifted my head and looked up at her. Was she talking to me? Her head was turned toward me. Through the gaps in the hair covering her face, I saw a look of fear in her eyes. I knew that look so well — I could feel it in my gut. I immediately felt an empathetic bond with her. I wondered what she was so afraid of.

"What?" I asked her.

"Please, don't..." she said in the same soft voice.

I didn't understand. "Don't what?"

"The fountain — it's broken."

I turned the chrome knob, and the water flowed just fine. "It works okay." I gave her a puzzled look.

She shrugged and lowered her eyes. "They told me to guard it."

"What?" I furrowed my brow. Someone was messing with her. "Who?"

She nodded nervously toward the main room. I looked over and saw two smirking short-haired punks sitting at a table thirty feet away, watching us. One was a white guy, and the other was a sullen-looking Native American kid. They looked about eighteen. I looked at her again. Now I recognized something I'd missed in that first glance: She knew fear at a level most people never experience, the kind of fear that never goes away, the kind that lives in the same house with you. I wanted to help her.

I looked over at the two guys watching us with smarmy looks on their faces. Rage boiled inside me. I wanted to get in their faces, teach them a lesson — maybe hurt them. I locked eyes with the white guy; he held my gaze for about ten seconds, then looked away, trying to laugh it off. Then I looked at the Native American kid. He glared at me and didn't look away. He was the alpha of the two. I could have left them alone and stayed with the girl, but I wanted to know what they were up to and why. I hated bullies who picked on weaker kids; it triggered a rage in me that made me want to go after them. I felt it now.

I quickly glanced around, looking for Bob. If something started, it wouldn't hurt to have him as backup, but I didn't see him. He was probably still out front with Annie. It was just me then.

"I'll be right back," I told the girl.

I walked over to the two guys, looking directly at them. I'd had plenty of experience dealing with punks. I never bothered to bluff; when you're short, you quickly learn that it only makes you look weak. A lot of guys would back down if they sensed you were ready to go all the way, that you weren't afraid to fight. When I was in that place, aching to hurt someone, guys could usually tell it was for real. I walked up to them and stared them down.

"Are you guys fucking with her?" I asked bluntly.

"We thought it was funny," the white guy said sheepishly. They both leaned back a little bit, which told me they weren't up for a fight.

It was already over. I'd won the battle without a fight, but I had to know more. I never trusted a situation if I didn't understand someone's motivation.

"She's pretty, and she wanted white cross," Alpha said.

That confirmed my suspicion. White cross was a potent meth-amphetamine. I was afraid this was a sick punk's test of what she might do for some speed, and I worried about what he might try next. Holding back my rage, I said, "Just fucking leave her alone. You ever even talk to her again and I'll find you. You understand?"

They didn't say anything, so I turned and started back toward the girl. It flashed through my mind that I was stupid for inserting myself into other people's problems when I couldn't even solve my own. I'd been doing it for as long as I could remember, ever since kindergarten when I started protecting the little co-op girl from her crazy John Bircher father.

The girl was still standing by the water fountain, watching me. When I reached her, she looked at me shyly and then averted her gaze, down to the floor. I stood close, but not too close, care-ful to respect her space. "Are you okay?"

"Muhmmm…"

It wasn't much of an answer. Maybe she'd thought those guys were going to get her some speed, and now I'd ruined it for her. I looked at her, but she didn't seem upset. She didn't seem much of anything. It was almost as if she weren't there. She had a ghostly presence.

"Are you sure you're all right?"

"Yeah."

"You won't look at me. Am I making you uncomfortable? You want me to leave?"

She looked up and made eye contact. "No."

Then I saw a little smile. The fear was gone from her eyes. They were soft now. My heart started beating faster. "My name's David. What's your name?"

"Donna."

Then I saw Bob and Annie coming down the stairs. They saw me standing with Donna and came over. I introduced them to Donna, and they exchanged casual greetings. Everyone seemed okay with one another so I decided to move things forward.

"Hey, Donna, Bob's parents are gone for the weekend. We're gonna go to his house and get high. You wanna come with us? I'll make sure you get home at whatever time you need to."

She looked at me shyly and said in a small voice, "Yeah."

I reached out and took her by the hand. We left the Coffee House and walked through the chilly evening air toward Bob's Volkswagen bug. I felt high and alive holding Donna's hand; my mind and emotions raced. I glanced over at her several times before we got to the car, and each time she looked more beautiful. Before getting into the car, I quietly asked Bob if he could make sure Donna got home on time.

"No problem," he said.

Donna and I got into the back seat of the Volkswagen. Annie and Bob got in front. We left the church parking lot with Sly & The Family Stone playing on the local underground radio station. I felt an energetic connection with Donna; there was definitely chemistry. I hoped she was feeling it, too.

Donna and I talked about music — rock bands we liked, albums we had, concerts we'd been to. At one point I impulsively told her how glad I was to have met her. She gave me a shy little smile and I knew she liked me. When I leaned in to kiss her, she responded willingly, without holding back.

"Bob, don't forget to stop at the drugstore," I heard Annie say.

"What for?" Bob asked.

Sounding somewhere between annoyed and amused, Annie said, "We need birth control gel, remember?"

"Oh, yeah," said Bob.

I was completely caught off-guard. Was Donna in on this? Was Annie just speaking for herself? I glanced furtively at Donna, and she gave me a sweet, shy smile. This was unbelievable. When had they come up with this plan? It must have been on the walk to the car. I found it easy to be with girls and talk to them, but I was still pretty inexperienced sexually. Donna was apparently relaxed and confident about sex, which surprised me, because she seemed so shy and introverted. She was only about a year older than I was, so her familiarity with diaphragms seemed un-usually mature. It made her seem more mysterious, and a little intimidating.

A minute later Bob pulled into a drugstore parking lot. Annie asked him for money, and he handed her a five-dollar bill from his wallet. I had a couple of ones, but not knowing how much Donna needed, I gave her a ten-dollar bill. When Annie saw it, she began razzing Bob about only giving her a five.

Bob grinned. "Well, I'm not a bigtime dope dealer like David."

I didn't like Bob saying that in front of Donna, but it was done. Besides, I didn't consider myself a dealer. I was very care-ful to sell only to trusted friends — I just happened to have a lot of friends. Annie and Donna went in together and came out ten minutes later, giggling and holding their purchases. I liked see-ing Donna lighthearted and laughing. When they got into the car, Annie was holding an instructional pamphlet about the con-traceptive jelly they'd just bought to use with their diaphragms.

"Hey, you guys need to make sure you know how much gel to use. Bob never does it right." She giggled. "David, read them to us — Bob's driving."

She waved the instructions in front of me, laughing as if it were a funny joke. But it wasn't funny, because I couldn't read them.

Then Bob said, "Come on Annie! You know David can't read."

Fuck! I cringed in the dark. That was the last thing I wanted Donna to know about me. I grabbed the instructions and stuffed them into my coat pocket.

"I'll read them later," I said tersely.

Annie saw how embarrassed and angry I was. I could tell she felt bad about it, but the damage was done.

"I'll read them," she said apologetically.

I just wanted the moment to be over and the subject dropped. I shook my head and said, "Don't."

"Okay," she said in a subdued voice.

Annie turned around to face the front. The laughter had stopped. The car was silent except for the music on the radio. I was afraid to look at Donna, afraid of what she must think of me now. Moments later I started the conversation again, trying to act as if nothing had happened, ignoring the anxiety churning in my gut. Donna seemed the same as before. When we were almost at Bob's house, she leaned against me and put her head on my shoulder. Maybe everything was okay after all. I put my arm around her, and she relaxed into me. As we pulled into Bob's driveway, I leaned over and kissed her again. She responded, kissing me warmly, her lips melting into mine.

Donna seemed different from any girl I'd ever met before. In the short time I'd known her, I hadn't detected any capacity for self-inspection, which was something that caused me to mistrust other people. But I also saw no signs of judgment or dishonesty or maliciousness in her. It was a combination I'd never experienced in anyone before. She also possessed a soft innocence. This was the kind of thing that meant something to me, but probably to no one else. She intrigued, intimidated, and fascinated me. I thought about her asking those guys back at the church for speed. I wondered if she was high on something now.

Bob pulled into the driveway of his house, and we went inside and sat down in the living room. In one corner of the room he had a cage with a rabbit in it. The cage seemed too small for the rabbit. I felt sorry for it having to live like that.

"Why don't you let the rabbit out for a while?" I asked Bob.

He just grinned at me and said, "Let's get stoned."

He pulled a bag of weed and some rolling papers from his pocket and tossed them to me. I took the two-ounce block of hash from my pocket, picked off a small chunk and crumbled it into the weed, then rolled it into a perfectly shaped joint. Donna watched the process intently, but she didn't seem impressed by my superior rolling abilities. I could tell she'd seen it all before. She wasn't naïve; that was for sure.

In the middle of smoking the joint, Bob got up and let the rabbit out of the cage. The rabbit hopped around, back and forth. For some reason it didn't hop like a regular rabbit. Its hind legs flew up and out, arching over its back. A couple of times it flipped over, landed on its back, then scrambled upright again, facing the opposite direction. We all watched in amazement through increasingly stoned eyes. At one point Donna said softly, "He said he's going to run away."

"Who said?" Annie asked.

"The rabbit," Donna said.

Bob and Annie laughed it off. I looked at Donna, staring sadly at the rabbit. I realized she wasn't joking. I didn't know what to make of her. Finally we all got up, very stoned, and headed for the bedrooms. I took Donna by the hand and led her down the hall toward the guest bedroom. I was excited, but the prospect of being with someone so much more experienced was intimidating. I entered the guest room, leaving the light off. The streetlight outside cast a dim light into the room.

Donna followed me into the room, dropping her purse by the door. In that moment she seemed way older than her years. She found the directions for the gel, and I suddenly felt anxious again, as if the moment was about to be ruined. Usually when someone found out I couldn't read they didn't know how to handle it; they acted incredulous, becoming awkward or condescending with me. But Donna didn't seem the least bit fazed by it. She took the instructions, went over to the window, and read them out loud by the glow of the streetlight. I joined her there. It felt so intensely intimate, standing next to this beautiful girl I barely knew while she read the birth control directions out loud.

"Annie's right to read this. I don't use that much gel," she said.

She gave me an impish smile. Suddenly everything seemed natural. The tension in me was gone. I was so relieved. I felt good about myself with her.

She asked about the bathroom and left with the diaphragm and gel. When she returned, she casually took off her shirt and pants, leaving them on the floor. She got on the bed in her bra and panties, her hair half covering her eyes. She was thin and her ribs showed, but she was incredibly beautiful.

I stripped down to my underwear, and we climbed under the sheet and blanket, escaping the cold. Her arms were covered with goose bumps. I made a joke about it, and we laughed together. Then we kissed.

Lying next to her, everything seemed uncomplicated. She

seemed to take things as they were, to accept them without analysis and move on. That was something I had a hard time doing. Of the two of us, I was definitely the complicated one. I couldn't let go of things that bothered me, couldn't stop my thoughts from racing, or just be in the moment. She didn't have any problem with me being an illiterate drug dealer, and now I was lying in bed with her, holding her, and fretting over her eccentricities. Things kept popping into my mind: *How much speed does she use? What does it mean that she thought the rabbit was talking to her?* I felt that I needed to know what was going on with her if we were going to be intimate.

"You like speed?" I asked, trying to sound casual.

"Yeah, I guess." She sighed.

I pulled her to me, and she kissed me again, but her body went limp. I sensed her ambivalence. Did she want to have sex? As I touched her more intimately, her body stiffened. She was giving off very confusing signals, but I wasn't going to press it.

"I'm on my period," she said softly.

I took that as a signal to back off. Now she seemed vulnerable and confused. I felt concerned for her, and I was happy just to lie there together and talk.

I still couldn't get the rabbit remark out of my mind. I knew if you did too much speed you started to lose touch with reality. It could even make you psychotic. I'd met some truly crazy speed freaks before. I liked Donna. I felt protective of her, and I didn't want to take advantage of her.

"Do you do a lot of speed?" I asked.

She brushed off the question with another kiss, so I decided to let it go. I stroked her hair, ran my hand down her stomach, and then let my fingers play lightly across her ribs. She instantly recoiled, as if I'd touched her with a lit cigarette. Suddenly she had her hands pressed together as if she were praying, and she was looking up at me with terror in her eyes, pleading, "Please don't…please don't…"

She was nearly in tears and repeated this several more times, even though I'd stopped immediately.

"Okay, I'm sorry." I wasn't even sure what I'd done. I pulled her gently to me and held her again. Her body was tense, and she was shivering.

"What's the matter?" I asked.

She relaxed a little in my arms and pressed her face against my neck. We didn't say anything for a while. Annoyed, I couldn't help but wonder if she was manipulating me. But I wanted to know more about her. She was reluctant at first, but finally she started talking about her life in a stoned stream-of-consciousness ramble. It made her more of an enigma. She obliged my curiosity by going on for well over an hour. I glanced at the clock periodically, knowing she had to be home by eleven.

I learned a lot about Donna that night. She had five brothers and sisters. Her parents were strict Italian Catholics. Her family was extremely dysfunctional and moved every year or two. As a result, Donna had never formed deep or lasting friendships and didn't trust people. It felt even more important that she seemed to trust me.

Her father drank and had to move his family a lot in order to get promotions in his high-powered sales job. He also emotionally and physically abused his wife and kids, and especially Donna. Because of him, she'd lived in fear most of her life. He flew into wild rages, hitting her with his fists and openhanded slaps, leaving large bruises on her body. Sometimes he punished her by tickling her and refused to stop until she passed out, ignoring her desperate pleas to stop. That's what had triggered her when I accidentally tickled her ribs.

Donna had been getting high since she was twelve, and she was high much of the time. As a result, her father thought she was straight when she was stoned, and stoned when she was straight. Because he beat her when he thought she was stoned, she got stoned as often as possible in order to avoid his beatings. She talked so personally, I could feel her, and what it all meant to her. I felt I was getting to know her — her head and her heart.

I thought about my older brother. I'd never found him capable of empathy. He would seem to act out of empathy if he had to, but it was strategic; nothing but his own self-interest ever seemed to touch him. I thought about other people more extreme than Emerson; they had no concern for others at all and were without a conscience, free of any self-inspection. I could recognize this kind of person immediately. It was like an odor in the air when they walked into the room. But I was fascinated by these people, and how their charisma, which seemed to come from being free of concerns about right and wrong, good and bad, could appear to be a healthy sense of self-confidence. If there was evil, this seemed to be a requirement for it. I thought about how most of the powerful people I knew had this trait, and I questioned whether it was a necessary requirement to be a strong leader. It seemed it was always the worst people who had the most self-confidence. I wished I were capable of their freedom from the constant self-questioning and judgment that were always going on in my mind.

Donna, on the other hand, was capable of deep empathy but not self-reflection. As I'd learn later, she was capable of deep devotion, even losing herself in that, but only with one person in her life at a time; all others were objects to manipulate. She could also get very confused, even delusional, and her vulnerability was real. I couldn't help it; she was totally fascinating to me.

Finally it was time for her to go home. Her story had disturbed me and filled me with both overwhelming empathy for her and anger about her abuse. It was so unfair and undeserved. I really liked her. I felt for her. And I didn't feel judged by her. Although she was still an enigma to me, a strong desire to protect her filled my heart.

We lay quietly for a few minutes, holding each other. The dim light of the streetlight bled through the blinds. My feelings were poignant and sweet. It was like the lull before a spring storm, when the air is cool, the sky turns dark, the wind is blowing gently, and the world takes on a magical glow.

Donna and I exchanged phone numbers in the car on the way to her house. She placed the slip of paper with my number into her purse as if it were a treasure. When Bob pulled to a stop in front of her house, Donna and I hugged and kissed goodbye. As she walked up to her front door, I saw the drapes part in the living room window. As she reached the front porch the light went on; the door opened, and her father was standing there. He didn't let her in right away. He stood there yelling at her while she cowered in front of him. Then he stepped aside and let her pass. I could still hear him yelling as he closed the door. The magical glow I'd been feeling wasn't the lull before a spring storm but the eerie calm that precedes a tornado.

A Life Raft

*A*fter I dropped Donna off at her house that first night, her father wouldn't let her go out after school for a week. I was going to Central Y every day and calling her when I got home. I couldn't wait to see her. She lived just a couple of miles away from me, so we arranged to meet the next Saturday afternoon a block from her house.

I got there a little early and waited for her down the street. I stood on the corner in the chilly autumn air, watching her front door. Finally it opened. She came out, and I waved from a block away. She started walking toward me with her head tilted down and her hands shoved in the pockets of her winter coat. Her bell-bottoms accentuated her long, slender legs, and her long brown hair hung down over her face. She looked beautiful, awkward, and mysterious.

As she drew near she seemed uncertain, so I went to meet her. I put my arm around her and pulled her gently to me, giving her a reassuring hug. It felt so good to hold her. We started walking slowly together, making small talk, taking almost an hour to reach the co-op. We came in by the back way, walking through the fields near the edge of the property until we got to my house. Donna was nervous about meeting my mother. It took a few minutes for me to make her feel comfortable about going in, but she finally agreed. My mother was sitting at the kitchen table drinking her coffee.

"Hi, Mom! This is Donna," I said, leading Donna past her toward my bedroom. "She's a friend."

"Hello, Donna!" Mom greeted her with a big smile. "Good to meet you."

Donna nodded shyly, mumbling "Hi, Mrs. Patten" to my mom, still with her head down and her hair hiding her face. We went through the family room and came to my bedroom door. It was large, made of thick, heavy wood, and afforded a sense of protection as well as soundproofing. I opened the door and let Donna in. My bedroom was actually two adjoining rooms, more a living quarters. I hung out mostly in the front room, and slept in the other room.

"This is my hangout room," I said as I followed her in. "My bedroom is through there." I pointed at the doorway to the second room. "Make yourself comfortable. That's my couch and chair, my desk, my stereo and record collection. You can check out my records if you want."

She went over to my desk and started looking through the clutter, seeing what was there. Then she went over to my pride and joy: an AR belt-driven state-of-the-art turntable and speakers, and my collection of almost a hundred rock albums. She looked through the albums and handed me *Buffalo Springfield*. I put it on, turned the volume low, and sat down in the big slouch chair. She sat down in front of me in the chair, and I softly pulled her back so she was leaning with her back against my chest.

"Finally we're alone together," I whispered in her ear, then kissed her ear and neck. She didn't seem to mind.

"I'm off my period," she said out of the blue. "It ended last Tuesday."

"Oh, good," I said, a little surprised. Then I felt as if I'd said something stupid. But she turned around and leaned forward, putting her arms around me, and we started kissing. She was so sweetly open. She maneuvered her body so that she was lying on top of me as I leaned back in the crook of the chair. We made out until the record stopped.

"I'll turn the record over," I said.

As I moved her off my lap to get up, I lightly bumped her lower back. She jerked away, cringing with a whimper, but trying to hide it.

"What's wrong?" I asked.

"It's sore," she said.

I carefully helped her to a sitting position. Then I lifted the back of her blouse to look. There were two bruises on her lower back, each one about the size of an orange — or a fist.

"What happened? You didn't have those bruises last Friday night."

"No," she said, almost apologetically.

"Do you have any other bruises?"

Hesitating at first, she pointed at her left upper arm. She was wearing a short-sleeve blouse with a scoop neckline. I lifted the left sleeve and saw the bruise around her skinny biceps, where someone very strong had grabbed her and squeezed hard.

"What happened?"

Donna replied sheepishly. "My dad got mad."

"Any more bruises?" I asked.

She shook her head no. I was furious at her father. The worst part was that she seemed to think it was her fault. She saw the anger in my face and looked a little frightened of me.

"When did he do this?"

"Last Friday night."

My heart sank. That was the night we met, the night I dropped her off. Her father had seen me — and he'd taken it out on her. It hit me hard. I knew it wasn't my fault, but I felt responsible. I didn't have any idea what I could do to help her, but it was at that moment I decided I'd do whatever I could to make sure he never hit her again.

"Why?" I asked.

"He said I was high."

I asked her more questions about her father, almost grilling her. She finally opened up and told me things that made me sick.

"When I was eleven he came into my room one night really drunk. He climbed in my bed and started…you know."

"What did you do?"

"I screamed and got out of bed. When he came after me I climbed out the window and onto the ledge. Then my mom came in, and they both started yelling at me to come back inside. They acted like I was the problem. He didn't try it again, but I never felt safe around him after that. And he started beating me more after that."

"Is there anything you can do to stop him?"

I felt like a jerk for asking. If there were something she could have done, she would have done it long ago. She changed the subject.

"Do you want to get some speed?" she asked with big puppy eyes. "Please?"

I didn't know what to say. I didn't like that she used speed, and I wasn't about to feed her addiction. I had mostly dealt non-addictive drugs, like pot, hash, and psychedelics. At the time, the kind of speed I was selling at Central Y wasn't considered any more addictive then coffee. Her big eyes bored into me with the anxiety of withdrawal.

"I don't think I can," I said.

"I can get some money to pay you back if that's what you're worried about."

"Do you have a job?" I tried distracting her by changing the subject.

"I model sometimes, like for catalogs."

"Really? How much does that pay?"

"Forty-five an hour."

"Wow. I think that's more than my dad makes."

"I don't work regularly. It comes and goes. So can we get some speed?"

"Look, Donna, I really don't know how I can get you any speed right now." I probably could have gotten her some, but I wasn't going to. "Let's just stay here. We can smoke pot, listen to music — just be together. Do you want to get high?"

She nodded, but I saw she was disappointed. I wondered how hardcore she was. Did she shoot up or just do pills? Was she really addicted or did she just really like it, or think it was cool? I loaded and lit the pipe, took a toke, and handed it to her. As she reached for the pipe, I scanned her arms, looking for tracks. I didn't see any. She took a long toke and handed the pipe back.

"Do you shoot up?" I asked her.

"Sometimes," she said, holding her toke. "Just meth."

"Where do you shoot? Your arms look clean."

She exhaled a stream of thick smoke. "My ankles. No one looks there."

"Can I see?"

She shrugged, then pulled up her bell-bottoms and pulled one sock down below her ankles. I leaned down for a closer look and saw tracks in the delicate area inside and just below her ankle. Some looked recent, and some were old scars. She was definitely a hardcore speed freak. I hated the idea of her shooting up. The more I learned about Donna, the more worried I became for her. She pulled her socks back up.

"When was the last time you shot up?" I asked.

"Yesterday morning. It was the last of my stash. It's all gone now. I don't have any money or connections here."

"Hmm…"

I took another toke and handed her the pipe. We finished it in silence. I was feeling anxious. I didn't know much about speed withdrawal, except that it could be real bad; the second day was a lot harder than the first day, and the third day was the worst. When I asked her if she was hungry, she asked if I had any sweets. I went to the kitchen and got a piece of white cake and a Coke from the fridge. I went back and put the cake and the Coke on the floor next to her. Then I went and lay down on the couch. A few minutes later she came and lay down next to me and put her head on my chest. We held each other for a while.

"Are you going to stay with me?" she asked plaintively.

"Yeah, sure," I said. Then I realized I wasn't sure what she meant. Tonight? Forever? "What do you mean?" I asked her.

"You can't ever leave me. I need you to always be with me."

"You mean by your side?"

"Yeah."

"I can't be with you every minute of every day. But I'll be there for you when you need me."

"I need you with me all the time."

She had a childlike way of drifting into unreality, the way she had with the talking rabbit, so I didn't want to promise her something that wasn't possible. But I wanted to be there for her. I saw it was pointless to argue with her about this, so I changed the subject.

"When did you start doing speed?" I asked.

"When I was twelve. My boyfriend Eric shot me up the first time. I didn't want to. He made me do it. But as soon as it came on, I loved it."

"How old was he?"

"He was twenty-one. My father hated him. He was always calling the police on him. He got busted for possession a year ago. They shortened his sentence on the condition that he join the army when he got out. He's in boot camp now. My father moved us here from Minnesota a couple of months ago. Partly because he got a promotion, but partly to get away from Eric."

"You're father moved out of state to get away from your boyfriend?"

"Eric's a pretty intense guy. I think my father's afraid of him. He didn't beat me nearly as much when I was seeing Eric." Then she dropped a bomb. "We're still engaged. He's coming to see me in a couple of weeks."

"What?" I said, completely astonished.

"He gets out of boot camp on leave in three weeks. He's riding his motorcycle out to see me." This was getting stranger by the minute. She spoke in a calm, matter-of-fact voice, as if it were all normal stuff.

"What the hell do you mean you're engaged? Why are you here with me?"

She cringed and gave me a worried look, as if she were afraid I was going to hit her.

"I really like you, David. I want to be with you."

"Then you need to break up with him! Or do you want to stay with him?" I was really confused.

"No, not anymore."

"Then call him and break the engagement."

"But…I still have the ring. He's gonna want his ring back," she mumbled, by way of explanation.

I looked at her in disbelief. "So mail his ring back."

She was getting more uncomfortable by the second. She stared at the wall, worry wrinkles creasing her forehead.

"It's not that easy. I'm afraid of him." I could see in her eyes that she really was afraid. "He gave me two miscarriages," she blurted out.

"What? How did he do that?"

"He kept punching me in the stomach and taking me riding on really rough trails on his dirt bike."

"Both times?"

"Yeah, over and over until I finally miscarried."

I couldn't believe what I was hearing.

"He said we couldn't afford to have the babies," she explained. "He didn't think they were his, and even if they were he could have gotten arrested for statutory rape."

Taken aback, I asked, "Whose else would they have been?"

Watching me intently she said, "I don't know. I don't want to say."

Pausing to think, I wondered what it could be that she wasn't wanting to tell me. Then it was obvious: He had made her a prostitute. Without thinking I said, "Shit. That fucking asshole!"

Frightened by my outburst, she became silent. Then she said in a small voice, "He made me," and began crying again.

"Why didn't you break up with him?"

"I tried to a few times. He just says no, and he always comes back. Besides, if I don't marry him, I don't know how I'll get out of the house before I'm eighteen. I can't live with my dad anymore. At least Eric takes care of me."

"Are you serious? He's worse than your dad!"

"No, he's not. He doesn't hit me as much. There's nothing I can do anyway; he's coming for me."

She seemed completely resigned. This was crazy. But she was so vulnerable; I couldn't just leave her in this situation.

"But…if you knew you were safe and Eric couldn't hurt you, would you break up with him?"

"Definitely! I want to be with you."

"Would you want to break up with him even if it wasn't for me?"

"Yes, but I want to be with you."

"You're absolutely sure?"

"Absolutely."

"Good. So now it's a matter of what it would take to make you safe. Look, Donna, I promise I'll protect you. I'll keep you safe."

"How?"

I didn't know how to answer that. It wasn't like I had a plan.

"I need a little time to think, but I'll figure it out. I promise. I'm not just saying this."

We lay there holding each other, her head resting on my chest. It was dusk outside and the room was getting darker.

I had a sinking feeling. This guy Eric was dangerous, as bad as the worst characters at Central Y. He was clearly a sociopath. Now I was virtually stealing his girlfriend, and he wasn't going to like it when he found out. I'd been in dangerous situations before, but this definitely upped the ante. I hated the war, but I hoped they shipped Eric straight from boot camp to Vietnam.

If I wanted to keep Donna safe, I'd have to come up with a plan. She would have to break up with this guy. She'd also have to kick her speed habit. I couldn't have a relationship with a speed freak. I couldn't tell if her bizarre behavior was just a result of long-term speed use or not. I hoped that was all it was. Maybe if she got clean, she'd return to some degree of normalcy. Or maybe she was screwed up before, and the speed just made it worse. Either way I still wanted to be with her. After all, who was I to judge her? I was as screwed up in my own way as she was. I felt like I had a problem too big for anyone to help me with, so people stood on the sidelines and judged me, as if that were help-ing. I wasn't going to do that to her. I knew how to stand beside a comrade and fight. I wasn't going to leave her stranded on Mars.

"Have you thought about getting off speed?" I asked her.

"Yeah, I will someday. But not right now."

"Why not?"

"I don't know. I'd need to be ready for that."

"How would you get ready? If you want to kick it now, I promise I'll stay with you the whole time. You're already one day clean, right?"

"I don't know. I don't want to think about that right now." I could feel her tense up again. We were silent for a few moments. "Are you going to leave me if I don't quit?" she asked anxiously.

"No," I reassured her.

"Good," Donna quickly replied.

I could tell she took that as a commitment. The idea of quitting cold turkey had to be scary. I didn't want to pressure her or freak her out. She was so fragile, and she was clearly terrified of abandonment, but I couldn't help her if she didn't quit. "But I don't see how we can have an ongoing relationship if you don't quit," I added.

This sounded like double talk even to me. She didn't respond, and I didn't say anything more. I wasn't going to leave her, but I couldn't, and didn't, promise forever.

"Can you stay the night?" I asked her.

"Yeah. But what about your parents?"

"I'll take you out the front door, and you can say goodbye to my mom. Then I'll sneak you back in through the back door to my room. What about your parents? Can you work it out?"

"Yeah. I'll say I'm staying at a girlfriend's. I'd better call soon."

Donna called her mom and told her she'd be staying over at a girlfriend's house. After she hung up, she told me that she didn't have to be home until the next morning. I took Donna out through the front door past my mom and back into my room through the back door. I left the lights off and we cuddled to *Buffalo Springfield*, side two. She seemed more relaxed again, now that she was spending the night with me. We made out a little, and then talked a little. At one point I asked again if she'd consider quitting speed. She immediately tensed up again.

"Why do I have to quit speed? I just want to be with you. Don't leave me alone. Please don't leave me alone." She started crying uncontrollably. "Promise you'll never leave me, that you'll always stay with me."

"I'm not leaving you, Donna. I'm right here. I'm not going

anywhere." I held her close and rocked her. "But I really want you to get clean. It'll make everything better. I promise."

Finally, she agreed. "Okay, I'll quit for you, as long as you never leave me."

"Don't worry. I don't know about never, but everything's going to work out."

It was growing darker outside. Her face looked so vulnerable and sweet by the faint light of the stereo in the dusk-lit room. I held her and stroked her hair, telling her everything was going to be all right. I half believed it myself.

After a while she got up to use the bathroom. On her way back she stopped at my desk. I saw her reach down and pick something up. Then I heard a familiar click. By the light of the stereo, I saw something metallic flash in her hand. I got up immediately with a weird feeling. She had opened my three-inch pocketknife. I went over and saw her calmly pressing the blade into the soft flesh just above the inside of her elbow.

I lunged for the knife, but the blade caught the edge of my palm with a sharp sting. I reached to stop her again, and she began to struggle with a ferocity and desperation that took me completely by surprise. I couldn't believe such a thin girl had so much strength. We had been so connected and intimate only moments before; now she was a completely different person. It was surreal. I was trying to stop her from hurting herself, and she was thrashing wildly as if I was attacking *her*!

She still held the knife. I gripped her hand and maneuvered it behind her, then reached my other arm around and pulled her to me. Now I had both arms around her, and control of the knife. My hand was still bleeding, and I was careful not to get any blood on her. I knew I couldn't let her go. If I did, I didn't know which one of us she'd use the knife on. I had to keep us both safe.

I managed to pry the knife from her hand and toss it away. She continued fighting. In the struggle, we both lost our balance. I tried to soften our fall onto the floor by landing on my shoulder and elbow, keeping my arms wrapped tightly around her. She continued to struggle furiously. Every few minutes she'd go limp; we'd lie there, panting, catching our breath, saying nothing. During one break I managed to tear off a piece of my sleeve and wrap my hand. Then she started up again. It went on like this for a couple of hours. She tried to kick and bite me; she hit her head against me and even hit her head on the floor. I did everything I could to restrain her, to keep her from hurting herself — and me.

At last she began to calm down. We were both exhausted and covered with sweat. I relaxed my grip but was still on guard. We lay there for a while, still not speaking. Over the next half hour she slowly grew softer, until I recognized the tender person I thought I knew. She was back. Then she gently wiggled around in my arms, turning to face me, and went limp again with her head on my chest, crying silently. We lay there for hours, holding each other, the open knife on the floor a few feet away. It was a relief when she fell asleep in my arms a little while later. I liked that. Eventually I drifted off, too.

Dawn came and the sun rose over the distant trees, shining through the long, vertical window in the outside door to my bedroom. I felt both desperation and intimacy in our embrace, and a new wariness inside myself. I didn't understand her. I also knew I wasn't going to abandon her. I realized I was in way over my head. Donna was more than a little scary. Yet, somehow, in our life-and-death struggle we had bonded. We lay like two shipwrecked survivors marooned on a life raft, watching the sunrise after a long, dark night at sea. Perhaps we were each other's life raft, maybe even each other's last chance. Maybe together we could make up one whole person.

Glimmer of Light

*A*fter our strange first night together, Donna and I spent all of our available time together. If we went anywhere, she was always at my side, leaning against me, or hovering just behind me with her right shoulder touching my left shoulder. She whimpered or cried every time she had to go home. She seemed to have motivation for only two things: being close to me, and getting stoned, in that order. Her father didn't approve of her seeing any boy, but for us, not seeing each other was out of the question. We kept things clandestine.

Each time we were together I learned more about her. By nature I was mistrustful of people. It seemed her stories where so extreme and unusual that I had trouble believing they were true. But as time went on I realized it was all true. She had a tragic air about her, and her resigned attitude toward life was surprising to see in a fifteen-year-old. She'd concluded that she had no control over anything; nothing was going to work out anyway, so we might as well just be together — and get stoned.

She was the most reckless drug user I'd ever met. She would use any drug, any combination of drugs, and any amount of drugs, with no reflection or hesitation. Yet with all of this there was an innocence in her depth of heart. She also loved me like no one else ever had before. She seemed to think that if she could attach herself to me and fulfill my needs, then she could finally be safe. Her primary need was to be as close to me as possible at all times. Sometimes it made me feel uncomfortable, but I also enjoyed the way she would anticipate my needs. She was there before I even had to ask. I loved the feeling of protecting her; it gave me strength. If I was worth nothing else, at least I could do whatever it took to protect someone I loved.

She was clearly addicted to meth. I knew that meth was addictive and could make you paranoid, violent, and potentially psychotic. I was never sure how much of Donna's bizarre behavior was a result of her speed habit, and how much was a result of her traumatic home life. At times I wondered if she were schizophrenic.

While Donna was extremely dysfunctional in some ways, she was highly functional in others. The oldest of six children, she'd been a surrogate mother to her five siblings, and the family's primary housekeeper since she was a young girl. Every day she cleaned the house, did the laundry, washed the dishes, and took care of her brothers and sisters. It was a heavy workload that she'd borne for years, along with her father's emotional and physical abuse. And despite the turmoil of her life she excelled academically, maintaining a straight-A average. Speed had helped her maintain her focus, but at great cost to her physical and mental health.

Now that we were together, I didn't see much of my friends. I tried hanging out with them and Donna a few times, but it didn't work. Donna was terribly shy and awkward in a group. She would get very quiet and tilt her head forward so her hair hung in front of her face. If you looked for her, you could just make out her eyes and a twitch of a smile, maybe her dimple. And her strangeness came out in unpredictable moments. She had a tendency to take off-the-wall jokes and put-ons literally, asking follow-up questions that made her seem incredibly naïve. My friends didn't understand her, or our relationship. They thought I was taking on way too much by being with her.

They were probably right. She was fiercely jealous and would erupt in fits of anger and hysteria, or collapse emotionally with little or no provocation. My walking out of the room, making an offhand remark, or talking to someone else for too long could trigger intense feelings of rejection and her greatest fear of all: abandonment. When this happened, I'd have to help her stabilize or she would start to panic or even hallucinate. At those times my instincts took over and I'd hold her until she felt safe and reassured. That could take a while, sometimes hours. It felt natural for me to comfort Donna in this way, and I couldn't help but wonder if this was anything like what my mother went through for me.

I more or less dropped out of sight to be with Donna. But we were getting to know each other and liked being alone together. There was a lot going on and a lot to figure out. For one thing, Eric, her sociopathic boyfriend, would be heading this way on his motorcycle, fresh out of boot camp. I still needed to come up with a plan to keep her safe, and I hadn't been able to think of anything.

One day, two weeks before Eric was due to arrive, Donna called and told me her father had decided to move to Texas in a week. They'd been living here less than six months. I couldn't get over the fact that she wasn't safe at home, or with this guy Eric. And we couldn't bear the thought of being separated. So I had the idea that maybe Donna could stay and live with us.

In the past, my parents had taken in troubled kids to live with us on a temporary basis. Of course, they'd all been boys. But I hoped we could work something out.

There had always been a rule in our family: We had to move out of the house at eighteen unless we were enrolled in college. But since college wasn't an option for me, I had less than three years to figure out how to make my way in the world. Until then, I could count on my parents to provide room, board, and whatever support they could. My mother still hoped I'd get a high school diploma, but it didn't look like that was going to happen.

My mother and I were close, despite a lingering strain between us after my suicide attempt. She treated me like a young adult, maintaining an emotional reserve with me. It was her way of protecting herself. Although I didn't tell her about my drug dealing, or some of my more dangerous adventures in Central Y, I could talk with her about almost anything else.

After learning that Donna's family would be moving in a week, I sat down at the kitchen table with my mother and told her what was going on. I told her about Donna's speed addiction and her strange behavior, about her father's abuse, and about her criminal boyfriend who got her hooked on speed and gave her two miscarriages. I didn't mention that he'd prostituted her or that he was coming in less than a week to claim her against her will.

My mother was as dependable and frank with me as I'd hoped she would be. She listened attentively and maintained her professional poise. When I was finished, she told me Donna needed treatment for her addiction. She added that I should be prepared; Donna might be schizophrenic. This echoed my own fears. In any case, she needed to be in a psychiatric hospital. Then I told her about Donna's family moving to Texas, and I asked about the possibility of Donna staying with us. She said absolutely not. I pointed out that she'd brought other kids into our home without our agreement. Now she was refusing to help someone who was in real peril and whom I cared about. I was desperate, believing Donna's life was at stake. I made it clear that if something bad happened to Donna, it would live with me, and I knew it would live with her, too. She tentatively suggested an alternate possibility. She said if Donna would go to a psychiatric hospital for a month and get clean, then afterward she might be able to stay with my aunt — my mother's sister — who lived a few miles from us. If Donna's father had insurance coverage, she could get her into a thirty-day treatment program. That was the best option. Donna's parents would have to agree, but my mother was willing to talk to them about it, and to her sister.

She told me that she would be doing this against her better judgment. She had serious concerns about Donna's psychological condition. She appreciated the fact that I cared deeply about Donna and wanted to help her, but she saw me trying to save Donna and that troubled her. She thought our relationship was unhealthy and probably wasn't good for either one of us. But she also knew that leaving Donna in her current predicament, addicted to speed with a physically abusive father and boyfriend, was the worst thing for her. She said she couldn't promise anything, but she'd try to help Donna if she could.

Afterward, I called Donna and told her about the conversation and the options my mother had offered. I asked Donna if she'd be willing to go to a psychiatric hospital and get clean to meet the conditions my mother had set. She said yes, as long as we would be together after she got out. So I told her that my mother would call her parents and talk with them. I also told her that she shouldn't talk to her parents about this until my mother had talked to them first.

I trusted my mother's plan. She was really good at this sort of thing — it was what she did for a living. Although she probably felt trapped by my involvement in the situation and felt obligated on that account, she truly was someone whose nature was to help others. Over the years she'd helped many local parents and kids resolve family conflicts. Neighbors and friends had always come over to talk with her about their troubles and to get her advice. That was something I'd always admired about my mother; she was willing to help just about anyone who needed it.

— ❋ —

Two mornings after our talk, I came out of my room to find a man sitting at the kitchen table talking to my mom. I immediately recognized him, though I'd only seen him from a distance, yelling at Donna in her front door. I quickly stepped back into my room and closed the door. *Oh shit*, I thought. *It's happening.* The plan was in motion. I just hoped that I'd done the right thing, and that he didn't go home and take it out on Donna.

I put my ear to the door but couldn't hear anything. For the first time I wished that the door wasn't soundproof. A couple of hours later I opened it a crack and peeked through. My mother was sitting alone at the table. So I went out to see her.

"When did he go?"

"A few minutes ago."

"How did it go?"

"We'll see," she said noncommittally.

She seemed neither confident nor pessimistic. She wouldn't tell me the details of their conversation because they were confidential. I'd have to wait until Donna called to tell me what her father said.

I didn't have to wait long. Donna called that evening and told me that her parents had agreed for her to go into treatment and then go to live with my aunt, to whom they would pay a minimal fee. Her family would still be moving to Texas.

My first thought was that they were only too happy to be rid of their problem child, and that their consent also had a financial motive — removing the expense of one daughter from their already-strained budget. Then it occurred to me that with Donna gone, they would be losing a maid and a nanny as well as a daughter. I began to consider the idea that maybe, even as screwed up as her parents were, they really did care about Donna in their own twisted way. Maybe the physical and verbal abuse was partly her father's sick, frustrated efforts to control and straighten out a wayward daughter. Whatever the case, he was letting Donna go, and that was all that mattered. Somehow, my mother had gotten through to him. My mother was savvy and she could be tough. I suspected that she threatened to expose his behavior and raised the issue that he could lose more than Donna.

Donna was apprehensive about going into an institution and quitting speed. But she was happy to be leaving her family and staying in Chicago with me. Over the next few days, plans were solidified. At the end of the week, Donna would go spend a month in Riveredge, a well-known psychiatric institute.

Riveredge didn't treat drug addiction or provide addicts with psychological counseling to address the root of their addiction. This was the Stone Age of treatment for drug addiction. Addictions were still considered a weakness of character, not a disease as they are today. Most drug addicts were shamed and left on their own without any help. Twelve-step meetings were for alcoholics only. Those who wanted help, and could afford it, entered psychiatric institutions to get clean. But these institutes only offered supervised warehouse situations where these patients would be unable to use drugs for the duration of their stay. Once they came out, technically clean, they were on their own again. This was the standard until the Betty Ford Center paved the way for a new model and a more humane approach to the treatment of addicts and alcoholics.

My mother helped facilitate Donna's acceptance into Riveredge. Her father's insurance would pay for her stay there. After that, his financial obligations toward Donna would consist of bare-minimum monthly payments for room and board to my aunt, who wouldn't be profiting from her altruism and had also agreed to become Donna's legal guardian.

Meanwhile, the situation with Donna's boyfriend was taking a new turn. I'd been urging Donna to call Eric and break up with him over the phone. Finally she did. He didn't take it very well. The next day, he called back to tell her his new plan. He'd told his sergeant that his fiancée had broken up with him and asked for emergency leave to go to see her. When his sergeant refused, Eric, as he put it, "kicked his face in" and went AWOL. He was on his way here and would probably arrive within forty-eight hours, on the day Donna would be going into Riveredge. He'd said he wanted to talk to Donna face-to-face. I told Donna I wanted to be there for that conversation, but she and her father both decided it would be a bad idea. They were probably right.

— ✦ —

On the day Donna was scheduled to enter Riveredge, Eric called in the morning, a couple of hundred miles away, to tell her he'd be arriving that afternoon. I went over to see her before Eric arrived, and to help her load her stuff into her father's car. Her father was going to give me a ride back to my house. Then he'd take Donna back home for her meeting with Eric, and after that, he'd take her to Riveredge.

Donna had said her father wanted to see me up close at least once before he and the family moved to Texas. I was a bit nervous about meeting her father, and about Donna's meeting with Eric, but I was feeling relieved that things seemed to be turning in our favor.

As I approached their house I saw a cop car parked across the street. Cops always made me nervous. I went up to the front door and rang the bell. A minute later her father opened it. He greeted me formally by name, and politely invited me in. I could tell he didn't like me.

Up close, he looked much younger than my parents. He was very handsome, looked strong and fit, and had a natural charm. I knew from Donna that her father had been the star quarterback in high school, and her mother had been head cheerleader; they had been voted king and queen at their senior prom. If I'd met her father anywhere else, I would've thought he was a dynamic, successful businessman. I never would have suspected him of being a child abuser.

I was still standing between him and the open door behind me when he looked over my head, smiled, and gave a friendly wave. I turned around to see the cop in the patrol car across the street wave back. Now I felt really paranoid. I remembered Donna telling me that her father had called the cops on Eric, and that Eric finally got busted and jailed for possession. Had he called the cops on me? Was he trying to get me busted? Then it occurred to me that the cop was probably there for protection from Eric.

"Please wait in the living room while we get ready," he said. "We'll be a few minutes."

But instead of going into the house, he went out the front door and crossed the street to talk to the cop. I went and sat down on the couch. A couple of minutes later he returned and walked past me through the living room and headed upstairs. When he reached the second floor I heard him say to someone, "I asked the officer to come back in an hour."

I sat there uncomfortably and looked around the room. There were boxes labeled and stacked in a corner, but the living room was clean and the furniture was nice. It looked like a typical, well-kept suburban tract house. A minute later Donna's mother came downstairs and into the room. She smiled and greeted me politely and asked if I wanted anything to drink. I told her no thank you. She also looked surprisingly young and quite beautiful. I could see why her parents had been voted prom king and queen, and where Donna had gotten her looks.

Her mother went back upstairs, and moments later I heard kids' laughter and loud footsteps. Donna's younger brothers and sisters came careening down the stairs and into the living room — three boys and two girls between the ages of six and twelve. They were all clean-cut and good-looking. They stopped at the bottom of the stairs and stood staring at me and giggling.

This was a classic American family — Ozzie and Harriet and a beautiful brood of kids. The only one who didn't make sense was Donna, the emaciated speed freak with needle marks on her ankles and dark circles under her eyes. It was hard to reconcile this beautiful picture-perfect family and tidy home with Donna's dark description of alcoholism and emotional and physical abuse.

I even wondered if Donna might have been exaggerating, until I remembered the bruises on her back and on her arm. Appearances could be deceiving, and in this case they had to be a lie. Donna was evidence of a darker reality behind this glossy exterior.

Just then, Donna's father came down the stairs carrying two suitcases. Donna came right behind him holding a large duffel bag by a strap. These were all of her belongings, at least those she would be keeping from now on.

"Let's go! We have to hurry!" her father called out.

I wasn't sure whom he was talking to. I went and held the front door open for them. Donna and her father walked out and continued down the sidewalk toward the car. The kids came and stood in the doorway, watching. Donna's mother appeared behind them.

"It was nice meeting you," I said to Donna's mother, and then added, "You have a very beautiful home and kids."

I wanted to be as polite as possible and make a good impression, for whatever it was worth. Donna's mother gave me a blank smile, and the kids just stared at me. I probably looked like Frank Zappa to them. I turned and followed Donna and her father to the car. He was loading the suitcases and duffel bag in the trunk. When he finished, he slammed the trunk and got into the driver's seat. I sat in the back on the passenger side, and Donna sat to my left, behind her father. Neither of us wanted to sit in the front seat with him. It was a little awkward, but the situation was already so weird it didn't seem to matter.

We drove the ten minutes to my house in silence, and Donna's father pulled into my driveway and parked in front of the garage. As soon as he parked he turned around in his seat to face Donna. Suddenly everything changed. The charming, handsome father disappeared, instantly replaced by an angry, red-faced, frightening man. He laid into her, starting off in an angry growl about how she'd better not take any drugs from now on, and if he found out she was taking drugs he'd come back from Texas and kick her ass, slap her silly, and beat her to a bloody pulp.

In less than a minute he'd worked himself into a wrathful frenzy. It wasn't only his words and tone of voice; even his body language was threatening. He seemed to be winding up, preparing to explode. Donna sat looking at him with a helpless, terrified expression. I was hoping he'd simply chew her out and the storm would blow over. I just wanted this to be over with, to get us the hell out of the car, and to have him drive off. Finally, he seemed to be finished. We sat there for a moment in silence.

"Donna, we should get going," I said, trying to sound casual.

She shot me a quick glance and gave a slight, pitiful shake of her head; then her eyes darted back to her father. I felt a sudden chill in the car. I knew I'd fucked up. I didn't know how badly. He looked at me, as if I'd insulted him.

"You're not going anywhere until I'm done talking!" he shouted at me.

He yelled a few other things at me, the gist of which was that he didn't trust me and that he thought I was trouble. Then he twisted halfway around in his seat and raised his right arm in a threatening backhand position. Donna instinctively put her hands in front of her face and started crying, "No, Daddy, no!"

Then he delivered the first blow, a well-practiced backhand that knocked Donna's hands out of the way and then smacked her across the side of her head. It was the first in a flurry of blows, each one making solid contact with a sickening thud. He started in on her knees and legs, and when she lifted her legs and curled in a ball on the seat, he leaned over and began swinging for her ribs and shoulder. The sounds of his blows were punctuated by vicious grunts. Donna gasped and whimpered each time he struck her. She covered herself as best she could, but he kept swinging at her and yelling, "Shut up Donna! Shut the hell up!"

I didn't know what to do. I was madder than I'd ever been in my life. I would have jumped on him if I'd thought it would have helped. Or even just put my body between them. But I knew if I interfered now, he'd change his mind and take her with him to Texas. Whatever he was doing now, he'd do worse when he got her alone. So I sat there with my guts churning, watching him wail away on this frail ninety-eight-pound girl I loved. I kept thinking, *She's still his daughter, but if I can hold out then I'll have her and I can keep her safe.*

Finally he stopped, breathing hard, his face red and contorted. Donna was curled on the seat in a fetal position. I thought it was over. Donna peeked out between her hands to look at him. Then, having caught his breath, he shifted his body around and started in again, now walloping the other side of her body repeatedly with his fist, striking her upper shoulders, back, and arms. Again came the sickening thud of his clenched fist against her body. Donna whimpered and moaned, jerking and twisting around, her body cringing in response to every blow.

We're so close, I kept thinking. If I could just hold back until he was done, it would all be over soon. Donna could stay here, her father would go to Texas, and he would never be able to hit her again.

Thud! Thud! Thud! It seemed to go on forever.

The whole time Donna never looked at me once. Finally, her father stopped again, completely out of breath. Then he turned to me with a look of pure hate. I thought he was going to start in on me. If he did, I'd have to sit there and take it. If that was the price of Donna's freedom, then okay. He glared at me and said in the most threatening voice, "If you ever hurt Donna, I swear to God I'll come back and make sure you can never hurt her again."

What a lunatic! He'd just pounded his daughter like she was a punching bag, and now he was telling me not to hurt her. I didn't know what to say, so I just nodded and kept my mouth shut.

"Now you can go," he said.

I stared at him, my mouth gaping wordlessly for a moment, and then I opened the door and got out. I didn't dare say anything to Donna for fear he'd start in on her again. He knew it, too, and so did she. I knew her beating was also a message to me. I shut the door, and he backed out of the driveway and drove off down the street.

We weren't out of this yet. After they dropped Donna's stuff off at my aunt's house, they went back to their house for the meeting with Eric. Standing in the driveway, I vowed that no man was ever going to beat Donna again. Not as long as I was around. I felt sickened by my inability to protect her from her father's beating. I knew there was nothing else I could have done, but it haunted me for years.

The next time Donna and I communicated was by mail, when she was in the hospital. She couldn't have any communication from outside for two weeks except by mail, and all her mail was being read. In her letters she said it went okay with Eric. I learned more when I called her two weeks later at Riveredge and we talked on the phone. She told me her meeting with Eric had gone surprisingly well. She'd given him back his ring and told him that she wasn't going to marry him, and that she was going into a hospital for a while to get clean from speed and then moving out of the state where he couldn't find her. After the conversation, he took off on his motorcycle and she never heard from him again. Donna didn't know, but I suspected, that her father had arranged for Eric to be arrested after he left. With Eric gone, Donna's father drove her to Riveredge. A few days later the rest of the family loaded their things into a moving van and headed for Texas. As much as I hated her father, I was impressed with the way he'd dealt with Eric. He'd done a better job than I could have done.

Knowing Donna was safe in a hospital, getting clean at last, allowed me to relax a little. I started feeling a sense of exhilaration at having helped Donna escape from an abusive situation. I knew something big had been accomplished. We were tied together now. I felt for her. I knew how scared she must be. I knew she was now completely depending on me, and my family. I also knew that my mother was uncomfortable with the arrangement and concerned for both Donna and me.

I also felt a nagging sense of unease. I wondered if Donna really could stay clean when she got out of the hospital. I wondered if I could really handle the situation I'd created. Our future now depended on me. Reality was setting in. I'd have to find a way to make money so we could get our own place when I turned eighteen. But now I had a purpose. I felt totally committed to standing by Donna and taking care of her. I was more fired up and determined than I had ever been about anything before. At fifteen, for the first time in my life, I was looking toward a future that might make life worthwhile. And I felt I was on a path to becoming a man.

Day of the Dead

*I*t was the strangest, saddest day of my life.

I was sixteen and attending Central Y. I wasn't making much academic progress, but outside of school things were good. I'd gotten my driver's license. Donna was doing much better. She was off speed and out of rehab. She was still clingy and fragile and had delusional moments, but other than that she was mostly clearheaded and very functional. Her family was in Texas, and she was living with my aunt, less than a mile away at the far end of the co-op. And we were hanging out a lot and happy to be together again.

We got high together a lot, but we only smoked weed and hash. Getting high didn't seem wrong. It seemed like a good idea; it helped her stay off speed. Speed was bad. It was addictive; it wired you for days, starved your body, fried your nervous system, and brought you crashing down. Over time it made you crazy and paranoid. But pot, hash, and even hallucinogens like acid, mescaline, peyote, and psilocybin were different. They were "natural" drugs. They weren't addictive. They mellowed you out, made you more real, and opened your mind and heart to a greater reality. At least that was what we all thought at the time, before the honeymoon period of the drug revolution ended and its darker side began to reveal its ugly face.

One November afternoon, Donna, Neil, and I went to visit my co-op friend Marsha, who lived a couple of blocks over the hill from my house. Donna and Neil really liked each other. Now twelve, Neil was still the same sweet kid he'd always been. He loved hanging out with us, and we loved being with him. But during the past couple of months I hadn't spent as much time with him as I used to. I'd begun to cut him out of my life, and we both felt bad about it.

It wasn't that we didn't love each other, or that I didn't want to spend time with him; it was because of my life, which had begun to increasingly revolve around smoking dope and dealing drugs. He looked up to me. I didn't want him getting into drugs, getting caught up in my world. He always wanted to come with me, and whenever I left the house he'd plead with me to let him come. But I was usually going places and doing things I didn't want him to be involved in. He was old enough to know what I was doing, but he still couldn't understand why I was shutting him out of my life after we'd been so close for so many years.

After hanging out with us for a while, Neil went to go play with a friend of his named Jan, the younger brother of my friend Don. A little while later Donna and I headed back home. We came over the hill and started down toward my house.

"David, look at all the people down there," said Donna.

A crowd of fifteen or twenty people gathered in the street below, a couple of blocks away. I knew my friends Toby, Don, and a few other co-op kids were shooting a movie about the Chicago riots that day for a class project. They had an 8 mm movie camera.

"They're probably watching Toby and Don shoot their

movie," I said.

"It doesn't look like they're making a movie to me," said Donna.

Suddenly I felt uneasy, as if something were wrong. "Let's go see what's going on."

I took Donna's hand, and we ran down the hill and cut across a couple of my neighbors' front yards. As we got closer, we started walking again. I was feeling really anxious now. I knew everyone there. They were all co-op people — neighbors, parents, and friends. They looked stricken. Some were crying. We reached the crowd, and I saw someone lying on the ground, shaking violently. It was Don. He was having convulsions. At first I couldn't believe it was Don. Then I recognized his father standing over him. Toby and the other kids who'd been part of the movie were all there.

He'll be okay, I thought. *His father is here. We're all here. Someone will help him.*

But his father looked distraught, even frantic. No one seemed to know what to do.

"He's not breathing," I heard his father say.

I heard snatches of conversation around me, something about a knife and part of a pen to stick in Don's throat. Donna was totally freaked out. There was nothing I could do to help Don, so I took Donna's hand and we started walking toward my house.

When we got there my parents weren't home. Donna and I were both in shock. We went into my room. I put on some music, and we sat down on the couch. A few minutes later I heard someone come in. I went out to find Neil and Jan, Don's younger brother, on their way upstairs to Neil's room. Neil said Jan's mom had told them to come stay here while they took Don to the hospital. I didn't know how much Jan knew about Don or what

I should do. I decided not to say anything about it. I wished my parents were home.

"Do you guys want something to eat?" I asked, not knowing what else to say.

Neil turned to Jan, and they both shrugged.

"Sure," Jan said.

Jan and Neil went upstairs. I knew he'd be okay with Neil. They'd spent a lot of time together. I kept wondering what had happened to Don, and if he was going to be okay. It was around one o'clock. I opened a can of soup, put it in a pot on the stove, and poured in a can of water.

Just as the soup was ready, my parents walked in. They were back from a co-op board meeting. They'd heard about Don and told me what had happened. Apparently they were filming a riot scene. Don had been lying on the top of the car, holding on by the sides. Another guy was filming with the camera from the street. The driver — it might have been Toby — swerved, and Don fell off the car and landed on his tailbone. He fell back, and a clear liquid, later determined to be spinal fluid, started coming out of his nose and mouth. Then he went into convulsions and his breathing stopped.

Dad hardly said a word. He looked exhausted. He kept rubbing his hand over his forehead — the way people sometimes do when they're tired.

"I'm not feeling well," he said. "I'm going upstairs to lie down a while."

My mother decided to make some sandwiches to go with the soup. She told Donna to go back to my aunt's house for lunch. Donna was still freaked out. I told her I had to stay with Neil and Jan, so she left.

I went into my room and sat on the couch, feeling as bad as I'd ever felt in my life. After a while my mother called us all to a late lunch. I went in and sat at the table. Jan and Neil came down. Dad didn't come. We assumed he was taking a nap. A few minutes later I heard his shrill whistle upstairs. Dad rarely whistled. When he did, it meant come right away. I knew something was wrong.

I dropped my fork on the floor, ran out of the kitchen, and headed upstairs to my parents' bedroom. Dad was sitting on the edge of the bed trying to button up a long-sleeve flannel shirt. His face looked strangely dark, and he seemed to be having trouble with the buttons. He looked up at me, and I could see he was scared.

"David," he said, "I need you to take me to the hospital."

His voice was weak and shallow. I'd never seen him look like this before. He suddenly turned pale. There was no expression on his face, just an anxious look in his eyes. I felt scared and sad at the same time. I went and stood in front of him.

"Dad, what's wrong?"

"I'm cold. Help me with my shirt."

I bent down and started buttoning his shirt from the bottom up. Everything was in slow motion, yet in extreme focus, like a movie close-up. I watched my fingers buttoning his shirt; its soft, cream-colored material with rust-colored stripes absorbed my gaze; it became an endless pattern.

I finished one button and started on the next. Suddenly Dad jolted upright and grabbed my head with his palms. Holding my face six inches from his, he looked into my eyes. I heard my mother come into the room behind me. I was lost in my father's eyes. I thought I heard him say, "This is it!"

Then my mother ran back downstairs to call an ambulance.

After my dad spoke these words, he pressed his hands tighter to my head, his face flushed bright red, and he fell back slowly, still holding my head, pulling me down on top of him. I slid off of him and looked into his bright red face. I heard myself say, "Oh, Dad, Dad…"

My father was still looking at me. As I looked back at him, I fell into his gaze. It was as if he were holding me with his eyes. I felt him struggling for life, yet he was incredibly present with me at the same time. I felt our connection. Then something began to fade from his eyes. I tried to hold him with me, but he slipped away. In a matter of moments they became vacant. They were still looking at me, but he wasn't in them anymore. I was looking in his eyes, but I couldn't find him there. I could feel that he was gone. Instinctively, I looked down at his body, and then around the room, as if I might see where he'd gone. I wondered whether if I had been stronger, maybe I could have kept him with us.

On a deep level I knew that he had died, but I couldn't admit it to myself. I didn't have time to process it. My mother came rushing into the room and threw herself on the bed beside him. She cradled his head in her arms and began sobbing hysterically, kissing him all over his face, saying, "No, Pat, don't go…nooo …please, Pat…don't go…"

My mother had always dealt calmly with difficult situations, but I could see that she was unable to deal with this. My father's face was now a dark-purplish color, but she didn't seem to notice. She kept on kissing him and begging him not to leave. He wasn't moving at all, and his eyes had the same glassy look. It seemed to me that his color was getting darker, as if it were approaching the color of death.

I stood there watching, feeling frightened and helpless.

I couldn't believe Dad was dead, so I believed he was dying instead. A few minutes later Neil and Jan came into the room. My mother told us we had to slap the soles of his feet and the palms of his hands. I didn't know what good it would do, but we started doing it. This was before people knew about CPR. Mom was crying and slapping one of Dad's palms. I was slapping the bottom of his left foot, listening for the ambulance. I was afraid they would have trouble finding our house. The roads in and around the co-op were confusing, and people coming to see us for the first time often had trouble finding us.

After a couple of minutes I went outside. I heard a siren approaching the co-op. As it got closer, I could tell it was on the wrong street, on the dead-end side of the neighborhood. It was exactly what I was afraid would happen: They were lost. They were only a few hundred yards from our house, but by the surface road more than a mile away. I heard the siren moving farther away. They were going back around to a main street to try to find their way here. I knew they could easily get lost again.

I ran back into the house, grabbed the car keys, got into my dad's car, and drove like a madman through the co-op to the crossroads they'd have to come through. Finally the ambulance appeared; I couldn't believe how slow it was going. I waved and yelled at them to follow me, then took off. But they were going so slow that I had to keep slowing down to let them catch up. I was furious. I knew every second counted, but they kept the same slow pace all the way to the house.

Two medics with a stretcher followed me upstairs to my parents' bedroom. One of them examined my father, felt his heart and throat, and checked his pulse. Dad's face was now a dark shade of gray. He wasn't moving and didn't seem to be breathing, but the medic looked at my distraught mother and said, "He's still alive."

The hopeful look on her swollen, tear-stained face was more than I could bear. Despite my father's appearance, we were all clinging to hope. Finally they put my father on the stretcher, took him downstairs, put him in the back of the ambulance, and drove off with the siren blaring. My mother followed them in her car. I stayed behind with Neil and Jan.

A few minutes later, Mike, one of our neighbors around Emerson's age, came over to find out what had happened. When I told him, he asked me if Emerson knew. I shook my head. Emerson was attending college in Ann Arbor, Michigan.

"You have to call him," Mike said.

"Yeah, I know."

"Do you have his phone number?"

"I don't know. It's probably somewhere around here."

"Where would it be?" asked Mike.

He was trying to help. I pointed to a pile of papers on the table near the phone. He rummaged through them and finally found the number of Emerson's dormitory. He dialed it and had a couple of brief conversations with different people trying to track down Emerson. Finally Emerson got on the phone. Mike told him Dad had had a heart attack. Then Emerson asked to talk to me.

"Hey, David, what's going on? Is it true?" He was in a state of disbelief.

"Yeah."

"Dad's dead?

"I don't know, but it's bad."

"What happened?"

"I think it was a heart attack. He just turned purple and… you have to come home now." I was crying.

"Oh my God!" Emerson burst out crying too.

"Emerson, you've got to come home. We have a lot to do, and I don't think Mom's doing too good."

"I'm getting on the next flight," said Emerson through his tears. "I'll get myself to the house. Don't worry about picking me up."

It was getting dark out now. Neil, Jan, and I went to the TV room. They sat down on the couch, and I turned on the TV. Then I sat down next to them. I remember the flickering light on their blank faces. *The Cosby Show* was on. Cosby played a high school teacher and football coach. I'd always found his show comforting. In this episode a woman was having a baby in a house during a rainstorm. Bill Cosby's character was there. It was raining so hard they couldn't go out, so he had to deliver the baby.

The woman was screaming, and he was trying to comfort her through the labor. The moment the baby was born onscreen, something cracked in me. The contrast between the new life being born into the world, and the mood of joy and wonder portrayed on the TV show, and the starkness of my father lying still on the bed with vacant eyes and a gray face, and the anguish on my mother's face — all broke through my denial and hopefulness. At that moment, I knew with absolute certainty my dad was dead. He had died when we were looking in each other's eyes. Then I knew why I'd been unable to find him in his gaze after it faded. I didn't say anything to Neil. I just sat numbly staring at the screen.

I can't remember exactly what happened after that. Mom came home from the hospital later that night. She told Neil and me that Dad had had a massive heart attack. He was dead before the ambulance arrived and didn't suffer long. She said that Don was dead, too. Jan was gone by now. I don't remember if his parents picked him up or if he went home on his own. My friend Marsha was there. So was Donna; she'd returned from my aunt's house. I remember all of us standing in Neil's room crying together and holding one another.

In the following days and weeks I realized how powerful my dad's presence in our lives had been to us, and to our co-op world. It was more than just the people who came to tell us how much Dad had meant to them, how much he'd helped them, how much they'd valued and loved him. It was also the vacuum created by his absence that revealed the impact of his energy and presence. We had taken him for granted. We didn't realize how profoundly his presence — his spirit — had colored and sustained our lives — until it was gone. But where had it gone? Could it simply disappear or be extinguished? I couldn't fathom this.

I felt a strange certainty that his spirit still had to exist somewhere, in some form. When a being with that much spirit and power collided with death, it had to continue, to go somewhere. As Einstein said, energy doesn't disappear.

I thought about how he was always making us laugh. Like the time when he and Mom got in a little argument at the kitchen table because he wanted to buy an electric knife and she thought it was a waste of money, so he tried to kiss her. And she said, "No, I'm mad, and I don't want an electric knife, and I don't want to kiss you." And he said, "Come on, let me kiss you." And then they were off, with Dad chasing her around the house. I remember how they passed by us in the kitchen, and Emerson and Neil and I were sitting at the table cheering and shouting, "Kiss her! Kiss her!" And how he finally caught her and they embraced, and he was giving her little pecks on her face, saying, "Okay, but I get to kiss you."

I remembered when Mom would want Dad to punish us, and he'd scold us. Then sometimes he'd turn to Mom and say, "All right, we're going to have to throw them away." Then he'd pick us up and take us out to the garage and drop us in the fifty-five-gallon paper trash bin. But we knew it wasn't really a punishment. And we'd rock back and forth in the bin until it fell over, and we'd climb out and go back to the table to finish dinner. And everything was fine.

And I remembered the time when all four of us ganged up on him. We picked him up and dragged him from the kitchen into the garage with his butt dragging on the floor. He was laughing so hard he could hardly catch his breath. Somehow we managed to lift him up and drop him butt first in the paper trash bin.

I also began to realize that my father had been a great man — a better man than I could ever hope to be. He'd always brought a special light, and a heartfelt humor, wherever he went. Almost everyone he knew had loved him and his laughter. Now I saw that his humor was his way of letting me know how much he loved me. Yet I hadn't told him that I loved him for several years. Only then did I realize how much I loved him. This struck me hard, and it would haunt me for many years.

I'd thought that when a loved one died, the survivors might question how much they were loved by that person. Yet the corollary had never entered my mind. All I cared about now, what I worried about and hoped for, was that my father had understood how much I loved *him* — even though I didn't fully know myself. I also feared that with his dying, I might have lost any chance of becoming the kind of person he'd been — the best person I'd ever known.

O.D.

*D*ad's death devastated our family. We'd lost the primary breadwinner, but more importantly, the center post of the family. His steady presence, his delightful humor, and his warmth had been the spiritual backbone of the family, its heart and soul. Now the humor and warmth that had nourished our family's spirit were gone, and the emptiness in the house, and in our lives, was palpable and painful.

Each one of us fell apart in his or her own way. Life seemed to be unraveling beneath our feet, and we couldn't stop it.

Emerson went back to college a couple of days after the funeral. I didn't see him much over the next couple of years. Neil was lost and bewildered. I started to let him hang out with me again whenever he wanted to.

Mom fell into a deep depression and started drinking. She quickly became a functional alcoholic. She'd been working three days a week, but now returned to working full-time. A large thermos filled with vermouth and vodka became her constant companion around the house. She'd have a drink immediately after returning home from work. Later she'd make dinner, and the three of us would eat together. That was very important to her. After dinner she'd sit in her favorite chair in the family room and disappear, knitting, smoking, drinking, and watching TV until late at night. Yet she still maintained all her responsibilities. Her commitment to managing the family and the finances, and to keeping Emerson in college and us in the house with virtually no support, was heroic. In the light of that, we overlooked her drinking. We all tried not to put any pressure on her. Neil and I were left completely unsupervised. I did my best to watch out for him, but I was also disappearing into my relationship with Donna, my drug use and dealing. Neil spent more time away from the house with his friends, or in the basement rec room my dad hadn't quite finished before he died.

Only fifty-two when he died, Dad didn't have much life insurance. We kids didn't know it then, but he and Mom had also been buying abandoned houses in depressed neighborhoods. Dad had hired neighborhood workers to fix them up and then sold them to local people who couldn't otherwise afford to buy houses. He helped them get financing and made no profit on the deals. This was just one of my parents' gifts of community service, their way of helping the less fortunate. They'd done this successfully a number of times over the years. When Dad died, Mom got stuck with a house she couldn't renovate and therefore couldn't sell. So we owned property, but it didn't do us any good. We also owned a portion of Mom's family's medical clinic, but that didn't provide us with any income either.

Now Mom's salary barely covered our living expenses. Our financial crunch motivated me to minimize my expense to the family and earn more money. But I still hoped to find a legal, less dangerous way to make a living than dealing.

A few months after Dad's death, I got a job with a waterbed

company making waterbeds and frames. As a sideline, I'd buy some at a discount and sell them. I made decent money, though not as much as dealing. But in the factory, my boss was getting on me for not staying focused on my work. The repetitive motion of the machines I was working on seemed to put me in a trance. I had trouble memorizing the names of the parts and sequences of the tasks. I attributed it to laziness. That's what I'd been told my problem was back in school. The waterbeds turned out to be made of inferior materials, and customers started returning them because they leaked. It was a fiasco, so I quit and went back to dealing.

With dealing I never had paperwork, memorizing, sequencing, or quality-control issues because I was my own boss. I never bought or sold anything I hadn't tried first, and I only bought quality stuff. No one ever returned merchandise. I understood the numbers, and I had the best weed at the best price along with the most consistent supply, so I always had repeat customers. Of course, no one ever tried to hurt me or rip me off for selling waterbeds.

My relationship with Donna was still much of my focus. When it was good, it was the most positive part of my life. We didn't have the money to get her counseling on an ongoing basis, and she didn't want it. Even though she was off meth, her personality remained indefinable and impossible to describe. She had phases when she would be disoriented and confused, and she'd hear voices. Sometimes, in the aftermath of one of these audible hallucinations, she would become like a different person — enraged for no apparent reason, accusing me of things that never happened, or not remembering things she did. Sometimes she would become shy and withdrawn, wanting no contact with the outside world, and at other times she became a wild woman who wanted to get stoned and do dangerous things. Watching her disjointed episodes, I got this picture in my head that she'd started out as a wonderful, kind little girl, but one day the person she most loved and depended on had decided that there were parts of her he didn't like. He threw her to the ground in a rage and she broke apart into distinct pieces.

The state of psychology at that time was simplistic, without refined diagnoses, so it wasn't all that helpful. When people were having hallucinations, they were considered schizophrenic. So, according to the experts, Donna was schizophrenic. I was told her condition would be called dissociative identity disorder — sometimes known as multiple personality disorder. That made sense to me, but I couldn't know if any of these defined her correctly. What I knew was that she would get overwhelmed by life and become very confused, and that she had a great heart, and loved me.

Giving up on someone never seemed right to me. At the time, I hoped many of the world's problems could be solved if we just cared enough. I wondered: *If I just cared enough, couldn't I help Donna put herself back together?* I thought if I could help her appreciate and accept all the different parts of herself, then she wouldn't have to swing between her extreme personalities. I hoped she could come together as a more whole, happy person. She hadn't been allowed to experience certain parts of herself, even the most basic needs such as hunger, or personal desires such as wanting nice clothes, had been unacceptable. These unacceptable parts of herself split off into separate personalities. For instance, anger seemed completely unacceptable unless it was caused by jealousy, so she would vent all her anger through outbursts of jealous rage. She was a puzzle. I felt that she could never be whole unless every piece of the puzzle was back in place. And nobody else in her life seemed to care about helping her put herself back together. Nobody was going to help her if I didn't.

It was working. As Donna grew in confidence, so did I in my ability to help her. I watched as she became highly competent, graduating from high school early, then getting work and starting to find her way through the social maze of life. I remembered how everyone else in my life had started out even with me, but they would learn in school and then surpass me, leaving me behind. But Donna wanted to stay with me. She knew my heart. I knew she was smart, and the more competent and plugged into the world she got, the more she impressed me. Despite the fears that it brought up in me that she would eventually leave me, I wanted her to succeed.

Over the next two years our life improved, but then things began to change. I'm not sure what happened. Maybe it was because I had started to imagine myself with a future, and so began to invest more of myself in our relationship. I started to take things more personally when she got mad or had trouble relating to me. I started to have expectations of her. Or maybe it was her desire to always do more drugs. I found myself wanting to control her drug use and suppress the wild-girl aspect. The more difficulty I had in accepting those parts of her, the more distinct and powerful they would become. After a few years I got a glimpse of a manipulative and amoral quality in her toward others and toward the world in general. She still included me in her inner world and seemed to remain heartfelt and honest with me. There were many pieces to her, and I had to accept that there might be a piece, or pieces, of her I never got to see.

Dealing was the only way I knew to make enough money

to get by. It was also a way for me to feel my independence and to prove myself as a can-do guy. Dealing gave me a rep and a certain prestige in the 1960s counterculture. I was buying hash, mescaline, acid, THC, and other popular drugs that came through Chicago. A couple of times Donna and I gave Mom money to help out. Each time I made sure I had a good explanation when she asked where it came from, such as when I had the waterbed job and Donna was working as a waitress.

Mom's drinking and my drug use escalated at the same time. We formed an unspoken agreement to ignore each other's addiction, or at least not to mention it to each other. I didn't mention her thermos of vodka and vermouth, and she didn't mention the smell of weed that now pervaded my room. One night, Donna, Neil, and I were hanging out in my room listening to music. I was sitting at my desk with a kilo of marijuana broken open in front of me, in plain sight. A large candle made from a green wine jug burned next to the open kilo of pot, which I was weighing on my balance beam scale and bagging into ounces. Suddenly the door opened, and Mom shuffled in, drunk. She looked at us and then at my desk. Her puffy eyes narrowed to slits and she looked at me. "That's a beautiful candle," she said. "It's late. Neil needs to go to bed." Then she turned and walked unsteadily out of the room, closing the door behind her.

A few times, bikers in leather jackets came over to buy a few kilos of pot. I'd casually invite them in and lead them single file through the house toward my room. Mom, sitting in her chair as they filed by, would stop them politely. She'd introduce herself and look each one in the eye. I was impressed that these heavy-duty bikers were so respectful of her and seemed to like her. She insisted that anyone who came into her house be introduced to her. It was her way of trying to maintain some kind of control in her home when our lives were spiraling out of control.

Meanwhile, Donna was still living at my aunt's house. I was sneaking into her room a lot at night to sleep with her. We were stoned most of the time. We did pretty much whatever we wanted, whenever we wanted, as long as we stayed in school.

Periodically there would be an "episode." Donna would fly into a fit of jealousy over an innocent encounter. One time we were riding in a motorboat in the middle of a Minnesota lake when she went into one of her fits of jealousy, screaming over a simple encounter I'd had with a store clerk while buying groceries. She jumped on me from behind, grabbed me by the hair, and began wrenching my head around. I lost my grip on the outboard motor, and we fell down in the hull while the boat veered in tight circles in the water. I finally managed to get ahold of her. After a time she relaxed in my arms, crying, and I was able to get up and steer us back to the dock.

She would have no memory of these incidents after they happened. Smoking weed at that point seemed to help; then I'd have a better chance of carefully coaxing her to remember. I stayed with her, and she eventually began to accept, in stages, what she'd done. She would remember a piece of it, or it might come back all at once. At these times she seemed very young and open, like a little girl. I was the only one who'd ever tried to help her like this. These were some of our most intimate moments together.

We knew we were screwed up, and it seemed that just when things began to improve to the point where we even dared to think we might have a future, they would turn in the wrong direction. Plus, the world itself was over the top, accepting the unacceptable. Witness King Richard Daley's Blue Knights cracking down on Chicago's antiwar protests; the Mississippi police brutalizing blacks and civil-rights protesters; and the U.S. bombing Vietnamese villages, supposedly defending America from communism. No wonder my generation didn't believe a word that came out of the mouths of the authorities regarding the dangers of drugs. Their lies, gross exaggerations, and heavy-handed tactics discredited any particle of truth their point of view might have contained. My generation wanted the truth. I couldn't be satisfied with half-truths from sources I didn't trust, whose purpose was to manipulate and control me, supposedly for my own good. Compared to the world's insanity, my compromises seemed minor.

It was easy to rationalize my own excesses in a world full of bullshit. Yet I knew that my life was heading in a bad direction. I wasn't doing anything to change its course for one very simple reason: I didn't know what to do. I felt powerless to change my life, and hopeless about my future and the future of the world. People would say to me, "You should graduate high school, learn to read." I'd think to myself sarcastically, *Yeah, I never thought of that.* Where had they been? I would've loved to graduate, but I couldn't read! Or, when pushed to think more deeply, they would say, "There must be something you can do." Why must there be something I can do? These were not stupid people. It seemed to me that when they couldn't find answers to problems, they resorted to platitudes that were only a reaction to their un-willingness to accept the truth. It was like being taught to hide under your desk when the nuclear bomb goes off. Thanks for the advice! It was too much for them to consider even the possibility that there might not be anything I could do.

This only intensified my conviction that for Donna and me

there were no answers. People's responses seemed so superficial that it was almost cruel. It seemed to make sense for us to stay reasonably stoned and self-medicated until I could find an answer for us. It seemed to me that people were rationalizing their own behavior. Donna and I were rationalizing, too, but at least we knew it. I wasn't sure which I was suffering more: what I did know and others apparently didn't, or what I didn't know and others apparently did. So we continued down the path we were on, self-medicating our pain and hopelessness by staying high, and moving deeper into a life of denial and disintegration.

One night Donna and I and our friends Nan and Todd went to buy five pounds of weed from a dealer named Jim. Jim was a tall, skinny guy who lived with his wife, Suzy. That night I also learned he had a fondness for speed. I'd bought weed from Jim before. I knew he had a gun, but he was dealing dope in large quantities, so it made sense. He and I'd never had any problems. A week before he'd told me he was getting in a large shipment of Colombian pot. I'd called him earlier, and he told me the shipment had come in. Now we had come to score. As far as I was concerned, it was just a weed deal like any other.

I parked in front of Jim's house, and we all got out and went to the front door. I knocked, and immediately all the lights in the house went off. We heard the sound of hushed voices inside. It was weird. Todd and I looked at each other. Then the front door opened a crack, and the porch light revealed Jim's haggard face peering out at us. I could see the paranoia in his eyes. I could see that he was strung out on speed, stretched to the limit and ready to snap.

"What do you want?" he asked suspiciously in a hoarse whisper.

He didn't seem to recognize me.

"Hey, Jim," I said. "It's me, David. We want to buy some pot."

He opened the door and waved us inside, then shut the door behind us and turned the lights back on. That was when I saw the gun in his hand, pointed in our general direction.

"Where the fuck is Suzy? What have you done with Suzy?" he asked in the same weird voice.

He waved the gun, gesturing randomly as he spoke. He wasn't trying to threaten us; in fact, he seemed almost oblivious to the gun in his hand. I decided the best thing was to ignore the gun and act as if everything was cool. I didn't respond to his paranoid questions about Suzy.

"Good to see you, Jim. Did you get the pot? We need some weight."

He perked up. "How much?"

"Five pounds?"

Then he looked at me suspiciously and asked again, "Where's Suzy?"

"Hey, man, we haven't seen her."

Suddenly he started crying. He stood there sobbing with his back to the door — still waving the gun in our direction. I didn't know what to do but steer the conversation back to the deal.

"So what about the pot? You got five pounds? How much per pound?"

He looked at me blankly. Then he said, "Yeah, sure. I'll get it. It's a hundred and ten a pound."

He walked past us, through the living room, and into the back of the house. We stood there trying to act normal. Just before he disappeared around the corner, he turned back to look at us, the gun dangling at his side.

"Don't any of you move," he said. Then he went into the back of the house to get the pot. I heard him rustling around in another room. At one point he yelled, "Don't you fucking move!"

Donna, Nan, Todd, and I looked at one another and didn't say a word. We all knew that even a whisper might trigger Jim's paranoia. I waved the girls to go, and they quietly snuck out the door. A couple of minutes later, Jim came back around the corner holding a big burlap sack, which he set down on the coffee table. He didn't seem to notice that half our group had disappeared. He opened the sack and showed Todd and me. There were two kilos of Colombia's finest, wrapped in dark paper, and a loose bag that I assumed made up the total of five pounds. I wasn't going to challenge him on it now. Jim put his hand out for the money, still holding the gun on us with the other hand.

I paused. "Is this shit any good?"

I wanted to keep a casual conversation going. I was afraid he might notice the girls were gone, or bring up Suzy again, who had probably split on him and his amphetamine psychosis.

"Definitely," said Jim. "It's real good shit."

"Cool."

I pulled a wad of bills from my pocket and slowly counted out 550 dollars on the table beside the open gunnysack. Jim nodded, apparently satisfied.

"Thanks, Jim," I said. "Good doing business with you."

Todd and I stood there facing Jim.

"You need to clean up," I said, looking into his crazed eyes, trying to sound as relaxed as possible.

He was still pointing the gun at us. "Yeah, get the fuck out of here," he said, as if now that I was confronting his habit he wanted to get rid of us.

"We'll see you later," I said.

I picked up the sack of weed and followed Todd outside, closing the door behind me. Donna and Nan were in the car with the trunk open and the engine running.

"Shit," I said to Todd. "I just bought five pounds of weed without tasting it or weighing it."

I threw the sack in the trunk and got into the car. Donna was behind the wheel and took off like a rocket. She was a really good driver even when she was stoned. I couldn't help thinking what a good team we were. I knew I could rely on her if we got into a serious scrape. A couple of friends joked about us being Bonnie and Clyde. If we were threatened and Donna had a gun, I was pretty sure she would use it without any hesitation.

It wasn't always like this. In my dealing, I'd met a lot of cool people I really liked. But it was inevitable that we would at times find ourselves dealing with paranoid crazies, low-life emotional cripples, or actual criminals — the kind of people I'd never wanted anything to do with. And I got used to it. One guy bragged to me about going to jail for killing a cop who'd tried to bust him. I was pretty sure he was telling the truth. I stopped dealing with him. If he got busted for killing a cop and he wasn't in prison, then he had to be a narc. It turned out I was right. I seemed to have a knack for this. Other dealers were getting busted, and I wasn't. Later this guy turned in an acquaintance of mine, who then tried, unsuccessfully, to set me up for a bust. It didn't stop me, but just made me more cautious.

For a while I didn't realize I was gradually changing into someone I'd never thought I'd become, and doing things I'd never thought I'd do. You can't help becoming like the people you're hanging out with. I thought I was separate from my business and better than the people I had to deal with to make money. I'd look at some of the people I dealt with and think, *I'll never be like that guy.* But only a few degrees, a series of choices and crossed lines, separated me from them. Gradually, I crossed one line after another.

I started doing things I regretted afterward. Once, a friend stole some money from the safe in my room. I figured out who it was and told him to pay up or suffer the consequences. He was scared, but he kept stalling and telling me he didn't have the money. Finally, I went over to his house with two friends and banged on his door. His mother answered. She knew me and had always liked me, but I could see she was scared of me now. She handed me a check for three hundred dollars, about half of what her son had stolen from me.

"It's all I have," she said. "Please take it…and don't hurt him."

But it wasn't enough. And I couldn't let him get away with it. I took the check and went inside. I took the phone off the hook and left one friend downstairs to keep an eye on things. Then I went up to his room. I found him there and pushed him around. I'd trusted him, and he'd ripped me off. We didn't hurt him too much. He was already apologetic and terrified, but he didn't have the money. On the way out, I picked up the amplifier he'd bought with the money. When my friends and I finally walked out of the house, his mother stood fearfully by the door, watching us leave.

I cashed the check, but I felt really bad about the whole thing afterward. I kept trying to justify it to myself. He'd stolen from me. He'd betrayed me. He deserved it. He made me do what I'd done. But I couldn't justify it. Eventually my conscience broke through. I'd scared someone's mother who was always nice to me. I'd pushed her son around in her house and taken her money.

She was a young widow with six kids and had fallen on hard times. I knew the three hundred was probably all she really had. I knew then I was heading in a bad direction. I was becoming the kind of person I despised. I had to find a way out of this. I had to find another way to survive. But I didn't know what else to do.

For years I'd felt a sense of impending doom, a certainty that sooner or later something bad was going to happen. Dad's death and the gradual unraveling of our family had intensified this feeling. Things were only going to get worse. My future held no hope or joy. There was no solution, no escape.

My accelerating drug use gave me no relief; it only made me feel more hopeless and estranged from life. My relationship with Donna no longer provided the sanctuary it once had. She was also unraveling. The part of her that wanted to do more and more dope was coming more and more to the forefront. My influence on her was slipping, and she was becoming less available and harder to deal with. Mom had warned me from the start. We were both sinking into our own private hells, and taking each other down. I couldn't imagine living this way indefinitely. It couldn't turn out well. Yet I simply couldn't stop.

The turning point came at the end of one of our drug binges. This time it was a week of nonstop synthetic mescaline use. By the end of the week Donna and I had consumed over one hundred hits, each day requiring larger doses to get off. That last day we had taken a megadose. An hour later we didn't seem to be getting off, and Donna suggested that we buy some acid. I knew a guy who had some, and I called him. He said it was sixteen-way acid. I'd never heard of such a thing and didn't really believe him. I figured he was exaggerating. I didn't want to do any, but Donna did. Her appetite for drugs was insatiable. She started talking more about speed, and it was getting harder and harder to discourage her. Against my better judgment, we went over and bought two hits of this guy's sixteen-way acid. I only let her take a third. I didn't take any.

We were both tempting fate. We were in a bad place before the run. After a week of tripping we both felt like crap, and everything seemed grim, horrible, and hopeless. We ended up hiding out in Donna's room at my aunt's house, lying naked in bed. The mescaline had finally kicked in, and I was as high as I'd ever been before. I was glad I hadn't taken the acid. But I was worried about Donna, who had. What if it was as strong as the guy said it was? She was more wasted than I'd ever seen anyone before. She couldn't talk. At one point she curled up in a fetal position and withdrew completely. I had a really bad feeling, but I was tripping so intensely I didn't trust my judgment. Maybe I was just being paranoid, imagining the worst, freaking myself out about nothing. I didn't want to focus on bad stuff that could trigger a bad trip.

So I lay there with my eyes closed while a nonstop flood of chaotic, scary, exaggerated mescaline-induced thoughts and visions pouring through my head. I swore I'd never get into this situation again. This was the last time. Every few minutes I'd open my eyes and examine Donna, and listen to her breathing. She was completely immobile, almost lifeless. Her skin looked a weird grayish color. Her breath seemed really shallow. But maybe I was hallucinating. I couldn't tell. I tried talking to her, but she didn't respond or seem to be aware of me. At one point I leaned over her and put my ear up to her mouth to listen for her breathing. I tried to hear her heartbeat, but my own heart was pounding so loudly in my ears I couldn't hear anything else.

I told myself not to panic. I was just tripping. Donna would be okay. People didn't die from taking LSD, unless they jumped out a window or something.

We lay there for hours, with Donna not moving, not responding to words or touch. My anxiety grew. The loud ticking of the clock on the wall began to drive me nuts. After a while the intensity of the mescaline began to fade, and I was able to think more coherently. I could see the time by the light of the lamp near the bed: 4:00 AM. I leaned my face close to Donna's again and whispered for her to wake up. I was sweating profusely, and my mouth was dry as sandpaper. I felt like a rock sinking to the bottom of a dark well. I started speaking her name and talking to her in a hoarse, desperate whisper, with my mouth right next to her ear. I didn't want to wake my aunt. She didn't know I was there, and I didn't want to deal with her in the state Donna and I were in.

"Donna. Donna," I whispered. "You have to wake up. Just tell me you're okay, and I'll let you go back to sleep."

She still didn't respond. I lifted her up again and shook her harder than before, fiercely whispering her name and begging her to wake up. Finally her eyes fluttered, and she let out a little moan.

"Donna, can you hear me? Are you okay?"

Then her eyes opened, barely a slit, and she mumbled, "Blood — there's blood in the streets...."

Then her eyes shut again, and she reverted to her previous catatonic state. At least she was alive. I decided to let her sleep it off. I lay down beside her and held her in my arms. I was relieved but still scared. I started rocking her gently. She always felt better when I held her like this. I realized I was rocking her as much for my benefit as for hers. At one point I began saying out loud, "Please, please, Donna, live. I promise I'll change. I'll do something different. I'll find a better way to take care of you. I'm sorry for everything. . . . I know we have to change. Just please, Donna, live."

Finally the morning light began to peek through the curtains. The mescaline was wearing off, and my head was starting to clear. I didn't know what I was going to do. But I knew I had to make a change.

Desperate Hope

9 left Donna that morning, burnt out from our weeklong mescaline run and shaken to the core by the experience. At one point I'd thought she was dead. I was sure she had come close to dying, or perhaps had retreated into a deep, catatonic psychosis. I couldn't imagine what my life would have been like if either one of those things had happened. I went home and flushed the rest of the acid down the toilet. I knew I had to change, but I didn't know what else to do, or how to become a different, better person. Over time I had let Donna's desires and needs define much of my life. I'd had enough. I'd rationalized my spiraling drug use and the chaos of my illicit life. We'd been together for over three years. I was seventeen now. Getting high every day since I was fourteen had numbed me to the gnawing sense of desperation I felt about my future. But that last bad trip and almost losing Donna were warning signs I couldn't ignore.

I felt again the sense of desperation over my troubled life. My severe limitations, which had set the course of my life and defined my identity, still seemed insurmountable. I felt the sense of hopelessness that had made me reach for drugs as a solution. I didn't see any solution, any real options, except for suicide. But now the idea of being institutionalized seemed more real than ever. The numbness and oblivion of drugs had seemed preferable to conscious anxiety and pain. But it wasn't working; it wasn't a solution. Something had to change. I had to get my life together. I had to graduate from high school.

I felt a new sense of urgency. Donna's thirst for drugs was more than I could control, and I was losing my ability to help her. I had to find something I could do that would make life worth the struggle — a self I could live with. I'd been hearing about Trans-actional Analysis, a remarkable new therapy pioneered by Dr. Eric Berne, and presented in his bestselling book *Games People Play*. TA was a big deal at the time, touted as a radical and life-transforming therapeutic method. Other authors had also written bestselling books based on Berne's work. Berne began organiz-ing weekly educational meetings for psychotherapists in the late 1950s called the San Francisco Social Psychiatry Seminars. I had a sense that maybe TA could help me. I thought this might be the answer for Donna as well.

I'd stopped selling drugs except for pot. Although I couldn't stop smoking pot, I still didn't consider it addictive. Meanwhile, Donna read *Games People Play* to me, and another bestselling book on TA by Thomas A. Harris called *I'm OK, You're OK*. The simple concepts of TA were making psychology accessible to a mass audience for the first time. I got very excited about it. TA was radical. Traditional Freudian therapy focused on patients ac-quiring a theoretical understanding of their inner drives, moti-vations, and dysfunctions. But the growing consensus, including the critique from TA, was that this didn't translate into healthy behavioral changes and transformed lives. TA focused on the drives, motivations, dysfunctions, and roles we play out in our relationships and in our lives.

Transactional Analysis sees the personality as divided into three ego states: *Parent, Adult,* and *Child.* These states operate on what Berne called *scripts,* formed through key relationship dynamics, or *transactions,* in childhood that become fixed patterns in adulthood. The Child's character, and the Adult that the Child grows up to be, are significantly formed by messages or scripts determined by the Parent. Healthy transactions result in healthy behaviors and ego states. Unhealthy transactions form unhealthy behaviors and ego states.

Berne claimed that understanding dysfunctional roles and scripts, making healthy behavioral changes, and learning to function in practical ways alleviated and even cured many emotional and psychological problems. He even created a contract, signed by the patient and therapist at the outset of therapy, setting an agenda of specific changes and results desired by the patient. It promised a bottom-line practical result that Freudian psychotherapy did not.

When my mother noticed my enthusiasm for TA, she gave me a pamphlet about a woman named Jacqui Schiff, a disciple of Berne, who had created a radical program for treating schizophrenics. Donna read me the pamphlet. I found it very interesting, so I got a copy of a book Schiff had written with Betty Day called *All My Children.* Donna read that to me, too. The book told how Schiff and her husband at the time, Moe, both psychiatric nurses, grew so frustrated by the inadequate care for the severely schizophrenic patients in the mental hospital where they worked that they resigned their jobs. They began taking schizophrenic patients into their home, inducing schizophrenic regression, and reparenting them through the developmental stages of childhood along the lines of Berne's theories. This even included an infancy stage, where they bottle-fed and diapered adult schizophrenics.

I'd experienced poignant moments with Donna when I felt the pieces of her coming together. In those moments she was always very open and like a little girl. I thought that Schiff's techniques could help Donna put her pieces together. I knew what I'd been doing instinctively was defending her against the bad conversations in her head and helping her replace negative messages she had about herself. As much as I cared for her, I was in over my head. We had made real strides, but here was a professional who might be able to help her.

Schiff's regression approach was radical and controversial. Psychiatry viewed schizophrenic regression as mere pathology, with no therapeutic value. To encourage or induce regression seemed grotesque and even harmful, like intentionally triggering a psychosis. Yet Schiff reported some remarkable successes, and even some cures, using her reparenting process. In 1969 she claimed that she had cured fourteen patients. Berne invited her to the San Francisco Social Psychiatry Seminars as a guest lecturer and enthusiastically introduced her by saying, "She takes people into her house that are very confused and unconfuses them, which confuses some people in the profession because it isn't supposed to work."* The *New York Times* published a feature about her that year too; she was mothering eighteen "children," whose real ages ranged from nine to twenty-nine.† A number of her patients apparently "grew up" and out of their schizo-

---

* "Theory as Ideology: Reparenting and Thought Reform," *Transactional Analysis Journal*, 24 (1) Jan. 1994.
† "An Approach to Schizophrenia That Is Rooted in Family Love," *New York Times*, 28 April 1969.

phrenic disorders and regained healthy, functional lives. Some of them became capable facilitators of Schiff's method, and began leading their own "families" of schizophrenics through the reparenting process.

I was excited by all of this. I saw some correlations between what I'd done with Donna and what Schiff had done with her patients. Instinctively, I'd given Donna a safe and caring circumstance, with functional demands and healthy messages about what was appropriate and inappropriate. I tried to show her that people could be trusted, and that she was worthwhile, lovable, and smart. Her most transformative moments came when she felt safe with me. At those times she seemed young and innocent, vulnerable, and very human. Over time I'd seen how she'd grown — still troubled, but so much more whole and happier. I thought if I'd been able to help her this much, think what a professional could do. And being a kid myself, and her boyfriend, I knew it was inappropriate for me to be a guide or parent figure for her. I also knew I'd taken her as far as I could. I sensed that Eric Berne's theories might hold some hope. And with modifications to Jacqui Schiff's methods for nonschizophrenics, this might offer me a new possibility for change, too. How could I help Donna to love herself if I didn't love myself? I didn't need reparenting, but I clearly needed new messages to myself.

When my mother found out that Jacqui Schiff would be presenting her theories at a meeting for psychiatric professionals in Chicago, she arranged for Donna and me to see her. One afternoon, we all drove into the city, where Jacqui would be speaking at a hotel. The event was held in a medium-sized room, and about thirty people showed up.

Jacqui Schiff didn't seem to be a very impressive figure when she walked to the podium that afternoon. She was a short, plump, professionally dressed woman in her forties. She had a soft, almost childlike voice, but with a blunt, almost mechanical style of speaking. She spoke in clinical terms without emotion or feeling. Yet despite her unimpressive appearance and odd style of speaking, it quickly became apparent that she possessed tremendous confidence, authority, and charisma. By the end of the evening I was completely under her spell.

Jacqui Schiff explained the details of her theories and methods in compelling terms. Her goal was to help severely dysfunctional people — schizophrenics — become functional, and rebuild healthy personalities. She spoke matter-of-factly about the current "family" of thirty-five schizophrenics whom she was reparenting, assisted by several recovered schizophrenics who had completed her reparenting program.

Jacqui Schiff believed that schizophrenics needed to confront the source of their psychosis or else they couldn't change. She described a process of regressing schizophrenics back to their Child ego state, mothering them through each developmental stage, and rebuilding their personalities. Her method was variously called *reparenting, attachment therapy*, and *healing the inner child*. She said that if you put schizophrenics in the right circumstance, they will often go into a natural regression, as if they instinctively know that they need to reprogram parts of themselves. She also said that most schizophrenics preferred to stay in their psychosis; they had to be confronted boldly, or they would continue choosing their familiar schizophrenic strategies of escape.

Jacqui Schiff's method was to induce a breakdown in her patients by confronting them with a highly structured environment and intense pressure to function beyond their capacity. This triggered all the dysfunctional defense mechanisms and faulty programming by which they avoided feeling and confronting the emotional traumas — such as severe neglect and emotional, physical, or sexual abuse — that underlie their schizophrenia. After regression was induced in them, they could be taken back to the places where the crucial decisions and patterns had occurred that led to their schizophrenia, and they could be guided to make new choices, write new scripts, and develop new behaviors that would enable them to function effectively in the real world under the normal pressures of life. Schiff used various methods to do this, including talk therapy, self-affirmations, self-forgiveness, anger management, self-discipline, the continued demand for practical functioning, and firm consequences for irresponsibility and acting out. After the crisis phase, she said the process became very nurturing.

The ability to function effectively and responsibly in the real world was a litmus test of recovery. And while Schiff's method was radical and controversial, it apparently made recovery possible — for some at least — from an otherwise incurable illness.

Hearing Jacqui Schiff speak, I sensed a brilliant and forceful personality at work, using highly unorthodox methods and apparently succeeding where others had failed. This could be exactly what I was looking for. She seemed to have no judgments about emotionally and psychologically disturbed people. She described them as nonfunctional.

Schiff's theories were radical and provocative. Some of the psychiatric professionals at her presentation that night were well known. When they aggressively challenged her methods during the question-and-answer session, she confidently dismantled their arguments with analytical brilliance. In the end, most of the audience seemed persuaded, and even the skeptics seemed impressed by her.

After Schiff finished speaking, two former schizophrenics named Eric and Aaron, who had gone through her reparenting process, came onstage and briefly told their stories. They were both articulate and handled themselves well onstage. They appeared to be high-functioning individuals who were working with other schizophrenics, taking them through the same process Jacqui Schiff had taken them through.

I was shaking by the end of the evening, almost euphoric. Jacqui Schiff's talk filled me with hope. It seemed perfect for Donna. And Schiff's ideas struck a chord for me, too, seeming to relate to my inability to organize or prioritize information in a linear fashion. This was one of the main causes of my inability to function in the world. Schiff had successfully applied her radical theories to severe schizophrenics who had been relegated to the wards of psychiatric hospitals for ten years or more. If she could help them, maybe she could help Donna, and even me.

After the talk, I went up to Schiff. I started talking excitedly to her and told her my story. It just gushed out of me. She listened intently, and then delivered insights into my situation that no one else had come close to. In her assessment, I had likely gone to school too early, before I'd fully mastered speech and before I was developmentally prepared, and that had intensified my developmental and learning problems. I was unable to deal with the normal curriculum because I was struggling in an environment that was over my head. This left huge gaps in my education and hampered my ability to learn and progress. She seemed able to pinpoint areas of the learning process that were the most problematic and underdeveloped in me.

Schiff seemed confident that she understood the dynamics of my lifelong struggle and failure to learn and to function in the normal world. And she seemed to offer a possible solution to my problems. Although the majority of her patients were schizophrenics whom everyone had given up on, perhaps her methods could apply to my situation. After all, like them, everyone had also given up on me a long time ago. Schiff wasn't promising to take me on, but she was speaking in a hypothetical way about how she would proceed if she did. She described the kind of circumstance she thought would serve me and allow me, finally, to develop and learn. When I asked her about helping Donna, she said it didn't sound like Donna was a danger to herself or to others, and so she would have to want her help.

For days after the presentation, I was excited about Jacqui Schiff and her work. I talked to my mother about the possibility of Donna and me working with her. My mother was also very impressed with Schiff and had gotten her phone number. She called her one afternoon, and they began a series of conversations about me, and the possibility of my coming to live with Schiff in her home and going through a program that she would develop specifically for my needs. I wasn't involved in any of these conversations. My mother reported to me after each one, telling me what they had discussed.

As excited and hopeful as I was, I had some doubts. Yet I had no alternatives. Donna was unwilling even to go to therapy, much less try something like this. In the past, therapists had criticized our mutual dependencies on each other, and so she had no interest in this. No matter how much I reassured her, she felt it was a threat to our relationship. I was still getting high every day,

I was no closer to getting a high school diploma, and I had no real job prospects for the future.

My mother was divided. On one hand she thought having me go to Jacqui Schiff's was a great idea. But there was a catch. When Jacqui Schiff reparented someone, she would, in some significant way, become that person's mother. And my own mother might be removed from that role in my life. A psychic bond would be created through the reparenting process that could supersede my relationship with my real mother. Sometimes this had to happen for the reparenting process to be effective. In theory, even though I would not be regressed, Schiff would be attempting to tear apart the "inner Parent" within me and rebuild it.

In Schiff's view, the inner Parent that reflected my mother represented the part in me that wasn't working. In the TA system parents were a primary source of children's dysfunctional scripts, with all the fears, judgments, strategies, and rules that went along with them. So a detachment from my mother might have to occur in order for me to form a healthy attachment to Jacqui Schiff. In any case, she wanted both of us to be prepared for that possibility.

This was all very disturbing to my mother. She was very reluctant for me to go through the reparenting process with Schiff. The bond we had established, especially in those first few years when she was connected to me almost around the clock, was still very deep. She also had doubts about the process, and worried that it might end up doing more harm than good. She talked to Schiff and expressed her concerns. Finally, after much consideration, she consented to the idea and Jacqui Schiff agreed to take me on.

Jacqui said she normally wouldn't select someone like me for her program since I wasn't schizophrenic like the other members of her family. But she was intrigued by the challenge I represented, and curious to see if her specialized program could benefit someone with my severe learning disabilities. When my mother talked to her about Donna, she said that over time Donna might come around, and we could revisit it then, but she couldn't take her without payment at that time. I'd pay a minimal fee with my Social Security income from my dad's death, and pay the balance by working in the house as an assistant. Although I didn't know about it, Jacqui would become my legal guardian. I wouldn't be part of the family, but I'd eat, sleep, and live at the house as part of the job of helping the others. It seemed perfect; I'd be getting a job, help with my learning, and help for Donna later on if it all worked out.

Jacqui was in the process of hiring professionals for a new school called Cathexis. She was creating this school based on her understanding of the stages of child development and the inner-child work of Transactional Analysis. I would attend this school while I was there. I would go back and review the developmental stages and relearn the basics I'd missed in each stage. Jacqui said she would be able to fill in the gaps and bring me all the way through to functional maturity at my current age level. She also said I'd be able to graduate high school with a GED in her school while I was there.

She cautioned me that some of the things I needed to relearn might seem stupid, but they would help build new patterns in me. I'd have to relearn simple things in order to learn more complex things. We'd identify the weakest areas, where the basics hadn't been properly integrated, work on those, and then move forward from there. These were huge promises.

I was convinced this was the answer. My mind was racing ahead, planning my future. The first thing Jacqui's program would do was get me off drugs. The intensive rigor and structure of her program would be like a boot camp. I'd be busy all day learning to function at a very high level under constant pressure. And I'd learn about psychology, a subject I was drawn to. Maybe I could go on to help others like me, people with learning disabilities, the way some of Jacqui's schizophrenic graduates helped other schizophrenics through the same process she'd taken them through. Maybe I could turn this into some sort of counseling career. Jacqui Schiff might have the solution to many of my problems.

My mother wasn't convinced this would work for me, but she also realized that it was the only option on my horizon. So she was very supportive as the time drew near for me to go and live with Jacqui and her family in Northern California. I think she convinced herself that this might be what we were looking for. We both needed hope. We needed something big and full of promise. And Jacqui Schiff seemed to fit the bill. And I believed that if this worked for me, Donna would eventually come around.

The House

9 flew from Chicago to San Francisco with only one suitcase packed with a few clothes and toiletries. We were allowed few personal possessions, and no medications or anything that could be used as a weapon. A "family" member named Jake met me at the airport and drove me to the small town of Alamo, about forty-five minutes away. We entered a suburban neighborhood and pulled into the driveway of one of the many large homes with half-acre yards. The house didn't seem so big when I remembered that I'd be sharing it with thirty-five other people, most of them severe schizophrenics. The ground floor had a big living room, a family room, a kitchen, and a dining room with a huge table. The upstairs was the men's dormitory, with six large bedrooms stacked with bunk beds, and a small bedroom at the end of a hall, where Jacqui slept. There was another large building behind the house, which Jacqui used as her office. It contained a meeting room, a kitchenette, and several more bedrooms, where the women slept. I never knew exactly how many lived on the property at any one time.

On my first day Jacqui came into the main room like a marine drill sergeant. She barely acknowledged me and started yelling at one of the kids who was waving his arms in the air, telling him to stop acting crazy. All of the family members were called "kids" regardless of their age. She told another kid to sit up straight in his chair, and shouted various orders to several others. Then she turned and left the room.

I was hungry when I arrived, but they'd just finished lunch so I didn't get to eat until dinnertime. The family members on dinner detail didn't make enough food, so everybody left the table still hungry. I went to bed late, totally exhausted and starving. I was ready for sleep, but Rudy, one of the "older" schizophrenics in charge of my room, saw that I could function at a higher level than other family members, which qualified me as an older family member, too. "Older" here didn't refer to birth age, but to emotional age, which was determined by your capacity to function responsibly and effectively, and to be accountable to the rest of the household and to Jacqui. Your chronological age was insignificant. If someone was in charge, you had to obey him or her. Period. If you argued or resisted, it meant you were acting out and there would be serious consequences.

So that night, before I had a chance to go to bed, Rudy put me in charge of Simon, one of my roommates. My job was to get Simon to do his bedtime routine — wash his face, brush his teeth, take off his clothes, put on his pajamas, and then get in bed and stay there. But schizophrenics need to feel safe, so they test you. They could be crafty. Simon saw right away that I was new and didn't know what in the hell I was doing. He began to passively resist me, talking strangely and making things as difficult as possible without getting into trouble. I'd learn that passive resistance was common behavior here. I didn't know what to do with Simon, or how hard to push him to get ready for bed. I was tired, hungry, and frustrated; now I was worried about getting in trouble with Jacqui.

It was midnight before I finally got to bed. I lay there thinking, *This is fucked up!* I repeated it over and over in my mind, like a mantra, as I fell asleep. I didn't have an alarm clock, and the next morning nobody woke me up, so I missed breakfast. I was given a warning and told that not having an alarm clock was no excuse for not getting up on time. When I asked for an alarm clock, I was told they didn't have one for me. I could see there was no winning in this place.

— ☥ —

From the start, it was go-go-go from morning till night — cleaning, serving, functioning, and responding in the moment to whatever the occasion required. Most Sundays, another guy and I would escort ten to fifteen of the best-behaved family members into the family VW van and into the family station wagon, along with packed lunches, and take them on day trips. We went to the beach, the San Francisco Zoo, Golden Gate Park, and any other place we could think of within driving range. It was grueling and required incredible vigilance.

You really had to be on top of things and nip the slightest misbehavior in the bud. Being in charge of schizophrenics not controlled by meds came down to establishing personal power and maintaining constant vigilance. So much of the communication was done with eye contact and body language. I'd had a lot of practice observing people. I'd learned how to know when Emerson gave even the slightest sign of hostility — a gleam in his eye or an upward turn of his mouth, a sudden movement or shift in the tone of his voice. Later through dealing drugs and surviving at Central Y, I'd learned the importance of expressing confidence and authority, both bodily and in the tone of my voice. My job was always to be aware of the room — correcting behavior and trying to look in charge instead of looking like the anxious and at-times-terrified person I was inside. I was continually engaging the "kids" verbally, talking to them, giving them directions and pushing them to function, establishing dominance, or trying to comfort or calm them down. So much of it depended on gaining their confidence and establishing a bond. Sometimes I could be friendly, but I always had to be firm; I couldn't be their friend.

Most people here were unpredictable, and some could be dangerous. Soon after my arrival, two of Jacqui's assistants taught me how to physically restrain someone. This was a necessary skill that every functional family member had to learn. The standard method required four people: two grabbed the person's arms, and the other two grabbed the legs; they pulled the arms behind the person's back and moved him or her into a corner. If there was still resistance, the feet were lifted up off the floor and the arms were forced back as far as they could go. It was painful but effective. If a person struggled too hard in that position, the shoulder could pop out of the socket. On occasion, if the resistance continued, you might have to intentionally dislocate a shoulder.

If anyone needed to be restrained, every functional family member in the vicinity knew what to do, and they had to do it quickly or be punished for negligence. The rule was that every-one in the room was responsible for what went on in the room, and everyone would be punished for anything wrong that hap-pened on his or her watch. We were all brothers and sisters, and we were responsible for one another. If you were in charge at night, you slept lightly, with your back to the wall. Any kind of rustling noise and you got up immediately. Many family members were handcuffed to their bed at night. If they had to get up in the middle of the night to go to the bathroom, the person in the room who was in charge had to go with them, which meant you lost sleep.

During my second week, a new schizophrenic named Timothy was brought into the house. Before he arrived, Jacqui took a small group of us aside. She explained that a paranoid schizophrenic would be arriving in a few minutes and that he was very agitated and potentially dangerous. He'd attacked several members of his own family, including his mother and father. She explained to me that she didn't use drugs to manage behavior because it prevented schizophrenics from learning from their experience, so he wouldn't be medicated when he arrived. We would be dealing with a full-blown, acting-out paranoid schizophrenic.

She said paranoid schizophrenics had two irrational states of mind, either scared and belligerent, or scared and submissive. Our job was to get him into a submissive role or he would see us as being weak. She said he would be dangerous to anyone he saw as weak, especially if that person held any position of authority. She said that paranoid schizophrenics know they are out of control and this makes them feel unsafe, so Timothy would be testing us to see if we could control him, and then he would feel a lot safer once he knew we could handle him at his worst.

A few minutes later, Timothy arrived from the hospital. Four of the strongest family members went to get him and brought him back to Jacqui's office, where we were waiting. He was twenty-five, around six feet tall, and weighed about 190 pounds, with wavy brown hair. Jacqui immediately got right in his face. She started provoking him until he exploded and tried to take a swing at her. The guys were ready.

Six of us piled on Timothy and started grabbing his arms and legs; then, while he was in the restraint position, we forced him onto a leather couch. I'd been in a lot of fights, but I'd never been involved in anything like this. Timothy continued yelling and fighting with unbelievable strength. But he was pinned down tight.

Now Jacqui really started in on Timothy, calling him a wimp, asking him who he thought was in charge here, and yelling in his face, "This isn't like anyplace you've been before!" He yelled back at her, and she slapped him hard on the face, saying, "Shut up! Is that all you've got?" He yelled at her again, and, *boom,* one of the guys socked him in the jaw and another guy slugged him in the stomach. More blows followed. Timothy was being pulverized, but he kept fighting back. Soon everyone was hitting him except for me. Then one of the other guys glared at me and snarled, "David!" So I hit Timothy a few times. I didn't know what I was doing. The others seemed to know when, where, and how hard to hit him — and when to stop. They'd all done this before. The whole time Jacqui stood by, overseeing the operation, talking to Timothy, and giving us directions. After a while, Timothy gave up and stopped struggling.

"You're good now, right? You're not going to pull anything?" asked Jacqui.

That just set him off, and the whole process started over again. Finally, Timothy was broken as if he were a wild horse. He went completely limp, just lying there, breathing hard with tears streaming down his face. When we let go of him, he was completely compliant. He just lay there while Jacqui talked to him. "You're safe here. We won't let you frighten or hurt anyone. We can and will stop you if you try. We can and will make you behave. You see we can handle you. You're safe." He seemed to take this in, and then he calmed down. Jacqui seemed to know what she was doing.

The incident freaked me out. I wondered if something like this could happen to me if I got out of line or into an argument with the wrong person. I swore to myself that I wouldn't be involved in an incident like this again.

But a few days later, Timothy started acting up and threatening some of the other kids. Jacqui ordered us to carry him into the bathroom and stick him in the tub. About six of us carried him to the bathroom, but we couldn't all fit inside. The four biggest guys brought him in and pinned him down in the empty bathtub. I stayed out in the hall, watching through the door. He was screaming and fighting the whole time. Jacqui yelled out to the younger kids to bring buckets of ice from the freezer. Then she came in and turned on the cold water in the tub while the four guys held Timothy down. The younger kids started bringing in bags of ice and Jacqui had them empty the bags onto Timothy as the water filled the tub. When they put the ice on him, he started screaming and fighting harder, but he couldn't get up. Soon he was covered with ice and submerged in frigid water.

"We'll let you out when you stop fighting!" Jacqui kept yelling at him.

But Timothy wouldn't stop fighting, even after he started shaking and turning blue. They kept dunking him down, holding him under, and then letting him up to breathe every so often. It didn't seem as if he was getting enough air to me, but what did I know? Jacqui seemed absolutely confident and in control of the process. After a while Timothy stopped struggling and became passive. Then, at Jacqui's command, he was lifted out of the tub, and they started drying him off with towels. As he stayed quiet, we all went back to our usual places. I chalked it up to one of the many freaky events I would find myself involved in at Jacqui Schiff's home.

— ⚘ —

Jacqui's three birth children lived with us in the house and went to public school each day. A handful of family members — high-functioning schizophrenics who had been "cured" by going through Jacqui's process — attended the local college. Only one of the family members didn't live in the house but came in the morning and left in the evening. And there were assistants, hired to do shopping and other household errands.

Jacqui was gone much of the time. There were two groups of people in charge of the household under Jacqui: family members who had gone through regression and come out the other side of their schizophrenia, and hired staff — psych majors who were getting some pay and college credit. There was always a designated Person in Charge, who made sure that everything ran smoothly when Jacqui wasn't around. The PIC could be either a staff member or a resident she considered responsible. The family members in charge were the most highly functional people I'd ever seen. They seemed totally together and not crazy at all. They were mostly men, but the women also commanded respect and had strong, confident voices.

Everyone started at the bottom. You worked your way up by demonstrating your ability to function under pressure and handle responsibility. The "healthier" you became, the more responsibility and freedom you were given. At the bottom to middle ranges there was little or no freedom and plenty of demand and responsibility; you were always under watch and had no privacy. At the mid- to upper ranges there was more responsibility, pressure, and stress, but, with permission, you could go to the store, the movies, and even on dates.

There was a lot of turnover among the hired staff. Most of them couldn't hold a candle to the older or recovered family members when it came to functioning, handling the pressure of restraining others, and dishing out consequences. If any family member acted out and needed restraining, the call would go out. Older kids within hearing range would come running, and the troublemaker would be taken down. Hired staff didn't always have the stomach for this, and they often quit if they had to do it more than a few times.

Within two weeks I was one of the high functioners, and at times I was made PIC of the house. At any given time one or more of the family could be acting out. When one acted out in response to another one's drama, they were called satellites. If more than a few went off at the same time, the entire room could escalate into total chaos. The pressure was indescribable. These situations often resulted in someone getting hurt, causing periodic trips to the hospital.

I soon realized that I'd been brought to Jacqui's house under false pretenses. I'd been told I'd only be there for a few weeks, that I wouldn't be a family member but just work there while I went through an evaluation process and set up a curriculum to get my high school diploma. But once I arrived, I was put in the same basket with the rest of them and treated like everyone else. I was angry about this. Then Jacqui told me she was now my legal guardian, and I had to do whatever she said.

After the initial shock wore off, I realized that as messed up as this was, it was my only real option, so I might as well give it my best shot. I was used to being in situations that were designed for people with different needs from my own. For this to work I had to be open and to try new things. I had to discern for myself what was useful and incorporate it into my life. And I had to recognize what wasn't helpful and be strong enough to throw it away, no matter how useful it seemed for others. I figured I'd at least get clean from drugs while I was there. I knew I couldn't do that on my own. But I realized I was on my own in a big way, which made me extremely anxious. I was given no parameters, no orientation, no formal schedule, and no emotional support.

For the first couple of weeks I kept asking to talk to Jacqui. I wanted to find out why our original agreement had changed, and ask her for some sort of schedule or program to follow. Finally, Jacqui agreed to talk to me. The conversation only lasted a few minutes. She listened briefly to my complaints, then interrupted me and told me that I was under observation, and I just needed more time to adapt to the routine. Then she left the room. After that conversation, she increased the pressure on me by giving me more chores and responsibilities. For the next few days she had me cooking dinner every night for as many as thirty-seven people. She ordered me to create a family vegetable garden in the backyard, and after I did, she came out one afternoon and tore it apart, yelling at me about doing a terrible job on purpose by planting too many carrots and not enough corn.

The last thing I wanted to do was piss Jacqui off. I realized how hard she could make my life. Besides, I needed her help. She'd mentioned that she was in the process of putting the school together. I just hoped it would start soon.

Jacqui was the most baffling personality I'd ever encountered. She was alternately angry and indifferent, brilliant and obtuse, and her attempt to control everyone around her inevitably resulted in chaos. I couldn't tell whether she didn't know what she was doing and nothing was under control, or whether everything was part of her cunning intention to frustrate, disorient, and trigger everyone. I was nursing grave doubts about her, and feeling increasingly anxious about having put myself so completely in her power.

Jacqui bragged about taking the most hopeless schizophrenic patients from hospitals that were glad to be rid of them, so she could prove her methods by curing them. The more bizarre the schizophrenics were, the smarter and more willful they seemed to be. Jacqui picked them smart and active. She said both of these qualities increased their chances of being cured, and that it was much harder to work with passive or dull schizophrenics. She wanted people who actively engaged rather than passively withdrew. Their resistance and acting out gave her something to work with. But if it gave them a better chance of recovering, it also made them more difficult to deal with.

One girl, Rachel, was a quiet, sweet-natured nineteen-year-old, the daughter of a famous couple. Rachel had taken on unusual qualities and mannerisms; she walked, talked, and behaved like an old lady. Jacqui successfully regressed Rachel's age identity until she reached her actual age of nineteen. At that point, Rachel ran away. For two weeks she managed to elude the police and the family members who went out daily and searched the neighborhood for her.

One afternoon, a man called the house saying he'd seen a girl acting very strangely who matched Rachel's description. He gave an address a few miles away. I was PIC that day and took the call when it came in. Jacqui was gone, so I left Rudy in charge and took the van to go look for Rachel.

I drove to the address the neighbor had given and found Rachel standing on the sidewalk. She looked extremely disoriented and grubby, and her face and scalp were red and peeling from sunburn. I got out and told her she had to come back to the house. She didn't want to go and started to resist. I couldn't just leave her there, so I grabbed her and started dragging her toward the van, and, just as I'd feared, she started screaming at the top of her lungs and fighting me as hard as she could. It looked as if I were kidnapping her. Then a man stuck his head out of the second-story window of a house nearby and yelled at me, "Let her go! I called the police! Leave her alone!"

I couldn't let her go, and I wasn't about to argue with the man shouting out of the window. I stopped, and just held Rachel's arm until the cop car came racing up the street, blue lights flashing, and pulled to a stop behind me. An officer got out and came over.

"What's going on?" he shouted.

"He's kidnapping that girl!" the man shouted from his window.

Rachel just stood there looking as crazed as she was. The cop looked at her and realized what was going on.

"You're from that house, aren't you?" he asked me.

"Yeah."

"Go ahead and get her into the van." He looked at Rachel and told her firmly, with full cop authority, "You have to get in the van and go with him." As the cop watched, she got into the van without any resistance. I tied her hands to the seat and drove her back to the house. Later on we learned that she'd been sleeping outside and supporting herself through prostitution. To Jacqui, this was a sign of improvement since it showed a boldness and initiative previously lacking in her character.

Some of the nonparanoid schizophrenics in the house could be a handful. Rob was twenty-three years old, extremely intelligent, and psychologically sophisticated. He understood the Parent/Adult/Child concept. He was also completely delusional. He had a habit of waving his arms around when he talked. When he was agitated, such as when I scolded him for not doing his chores, he'd wave his arms wildly in a very threatening manner. I didn't like it, it wasn't acceptable, and we discouraged him from doing it. Acting crazy and aberrant behavior weren't tolerated in the house. Persisting in such behavior after being told to stop was official grounds for punishment. That could mean being told to stand in a corner, being restrained, being whipped, being given an ice bath, or any other punishment Jacqui deemed necessary. Rob took the whole TA Parent/Adult/Child thing literally. When we would have a normal conversation, he would talk to me as my Adult self and call me David. But when I'd scold him, he determined that I was talking from my Parent state and would refer to me as either Mr. Patten or Mrs. Patten.

Whenever Rob started acting out, I'd say in a firm voice, "Rob, stop acting crazy."

"Okay, Mrs. Patten," he'd say, and then start waving his arms.

— ⚙ —

Jacqui said it wasn't her job to be loving. Her job was to make demands, push people to their limits, and deliver any necessary blows to force them to confront the roots of their illness and grow beyond it. She was a fearsome presence who insisted on total obedience and had absolute control. She'd walk into a room and size it up in a flash. She was amazing that way. She'd know in moments what everyone's game or strategy was, where people were at in the moment and how to deal with them. She could see right through people. The moment she entered a room, everyone, even full-blown schizophrenics, straightened up with some form of attention to her. When she started yelling, everyone was afraid — schizophrenic or not. She also had a way of speaking only a few words, very quietly, yet causing tremendous stress. She seemed to have an energizing, almost intoxicating effect on people around her. But her bottom-line demand was absolute loyalty and obedience to her, her methods, and her work.

According to her theory of regression for schizophrenics, every year of life required about a month of regression at that age. In practice, it was more random and flexible, and varied from person to person. Each person in regression got time alone with Jacqui. Depending on their phase of regression, she might feed them with a bottle (I even bottle-fed some family members), let them crawl or teethe on things, play child games, or read picture books. These were the few times she demonstrated anything that even remotely looked like love.

A full regression took the "kids" back to infancy, but some only had to go back to a particular stage in their lives, perhaps when a decisive trauma occurred, to address and heal the damage. They might need to be that age for only a day or two in order to come out of it cleansed and return to the functional world. Some really did come out of regression noticeably improved. I could see and feel the change in them. Something remarkable had clearly happened to them in the process.

I wondered if part of Jacqui's success was a result of her charismatic personality, which inspired a great deal of faith in her. In a way, maybe she was also a kind of hypnotist or faith healer.

We weren't allowed to identify others as crazy or insane. We could only refer to their behavior. They weren't said to be crazy, only that they acted crazy. The pressure was intense due to the general insanity of the environment, the relentless demands to function, and the serious consequences for nonconformity and resistance. Jacqui wanted us to be overwhelmed and anxious, and she was always looking to get someone in trouble. This created a hypervigilance that Jacqui felt made us more observant and made us try harder. Everyone got into trouble at one point or another for minor infractions. Jacqui frequently made patients stand in corners. She considered "corner contracts" a form of "passivity confrontation."

At times Jacqui and her assistants would focus on different people and make sure they repeatedly got into trouble. It did sometimes trigger regression. It also created a great deal of fear and anxiety in the house. I didn't want to become a target, so I stayed vigilant and tried harder. Because Jacqui was so powerful and bigger than life, when she broke patients, it triggered in them a kind of submissive adoration of her. Then they seemed to crave being regressed and mothered by her. It wasn't just that the alternative to submission was punishment, rejection, and ostracism, though that was part of it. I didn't fully understand it. I wasn't comfortable with Jacqui — I didn't like her, and I didn't trust her — but I still craved her approval. This was partly practical, because she had so much power over me, and partly a mysterious effect of her personality, and the influence it had on all of us.

Finding myself under more stress than I'd ever experienced before, I exerted myself more than I had at any time in my life.

This was boot camp, my last chance to get somewhere in life, and I wasn't going to waste it. In the crucible of Jacqui's madhouse, I began to tap into inner resources I didn't know I had. As I learned to do the tasks I was assigned to do, and began functioning consistently under intense pressure, my self-esteem and confidence grew. And I earned the respect of others there, including the respect of Jacqui, who kept giving me more responsibilities.

I came to believe that the demand for high functioning was good for me, and for everyone else in the household. But I never believed that the component of terror was good for anyone. I didn't think it needed to be there. But it was. And I saw that, despite its negative effects, terror made people stretch to be their most genius selves. It definitely made me function at supernormal capacity.

The high-functioning schizophrenics who had successfully completed Jacqui's reparenting process didn't seem mentally ill, but they did seem oddly mechanical and emotionally detached. At first I thought it was a leftover part of their schizophrenia. But later I found myself becoming mechanical and detached in a similar way. I realized that I was shutting down emotionally to avoid feeling the intensity of the stressful environment, all the while maintaining a constant vigilance to avoid getting into trouble. This happened to everyone. Our common goal wasn't recovering, but trying not to get into trouble.

Jacqui's high-functioning graduates made up her inner circle and her evidence that her methods, as chaotic and dangerous as they were, produced results. Jacqui held these graduates in special regard, and they had special status and privileges. We had to obey them as if they were Jacqui. They were less scary than Jacqui, yet I felt they were at the same time potentially more dangerous. I saw in them the danger of acting by proxy, trying to duplicate the judgment and authority of their leader, whose limits were unclear.

The uncertainty of my situation, the bizarre intensity of the environment, and my doubts about Jacqui and the craziness of the people I was surrounded with gradually took their toll on me. I was tense and hypervigilant all day and didn't sleep well at night. Everything was a struggle — getting enough sleep, getting enough to eat, getting a turn in the shower, and just getting through each very long, very stressful day.

I didn't want to be there. But I didn't have any other options, or any life to return to that held meaningful possibilities. It seemed like my only chance. I clung to that hope while nursing fears that this wasn't going to help me, that I wasn't going to get my high school diploma, that none of the things I'd been promised were going to pan out. I thought seriously about running away, but where would I go? I was living in a small California town two thousand miles from home with no cash and no friends, under the legal guardianship of a very powerful woman who meted out physical punishment and restraint like a prison warden.

Also, I didn't trust my own assessment of things any more than I trusted Jacqui. I had no clarity, and my personal track record was one of chronic struggle, bad choices, and failure. I was never really sure if Jacqui was right or wrong. Her absolute certainty about her methods and her supreme self-confidence made me doubt myself and my own perceptions. It seemed she could always sway anyone to her point of view. No one could argue with her or make the slightest dent in her certainty. And she tolerated no dissent. She seemed extreme to me, and I often thought she went too far. Yet some people did get better. Her methods often seemed to work. But I wondered at what cost.

Charismatic people had always fascinated me. They seemed to have a freedom and intensity, a dynamic drive and sense of purpose that ordinary people lacked. They were not constrained by self-doubt, a conscience, or social inhibitions. Some seemed indifferent to the feelings and opinions of others. Often their compelling personalities seemed to transmit an exhilarating energy that drew others to them, but also kept them separate and made them different, special.

Many of the charismatic people I'd encountered were criminals, political radicals, or sociopaths. A few of the major Central Y players had this quality. You couldn't take your eyes off them. A few of my biggest dealers had that quality. So did Yellow Shirt, the Blackstone Ranger who had almost thrown me down the stairwell. I felt something similar in Jacqui Schiff. She wasn't willfully cruel, but she was ruthless in her purpose and indifferent to the feelings of others, and she frequently hurt people in the course of going about her work. And we were all subjects in her surreal little kingdom.

Like everyone else there, I was only getting about four hours of sleep at night. I was functioning from the minute I woke up in the morning until the minute I went to bed at night. My job on any given day could include single-handedly wrestling a guy nearly a foot taller than I was into a corner and making him stay there; changing a diaper on a large man with a three-day growth of beard who had regressed to the level of a two-year-old; or calming down a roomful of frightened and hysterical schizophrenics. I was cooking meals for thirty-five people when I'd never cooked a full meal before and couldn't read a cookbook. While I cooked, I also had to keep an eye on my paranoid schizophrenic kitchen assistant, Timothy, who was tied to me with a rope and who wasn't supposed to be around knives. Because Timothy could read much better than I could, I had to rely on him for the cooking instructions. He liked to mess with me by changing the recipe ingredients and amounts without telling me, which, on more than one occasion, ruined a meal and got me into trouble.

One evening, a large group of us were sitting in the living room watching TV when we heard the sound of shattering glass in the bathroom down the hall. A bunch of us older kids immediately jumped up and ran to see what had happened. When we got to the bathroom, we saw a girl named Francine standing in front of the sink with pieces of shattered mirror lying all around her. Francine was one of the "cured," mature schizophrenics who had successfully gone through regression and grown up to her real age. I'd only just met her because she was now living on her own, holding down a real job, and had come home for a visit. She was holding a shard of broken mirror in one hand; her wrist was slit open, and there was blood all over the floor. I let some of the older kids she knew go in to deal with the situation.

Francine fought them off using the shard as a weapon. Her arms were flailing wildly, and blood was flying everywhere. By the time they got the shard away from her, she had cut herself in several more places on her arm. They wrapped her bloody arm in a towel, and Jacqui and a couple of her assistants took Francine to the hospital. I went into the bathroom to clean up the mess. Blood and broken glass were everywhere — on the floor, in the toilet, the sink, and the bathtub, and on the walls. It took me almost two hours to clean it up.

Later, Jacqui returned with Francine. I could tell Jacqui was shaken. I'd never seen her that way before. I guessed that having one of her "cured" kids attempting suicide got to her. She immediately started yelling at people, giving orders and appearing confident. Oddly, that seemed to calm everyone down. I didn't know Francine very well, or what had triggered her suicide attempt, but it upset all of us for a few days. It definitely shook my remaining confidence in Jacqui.

— ⚘ —

Unexpected delays prevented the opening of Jacqui's new school for weeks after my arrival. I was incredibly frustrated. I'd come here thinking Jacqui was going to help me deal with my "issues," relearn things I'd missed in my early developmental stages, and also learn to read and get my GED. But so far, none of that had happened. I was basically an unpaid, highly functioning assistant — a captive, subject to family rules. I'd been getting some benefit in terms of discipline and improved functioning, but I would have gotten as much if I'd joined the army. It was starting to look as if I'd never get my diploma.

Finally, Jacqui's school started up in a small two-bedroom house she'd rented in Danville, a few miles from the main house. I was the only student attending the school from the house, with five other kids from the surrounding community, who, for one reason or another, had been kicked out of public school. No one was schizophrenic. Jacqui received money from the parents of these five students and from the public school system.

There were three teachers: Robert and Jane, who were a couple and also ministers of some kind; and Dee Dee, who was very nice and had been trained by Jacqui, though I never knew much else about her. Robert and Jane were both studying psychology, and were I think getting credit toward their degrees by working with Jacqui. They were familiar with the dynamics of the main household, where they'd worked as paid assistants and undergone training with Jacqui. They were considered part of the family. I'd find out later that they had their own misgivings about Jacqui's methods.

After the first month, I went to Jacqui's Cathexis school six days a week, twelve hours a day. I liked it. I was excited to begin the curriculum Jacqui had promised, and it was a relief from the pressure of the main house. But all I studied was the California GED study guide to prepare for the high school equivalency test. The teachers were very encouraging at first, and assured me I'd be able to learn enough to pass the test and get a diploma, but that encouragement faded as I struggled with the same insurmountable disabilities that had always held me back.

I really liked the encounter groups we had, guided by Dee Dee, who was a trained counselor. I'd been instructed by several family members not to talk with the teachers or other students about what happened in Jacqui's house, since most people wouldn't understand and it could cause a lot of trouble. But in the encounter groups I discovered that I had a knack for counseling kids. I had a lot of experience and insight, and the other students seemed to trust me and look to me for guidance. For one of the rare times in my life I felt useful, as if I was really helping people and doing some good. The teachers confirmed this to me privately, and I was encouraged by them to think about counseling as something I could do for a living. But the learning issues still stood in my way.

After I'd been at the house for a few months, Jacqui found a dormitory-style building a few miles away; almost all of the guys moved there. We called it the "cabin," or the "boys' dorm."

Now, every morning before heading to school, I had to get every-body awake and cleaned up. I had to make sure they cleaned the cabin, and I had to deal with whatever the crisis was that morn-ing. Rudy and I would drive everyone to the main house, where they would spend the day; then I'd go to the Cathexis house for my twelve-hour school day. In the evening we would drive ev-eryone back to the cabin, get everyone to do evening chores, get everyone cleaned up and deal with more flip-outs and crises, then get everyone into bed. Depending on how it went, I'd get to bed between midnight and 2:00 AM.

— ⚬ —

I'd been in Jacqui's program about six months. I missed Mom and Neil so much. I still missed Dad. But I missed Donna most of all, especially at night when it was quiet. I missed her laughter, her face, her body lying next to me, and her arms around my neck. I had never left her alone before, and I was unable to find out how she was doing. I felt so alone. I was constantly surrounded by other people, but there was no one I could talk to and no one I trusted. There was no sense of love or closeness with anyone, especially Jacqui. It wasn't a family in any sense of the word. I just kept hoping this would all be worth it. Sometimes I wished I were home again, but then I'd remember how awful it was for me there. I didn't want to sell dope anymore. I didn't want to end up in prison or on the street.

When things got really bad, I'd think about Eric and Aaron, the two men who had spoken at the first presentation I'd attended with Donna and my mother back in Chicago. Eric had a real job and his own apartment in the outside world. Aaron ran his own family in another house, using Jacqui's methods to reparent and retrain other schizophrenics. I'd met them both, and they didn't seem crazy at all. This gave me the trace of reassurance I needed to keep going. And above all, the one simple reason I stayed with Jacqui under these insane and frightening conditions was the promise of a GED. I was truly desperate. I saw this place as my only chance for a future. It seemed to me that if I could succeed here, I could succeed anywhere. And if I failed here, it was the end of the line.

Madness Treating Madness

*A*fter a few months I was allowed to talk to Donna on the phone every week or two, but I wasn't allowed to talk to my mom. One day while I was at school, I snuck out and called my mother from a payphone. I tried to tell her that Jacqui and her place were nothing like what we thought they would be. She said that she was glad to hear from me, but told me she had promised not to take calls from me and not to call her again.

At Cathexis each day, I was the only student from Jacqui's family. The other students came from town. The schoolhouse was very different from the main house—more relaxed and comparatively casual. It had two bedrooms and was comfortably furnished, except there were no beds. I liked it there. Each day we had a group session sitting on the couches and stuffed chairs in the living room. One afternoon I was expecting a phone call from Donna. The other students and the teachers all knew about Donna, and her drug use; I'd shared this in our sessions. The phone in the kitchen rang during one of our sessions, and I ran to get it. It was Donna. I stretched the long phone cord to the nearby bedroom and closed the door for privacy.

When we'd first planned for me to live out here, we'd understood it would be two weeks. I'd been gone far longer than we'd ever imagined. Our conversation was very disturbing. Donna told me she'd gone through an ounce of MDA over the past few weeks and was crashing hard. She was a mess. I flipped out and started screaming at her. MDA was new and a heavy drug that trashed the body—a harsh predecessor of MDMA, or ecstasy. I was told it combined the effects of speed, cocaine, and LSD. I'd never done it myself.

I hung up and returned to the group, visibly upset, and shared with them what was going on. Word got back to Jacqui, and the next day she came to see me. She suggested that Donna come out here and get evaluated, to see if she should get into the program. At the very least, it would get her away from her drug connections.

I was worried about Donna and missed her terribly, so I was thrilled with the idea. This way we'd be together again. But I tried to hide my excitement, concerned that Jacqui might use this as leverage against me later. I was also afraid that Donna was spiraling into addiction and the resulting mental dissolution. I knew Donna wouldn't want to be part of Jacqui's household. I told Jacqui I would encourage Donna to come, but I insisted that she wouldn't become a family member subject to the rules, pressures, and consequences the rest of us lived under. She just needed enough support and supervision to get clean.

Donna had just turned eighteen and didn't need her parents' consent or Jacqui's legal guardianship. Jacqui and I negotiated an arrangement, subject to Donna's consent. She would work eight hours each day as a housecleaner in the main family house in exchange for counseling with Jacqui, lunch each day, and her own room at the house of a third party. Jacqui said the parents of one of the schizophrenic kids undergoing treatment might take Donna in.

I called Donna later that afternoon and told her the plan. She was totally into it, and the plan was set in motion. Jacqui arranged for Donna to sleep in a spare room in the house of John Hartwell's parents. John, a schizophrenic, had a special arrangement with Jacqui. He spent every day at the main house as a family member and went home each night to sleep. No one else in the house was allowed that kind of liberty. The Hartwells agreed to give Donna a room plus breakfast and dinner at no charge. They were doing Jacqui a favor in gratitude for her taking their son into her program. Donna would be half a mile from the Cathexis schoolhouse.

When Emerson learned that Donna was coming, he also decided to come out. He knew, from my reports to my mother, that my situation at Jacqui Schiff's was not at all what had been promised. He told Donna it didn't sound good, and he decided to come out and see what was happening for himself. He had been planning to visit a friend of his who lived in South San Francisco, a Romanian poet named Andrei Codrescu, whom he had gotten to know at the University of Michigan at Ann Arbor. Emerson was an aspiring poet, and Andrei was going to help him publish a small collection of his poetry while he was here.

Emerson contacted Jacqui Schiff beforehand, and she invited him to assist part-time at the house, buying groceries for the family members and running occasional errands. He would receive no training, he would interact only with Jacqui or her staff, and he wouldn't have any responsibility or direct contact with family members. But all of this was going on behind the scenes for me, without my participation.

I was so happy to see Donna when she arrived. We hadn't seen each other in more than six months. Each day she'd hitchhike from the Hartwells' house to Jacqui's house, put in her morning hours of cleaning, and then hitchhike to the schoolhouse in time for lunch. After lunch we'd walk to the Hartwells' house. Both of the Hartwells worked, so Donna and I could hang out in her room and be intimate. Then she'd hitchhike back to the main house and I'd walk back to school.

When Emerson arrived two weeks later, I wasn't allowed to see or talk with him. But after seeing the house and the "kids" and meeting Jacqui, it didn't take him long to assess the situation I was in. He told Donna it was bad and that I needed to get out of there. But I was still hoping to stick it out and get a high school diploma.

Donna and I were surprised by how accepting and open people in California were about marijuana. It was 1971. The kids at Jacqui's school all talked openly in our groups and in front of the teachers about getting high. They said smoking weed was a common public school pastime, so we figured getting weed wasn't a problem. I hadn't gotten high in California until Donna arrived. I didn't think weed was so bad. And for Donna to stay off hard drugs, I figured she'd need to get high. I knew by now that she couldn't do without drugs completely, but maybe working with Jacqui would change that. In the end, however, nothing happened. Donna never got any formal counseling with Jacqui. She only had a few conversations with her and never got a/**./******** help. The teachers at school had to know we were getting high because they could smell it on me, and all the other students were getting high, too. I'm pretty sure Jacqui also knew but didn't think it was a big deal either.

Our new routine ran smoothly for a while. I was more relaxed about things now that Donna was with me and I didn't have to live in the main house, where all the real insanity was happening. But a few months after Donna came, things took an unexpected turn. The Hartwells found a stash of weed in Donna's room and got very upset. They called Jacqui, and a strange chain of events was set in motion.

Jacqui talked the Hartwells out of kicking Donna out of their house, but someone had to be punished. Since Jacqui had no authority over Donna, I was that someone. I don't think Jacqui was particularly upset with Donna for smoking pot, or getting caught for that matter. I think she was really looking for a way to temper the Hartwells' anger and push me to my next edge. I knew I was in trouble when Jacqui called and told me to come over to the house the next day.

When I got there, Jacqui told me that Donna had put her in a difficult spot with the Hartwells. She said it was my fault because Donna was my girlfriend, and if I was going to break the rules, then I would have to take the heat. It was clear that I was in more trouble for getting caught than for doing the deed. She told me that I had to be punished, and she sent me to the living room. I sat there with a group of the least functional family members, reflecting on my situation. I hadn't gotten into any real trouble since I'd arrived, and I'd shouldered a lot of responsibility, so I figured I'd get off relatively easy.

A while later Jacqui came in with two of the big guys, Rudy and Narrow. She told me to come with them to her bedroom, where I was going to be whipped. Then she ordered one of the family members to get the willow branch. This was a big branch, with a whipping tip about as thick as my forefinger. I pretended to go quietly until we got to the stairs; then I broke away and ran for the front door. Before I could reach it, Rudy tackled me from behind, and I went down hard. Both Rudy and Narrow pounced on me, and a couple of others joined in. Now there were four of them holding me down, twisting my arms back and bending my elbows so that my shoulder felt like it was going to pop out of the socket. Once they had me in this position, I made no resistance; it would only get me a dislocated shoulder, and an extra beating.

They lifted me to my feet with my arms twisted back in the control position, then walked me down the hall and up the stairs. When we were in Jacqui's room, they took off my shirt. Jacqui had them pull her dresser out a couple of feet and tilt it back against the wall. She had Rudy, Narrow, and the other two guys lay me out on the dresser while they held my arms and legs. They pulled down my pants and tied my wrists and ankles to the dresser with my back exposed.

Jacqui gave the branch to one of the guys — I couldn't tell which one — and told him to whip me as hard as he could. The whipping began. It hurt like hell; the beater was wailing on me with the branch and Jacqui was yelling at him: "Harder!" I tried not to make a sound, but the impact of each lash forced the air out of me in an involuntary grunt. The sound of the whip whistling through the air and the thud as it sliced into my back were so loud that I was sure everyone downstairs could hear.

I had no idea when it would stop. I just took it. With each blow, the whip cut into my back, and I saw myself running away and never coming back. Finally Jacqui told them to stop. I felt blood dripping down my backside. I don't remember things clearly after that. Someone washed off my back with a damp cloth; some spots felt like raw meat. They untied me and stood me up naked in front of Jacqui. She told me to pull up my pants and underwear; then someone gave me a clean T-shirt, and I put it on. I did my best to wash my backside before going to sleep that night, but my T-shirt and sheets were bloody when I got up the next morning.

The next day I went to school. I was so ashamed I didn't talk about the beating with anyone. I was now demoted, with no authority in the house. The older kids at the house and the teachers at school were watching me closely, on Jacqui's orders. That was how it went when you really fucked up.

Donna came over at lunchtime, and we went on the back porch to talk privately. I told her what had happened. When she pulled my T-shirt up and saw the bloody, swollen welts covering my entire back and butt, she totally freaked out. I'd never seen Donna feel so guilty about anything before. It ripped her apart knowing I'd gotten whipped because of her. At that point, she became completely committed to my escape.

But if I escaped, where would we go?

We had a long talk. My relationship with Donna was wonderful and problematic. I gave her the anchor she needed to keep her delusions at bay, and at times she counted on my reality as her own. But this put a great weight on me, a pressure I wasn't certain I could maintain. I was unable to keep her off dope before. I couldn't protect her from herself. I knew I didn't have the clarity or purity that was required to be someone else's reality. I was the first intimate person in her life who didn't want to exploit her, and yet I needed her to function for my own sake. Donna stabilized, often through my constancy of attention and through the demand that my disability made on her. She became highly functional, in a manner similar to what we surmised was the benefit of Jacqui's program for the others. Give a schizophrenic or anyone a lot of structure, and they tend to stabilize and strengthen. This demand from me helped Donna in some ways, but we both knew it might prove to be the catalyst for the end of our relationship.

Another big concern was my education. Where else was I going to get the tutoring at my level? I still wanted a diploma. Even the military wouldn't take me without a diploma. Still, we both knew we had to escape.

That night Donna went to see Emerson. The next day she told me she and Emerson had come up with a plan for me to escape that night. She gave me a scrap of paper with Emerson's phone number on it. I wasn't sure I could pull it off, certainly not at night. Family members in charge in each room slept with virtually one eye open all night. I'd have to seize an opportunity in the moment. As soon as they discovered I was gone, they'd have a team of family members out on the streets, and Rudy and Narrow driving the van through the neighborhood looking for me. If they didn't find me within an hour, they'd call the police.

If and when I did run, Donna and I would have no way to communicate. Emerson, who was staying at Andrei Codrescu's house, would be our mutual contact. Andrei was in on the plan.*

I wanted to leave as soon as possible, yet I was overwhelmed by feelings of disappointment at not having gotten any of what Jacqui had promised. I'd come with such high hopes but would leave more or less the same as I came, with no diploma, no

---

* Andrei Codrescu later wrote a wonderful fictionalized account of my escape from Jacqui Schiff's entitled "TP: A Case for Sanity," which appears in his memoir *In America's Shoes* (City Light Books, 1983).

healthy reprogramming, no improved learning or work skills, and no new plan for my future. I'd improved my ability to function under incredible pressure and stress, but at great emotional and psychological cost.

The realization was sinking in that I'd gone through all this craziness for nothing. My escape wouldn't be a move forward but a flight backward, to my old life of insanity, drug deals, paranoia, and a struggle to survive. At least I'd have Donna, and I really had no choice. I decided to do it.

The next day at school I acted as if it were just another day and I wanted to get back to work on my GED. At one point when no one was paying attention, I snuck into one of the empty rooms and opened a window, then came back into the main room. A little while later, I asked the teacher if I could go and study in that room. He said it was okay, but I had to leave the door open. I went in with my GED book. Seconds later I'd climbed out of the window. I took off running across the front lawn and down the street. I figured I had twenty minutes, maybe less, before they noticed I was gone.

Soon I was standing on the main road with my thumb out and my heart pounding. The first few cars passed me by. I kept looking back to see if they were coming after me. Finally an elderly man picked me up and gave me a ride to downtown Danville, a few miles away. I found a payphone outside a small market and called the number Donna had given me.

When Emerson answered, I was never so glad to hear his voice. He said he would call Donna at the main house and call me right back. I hung up and stood in the phone booth for twenty minutes. It seemed like an eternity. I'd been gone over an hour. They were probably out searching for me by now. I kept scanning the parking lot and the street for cops or the family van. Finally, the phone rang. I picked it up.

"Goddammit, Emerson, that took way long!"

There was a pause on the other end of the line.

"David, there's a problem," Emerson said.

I felt my heart beating hard and fast, and a chill passed through me as if all the blood were draining from my face, down through my body toward my feet.

"Shit! What kind of problem?"

"Jacqui has Donna."

"What do you mean, she has Donna? Donna's not part of Jacqui's family. She can't hold her there."

"I know! I told her that. But she just says she's holding Donna until you come back to the house."

"She can't do that, can she? That's false imprisonment or kidnapping or something. That's a federal offense."

"I know," Emerson said. "But she's not letting her go."

I realized he was right. Jacqui didn't care about such things. Jacqui did whatever she wanted. I knew there was no way she would let Donna go. I licked my lips. My mouth was parched, and my hand was shaking. "Shit. I have to go back."

"I know it's fucked up, David," Emerson said. "I'm sorry it happened this way."

The reality of it was sinking in. I fought back tears of disappointment. "Oh, man, I bet they beat the shit out of me for this."

"What do you want me to do?"

"Nothing for now. We'll have to try this again later. I'll call you when I can. It may not be for a while."

I hung up, walked back to the main street, and stuck my thumb out. I caught a couple of rides and made it back to the house. I walked slowly up the driveway as if I were going back to prison, savoring my last moments of freedom. Before I reached the door, Rudy and Narrow came out to meet me. They escorted me around the back of the house.

"Where's Donna?" I asked.

"She's going out the front door right now," said Rudy sternly, "and she's not ever welcome back here again." *Well, at least she's safe from you assholes*, I thought.

"Mom wants to see you," Rudy said, meaning Jacqui.

Rudy led me to a recently constructed outbuilding that was Jacqui's new office. I didn't get the feeling that I was about to be whipped, but I was still very nervous. I'd never pulled a stunt like this before. Rudy knocked on the door.

"Come in!" Jacqui's high, childlike voice called from inside.

Rudy opened the door and nodded for me to enter. Then he turned and left. Jacqui was alone, sitting behind her desk. It was hard to reconcile her dumpy housewife look with the power and authority she wielded so completely. She invited me to sit down on one of the couches. I sat down cautiously.

"Would you like a drink — maybe some soda or water?" she asked in an almost friendly tone.

I didn't know what to think. She'd never been this nice to me before. Knowing Jacqui, there had to be some psychological strategy behind it. She and her little kingdom were so bizarre I couldn't rule anything out.

"No, thank you," I finally said.

She got out of her chair and started doing office stuff, as if I weren't there. She tidied up her desk a bit, went over to her filing cabinets, and rummaged around for a minute, then rearranged some papers and other things stacked on the wall shelves. It was odd. I couldn't tell if she was trying to make me nervous, if she was killing time, or if she was gathering her thoughts. Finally she returned to her desk, sat down, and looked right at me. Her eyes were steady and showed no feeling.

"David," she said, "why did you come here?"

I figured I had nothing to lose at this point, so I might as well be completely honest. I wouldn't know how to manipulate her anyway; she was way out of my league.

"I really wanted to get the GED you said I'd be able to get. And I wanted to get some help understanding myself. I wanted to learn how to learn better, or at least understand why I have trouble learning."

"Is that really it?"

"Yes. I also wanted to know why I'm always depressed. And why I can't feel happy the way other people say they feel. I don't ever remember really wanting to be alive. I've been happy a few times. I get excited about getting things or doing things sometimes. But it never lasts, and there's always this feeling of hopelessness deep down, like I'm doomed. I don't see a future for myself. I was hoping coming here would change that somehow. But it hasn't."

"I have you in my school studying to get your GED."

"I've been working with that book, and I don't see ever getting through it. What about all the other stuff you were going to work with me on? Even if I get my GED, what kind of job can I get? I'll probably have to live in a flophouse and get by on menial work. You knew I was coming here because I was desperate. You said you were going to be able to help me. But you haven't. This hasn't worked out at all. And I don't know what else to do."

"You know what I'm about here, David. We're devoted to

helping people truly change — the ways they want and need to."

"That's great, but I don't see it. I'm afraid of you, and so is everyone else. So if you're supposed to be our mother, how does that help? Nothing has changed for me, and I've been here nine months."

"I've told you all before, my job isn't to be loving or to teach anyone else how to love. All I can do is help people change and learn how to live responsibly. And if they have to be afraid of me to get there, then so be it. I show my love by helping them get better, not by being nice. Look, David, I know Donna and your brother have been trying to get you to leave. Before you decide whether or not to try to leave again, you need to consider the people who want you to leave and their motives."

"What do you mean?"

"Donna is a very sweet girl, David, but is she good for you? Does she have your best interest at heart, or her own? You have to look inside yourself to answer that."

"What do you mean? Both of them are out for themselves?"

As always, she'd somehow thrown me off balance and into confusion. I didn't really understand what she was telling me. I thought she was trying to make me mistrust Donna and Emerson and trust her instead. She fixed me with that cool, penetrating stare.

"I'm talking about people lying and manipulating you in order to get what they want from you."

"You mean Donna? I think I could tell if she was doing that."

"No, David, I don't think you could," Jacqui said with absolute certainty. "With someone like Donna, no one can ever tell for sure. Even lie detectors can't tell if she's lying or telling the truth. She doesn't even know herself. She may or may not be schizophrenic, but she definitely has a character disorder. People with character disorders don't know the difference between right and wrong. They have no ability to empathize. They're capable of just about anything when there's enough at stake, or even just to get what they want." Jacqui paused. I stared at her in disbelief. "I'm not saying Donna's malicious," she continued. "I don't think she is. But because of how she grew up, she hasn't developed a conscience or a sense of morality — a guiding sense of right and wrong. She's a sociopath. She wouldn't hurt someone for no reason, but she will use people to get what she wants or thinks she needs. That includes you."

Jacqui paused, giving me a chance to respond, but I had nothing to say. I knew that Donna could be crazy at times, and that she was driven by deep fears and an incredible neediness, but Jacqui was missing something about her. Jacqui didn't say anything about her personality being fragmented into pieces. I knew that I really loved Donna, and she really loved me. I couldn't say this to Jacqui; to try to explain it would only make me look naïve or stupid. And I didn't want to look stupid to Jacqui.

"You know I'm right," Jacqui continued. "Donna desperately needs you, and she'll do anything to keep you, even if it destroys you. This kind of relationship is one of the worst things for a person as paranoid as you are."

I could understand Jacqui saying that Donna would do almost anything, but this last statement shocked me with a kind of physical impact. I didn't trust Jacqui, but when she made psychological observations I couldn't just shrug them off. She had penetrating insight into people and their motivations. I'd seen it many times before. And she had a way of making you doubt yourself and lose all of your confidence.

"What do you mean?" I asked, reluctantly. "I thought para-noids were delusional. Do you think I'm delusional?"

"No, of course not. You're not clinically paranoid," she said. "But think of the definition of *paranoid* as becoming what you're afraid of. That's you. You live in fear of what you might become, and that's what you do become. It's something we all do, but for the last few years it's been the dominant pattern of your life. You practice paranoia without knowing it. In times of crisis, you let your fear determine your response. Every time you tried to be as tough or as scary as the people you were afraid of, you were practicing paranoia."

Her argument was compelling and seemed so accurate that I couldn't deny it.

"Well...then I'd better stop doing that" was all I could say.

"That's easier said than done, David. Bad habits are much harder to break and take longer to unlearn than they take to learn."

I pondered her words, trying to understand their true mean-ing. Was I really paranoid? Was I doomed to live out this pattern she was describing? I didn't know how to even begin to change — that was why I'd come here. She was supposed to help me. Now she seemed to be telling me I couldn't do it. Or maybe I was be-ing paranoid right now. I couldn't tell.

"Emerson is your brother, and I know you love him," Jac-qui said. She was starting on Emerson now; she dissected and pathologized everyone. "But you know he has trouble taking other people and their feelings into account. Emerson is a nar-cissist. He can act sympathetic, but he's all about himself. He's not capable of empathy. He lives as if he's the only person who matters. His needs, his opinions, his feelings are more important than anyone else's. He thinks he's right and everyone else in the world is wrong."

"But everyone's like that," I said weakly.

In a way she was right, but I couldn't help seeing that Jacqui herself was exactly the kind of person she was describing Emerson to be. But I couldn't say that to her. There was no way to argue with her; you only dug a deeper hole for her to bury you in. The problem with Jacqui was that she was always right in some essential way.

This was a lot to take in all at once. I'd never thought about Donna in the way Jacqui was describing her, but now I could see the possibility that she might be right, the way she was right about Emerson. Still, something felt wrong. Donna heard voices in her head. This seemed real to me. Yet I had to take seriously what Jacqui was saying. Was I being manipulated by Donna? Was I just supporting her delusions by taking care of her? Now I wondered if Donna had been lying to me and I just wasn't able to tell. Or maybe Jacqui was triggering my paranoia and directing it at Donna, to separate us so that she could control me. That fit with my picture of Jacqui. She really was everything she was accusing Emerson and Donna of being. But she was also brilliant and powerful. I was so confused.

"So should all people with character disorders be put in prison?" I asked, trying to defend Donna while also trying to gain more understanding.

"No, not at all. They're not necessarily criminals; they're just not capable of distinguishing and functioning stably within conventional social norms — like appropriate and inappropriate, right and wrong. Nonmalignant character disorders function best in highly structured environments. They do well in prison, either as inmates or as guards. They do well in the military, in the police force, and in other strict environments that give them clear rules and guidelines of right and wrong. My father had a character disorder, and he was a police sergeant who did very well."

"Can someone have a healthy relationship with people who have character disorders?"

"Well, yes, with some character disorders, if they're generally well-balanced, productive people. I also have a character disorder."

I couldn't believe my ears. I couldn't believe Jacqui was admitting this to me. I fucking knew it! I should trust myself. I can always tell with certain people. Carefully, I asked, "How is your environment highly structured?"

"Well, I have an outside psychiatrist who oversees me and regularly reviews my work with me. This way I can continue my work within appropriate limits, under qualified supervision."

I'd seen a guy with curly hair come to see her sometimes. I thought he was just a friend of hers. He never came in or looked around; he just went with her into her office, and they spent time talking together. At one point a few of us speculated that he might even be her lover.

"The point is that neither Donna nor Emerson has any kind of structure or accountability for their behavior, especially where you're concerned. And I don't think they're capable of having your best interests at heart. I can say that I do, because I don't need anything from you. I only want to help you, and I know how. I think you know it's true. This place is your best chance, David. You're not going to be punished for now. But I'm putting you under twenty-four-hour one-on-one supervision for the foreseeable future. Do you have any questions?"

Yeah, thousands, I thought, *mostly about you.* By now I didn't trust anything she was saying. Maybe she believed she could help me. But I didn't.

"I don't know." I shrugged.

"David, if you really want to get better, you need to seriously consider what we've talked about."

"I will."

What else could I say? I didn't know what to do. I didn't know what to think. I left Jacqui's office with my mind spinning. Was I really paranoid? Was she trying to *make* me paranoid? After spending half an hour alone with Jacqui, I left not trusting myself. I half believed everything she'd told me, and I was feeling paranoid about Emerson and Donna. Jacqui clearly wanted me to mistrust them and trust her instead. But they were trying to help me escape, and she'd taken Donna hostage and was now holding me prisoner.

I was shaking when I got back into the house. My mind was racing. I couldn't think straight. I felt my body lose all sense of coordination. The only thing I had to hold onto in this world, the only thing that meant anything to me right now, was my love for Donna. I'd always thought Donna needed me more than I needed her, but maybe it was the other way around.

I went into the family room and sat down on one of the couches with the other kids. I'd lost all my privileges and was back at the bottom of the pile. Rudy was in charge and therefore keeping an eye on me. I looked around at the others. I'd been responsible for many of them for months now. They were all pains in the ass, but there was something about each one of them that I loved. At times I'd seen the human beings trapped behind their madness. I felt a connection to them, a feeling of empathy. With all the pressure of managing them, it was hard to feel that. But I felt it now. I felt as if I finally understood them.

Their minds were out of control, firing off distorted thoughts and lying to them, leading them off on wild fantasies they mistook for reality. It wasn't their fault. Their schizophrenia was like a misfire or an explosion going off randomly in their heads, shattering their minds' continuity of reality, sending bizarre fragments of thoughts, ideas, and images flying like shrapnel in all directions. To many of them it seemed that their thoughts were actually voices coming from outside of them. Their strategies and strange behavior were misguided efforts to find meaning and stability in a maelstrom, to patch the fragments together into a whole that made sense. But the whole they constructed was meaningful only to them, and it looked like insanity to the rest of the world. How can a broken mind fix a broken mind?

Jacqui constantly confronted her schizophrenics with terrible consequences for their abnormal thinking and behavior; she thereby forced and motivated them to want to see reality as it was, and how it might be different from their own perceptions. I realized that Jacqui hadn't stopped their delusions at all. But, over time, some did start to distinguish better and better between their delusions and reality. It must have taken profound humility and desperation to get to the point where they would be willing to give up confidence in their own perceptions. Jacqui had motivated them profoundly, and what they'd been doing hadn't been working for them at all. To begin to trust in their ability to judge what was real from what was not had to be profoundly difficult. I can't know exactly what that would be like, but I do know that it would take a lot for me to believe that what I see and hear isn't real, and try to ignore what my mind and senses seem to be telling me.

We all naturally have to believe there's special truth to our own perceptions. I'm not sure I could step out of the house if I knew I couldn't rely on my own perceptions.

Jacqui had tried to use force to motivate the schizophrenic mind to do the hard work of first questioning its perceptions, then distinguishing between them, and then choosing reality. I'd tried to do the same thing for Donna with trust. Together we had done the hard work to establish trust. But Donna needed me to be with her at all times, and by my being there she wasn't forced to perfect her own ability to distinguish reality. She didn't have to build the necessary confidence to rely on her own ability to perceive the difference between delusion and reality. She'd been so broken by life that she was willing to not trust her own perceptions and instead trust mine. Seeing the profound innocence in that depth of trust would always break my heart, and knowing the absolute necessity of that trust I was willing to forgive her jealousy. The predictable, simple, and structured environment that Jacqui provided the schizophrenics helped them to distinguish the differences in the qualities between reality and delusions, and was something I was unable to provide for Donna. But this had been a big part of what enabled them to become more comfortable in ignoring the delusional qualities. I don't believe the misinformation ever stopped, but maybe it quieted down.

I always knew that it was inappropriate for me to be both Donna's boyfriend and the one she relied on for reality. I always knew my primary responsibility was defining her reality, but my personal desire was to be her boyfriend. The only hope of me being her boyfriend and not her therapist was for her to take responsibility for her own reality.

I looked around the room at the schizophrenic family I'd been responsible for, stressed out by, and frustrated with. I wondered who they would have been if their minds didn't misfire. I wondered who I would have become if I hadn't been broken in my own way. Maybe it was no accident I had ended up here in this "family." I had a lot in common with these people. We were all lost in our own orbits, out of place in the world. Our only hope was Jacqui. And she was mad and broken in her own way.

Why had Jacqui created this environment and made herself a dictator in a family of lunatics? Was she trying to heal herself by healing us? Was she trying to control her own madness by managing ours? Did she need to force others to see reality in order to stay in touch with reality herself? Maybe she needed all of us as much as we needed her. To varying degrees, maybe everyone is mad and broken.

For months before the whipping incident, I'd had a bad feeling that someone was going to be seriously hurt or killed one day. I didn't want to be there when it happened. I was scared. I wanted out. I didn't belong here. But now I was concerned about how and when I could try to escape again. If I got caught, my punishment would be something worse than being whipped on the back with a willow branch.

I lay in bed that night churning with anxiety. How long would I be here? Where was Donna? Was she with Emerson? Was she wandering out there by herself? She had an uncanny knack for finding bad company. I hoped she was okay. She had Emerson's number. I hoped he was helping her. Lying there worrying, unable to fall asleep, I knew I couldn't stay here one more day. I decided to sleep lightly, if I could sleep at all, and get up just before dawn. I knew I couldn't hitch a ride out before then.

I drifted off and woke up several times. Each time it was still dark. I drifted off again, and when I woke up this time it was light out and a few birds were singing. I freaked out for a minute. Rudy had taken my watch along with my clothes, so I had no idea what time it was. I lay there for a minute, listening quietly. Everyone was asleep. I hoped that I had an hour or so before they woke up. That should give me enough time.

Rudy lay on the floor next to my bed, facing me and directly in front of the door that opened to the backyard. I quietly got out of bed. I stood over Rudy, staring at the space between his head and the door. I wondered if there was enough room to open the door and slip out without bumping his head and waking him. I looked around for my clothes. I was naked because Rudy had taken my clothes when I went to bed so I couldn't run away. They had to be here somewhere. I looked around but couldn't see them.

I tiptoed to the laundry basket fifteen feet away. He hadn't thought of the laundry. I looked inside and found a pair of my pants, but nothing more. The pants would have to do. I grabbed them but didn't put them on. I had to slip through a narrow space and every fraction of an inch counted. I tiptoed back to the door. I turned the handle very gently and slowly pulled the door open, stopping each time it made the slightest noise. The open door was about an inch away from the back of Rudy's head. It looked just wide enough for me to slip through.

I took one last breath and silently exhaled, pressing my chest and stomach in as far as I could. Then, as carefully as I've ever done anything in my life, I stepped sideways, into the gap, and slid through the door. I felt the doorknob press against my stomach, and then I was on the other side. Slowly, gently, I pulled the door toward me, almost but not quite closing it. I was afraid it might click into place and wake Rudy. Now I was standing outside in the dawn light, stark naked. I quickly slipped the pants on and put Emerson's phone number in my hip pocket. I had slipped it under my pillow before Rudy took my clothes the night before. Then I crept around the side of the house and through the dewy grass, and came out in the front yard. When I hit the sidewalk, I took off running.

I could feel the house receding behind me, like a heavy weight being lifted off my back. A newspaper boy rode past on his bike and stared at me. I realized I must look strange running barefoot down the street with no shirt on. I didn't care. I just wanted to get as far away from that house as I could and as fast as I could. I ran for several blocks, my feet pounding the sidewalk while I breathed in huge gulps of air. I felt alive, hopeful, and scared. As I ran, I scanned the sides of the road for places to hide if I needed to, glancing back a few times over my shoulder. I passed a couple of guys in suits getting into their cars to go to work. They looked so normal. They glanced curiously at me as I ran by, but they didn't seem alarmed. I tried to look casual, as if I were out for a morning run.

I heard the rushing sound of cars on the freeway up ahead. I was only a couple of blocks from the underpass that led to the freeway on-ramp. Before long I was jogging onto the on-ramp, gasping for breath. I stood on the asphalt shoulder facing the approaching cars. As soon as a car turned onto the on-ramp, I stuck out my thumb.

Within a few minutes a guy in a Volvo picked me up. He didn't comment on my clothes or ask questions. He didn't say much, except that he was only going a few exits, to Walnut Creek. When we got there he pulled over to the shoulder of the exit and let me out. I ran back to the freeway on-ramp and stood waiting for the next car to come by. I stood with my thumb out, feeling like a neon sign. None of the cars driving past me onto the freeway stopped to give me a ride. The longer I stood there, the more anxious I felt. I was sure they were after me by now, and worried they might drive by and spot me. I kept seeing cars that looked similar to the family cars, but none of them were.

I'd been standing there for about fifteen minutes when I saw a green van approaching in the distance, driving in the middle lane. It looked like the family van, but I couldn't be absolutely sure. I hunched down and kept my thumb out, but all my attention was on that van. As it came closer, I saw that it was Rudy. He was looking over at me. He tried to change lanes and almost hit a car in his blind spot. The angry driver honked and Rudy swerved back again, narrowly avoiding a collision. As he passed by me our eyes locked on each other's across the lanes. I could see his intense expression like a perfect snapshot.

I figured he would get off at the next Walnut Creek exit and take city streets back to this entrance. He'd be back around in less than ten minutes. I was desperate. Several more cars passed me on the ramp. I began looking around for a place I could run to or hide. I started running on the asphalt, the stones digging painfully into my feet. Then I noticed that one of the cars was slowing down. It came to a stop, and I ran toward it. A woman was driving, and a man was in the passenger seat. He rolled down the window a few inches.

"I'm sorry — we didn't mean to make you think we were giving you a ride," he said.

That was unusually nice of them, I thought, *pulling over to apologize and explain the misunderstanding for not being able to give me a ride.* I felt like a salesman about to close a deal.

"Where are you going?" I asked, trying to sound friendly and nonchalant.

"We're just going two more exits up," the man said.

"That's perfect!"

Without missing a beat I'd already opened the back door and was getting in. It was either that, or wait for Rudy to come and get me. They both look startled.

"Well, where are you going?" the guy asked nervously.

"Berkeley, but you can drop me off wherever you get off. It's not a problem. Let's just get going."

They glanced at each other, and I couldn't tell if they were annoyed or afraid. I didn't care; this was my only chance. I slid down low in the seat, hoping Rudy hadn't reached us yet; then the lady pulled onto the freeway.

"Well, I guess we could drop you off at the first exit headed for Berkeley," she said reluctantly.

"That's great. Thank you very, very much for the ride."

Nobody said a word for the next few minutes. They slowed down and pulled off at the exit. As they pulled over to the side of the road to let me off, I said, "I can't tell you how much I appreciate the ride. Thank you. I hate to ask you this, but do you have a dime to spare? I need to make a phone call."

"I think so," the guy said. He reached into his pocket, pulled out a few coins, and handed me a dime. "Good luck," he said.

The woman glanced back at me and nodded. I could tell they meant it. They knew I was in some kind of fix.

"Thanks; I need it," I said, and got out.

I ran down the exit ramp and across a road over to the on-ramp. When I got to the entrance ramp, I saw them wave as they drove off. I wondered what they might have been thinking, particularly when I realized they probably saw my back as I turned and ran. I was in a much safer spot now. The pillars of the underpass completely blocked me from view of freeway traffic. Rudy wouldn't be able to see me even if he did drive by. A few minutes later a guy in a station wagon stopped and picked me up. In the back there was a cage with a dog in it. It looked like the guy and his dog lived in the car. I think he wanted money but quickly realized I didn't have any. He dropped me off in Berkeley. I found a payphone and called Emerson. Luckily he was there.

"Is Donna okay?" was the first thing I asked him.

He told me she was safe, and that he'd found a place for her to stay with Jacqui's former house manager and her boyfriend. Emerson didn't have a car, but he said he'd send some friends to pick me up.

"Have them bring me a shirt and zoris," I said.

Zoris was the Japanese word for flip-flops we'd always used in the co-op. We hung up, and I sat down near the payphone to wait. I was still feeling nervous about being in public with nothing on but a pair of pants, and with Jacqui's assistants still looking for me. About an hour later a car pulled up to the payphone. A man and woman in their twenties sat in the front, and Donna was in the back. That was the first moment I felt I'd actually escaped.

I got up and went to the car. Then I recognized the woman in the front passenger seat. She'd been Jacqui's house manager. Emerson had met her during his brief time buying groceries for the household. She had quit a couple of months previously. We looked at each other and shared an awkward greeting. It made me uneasy. Later, I learned that she strongly disagreed with Jacqui's methods and had agreed to help Donna and me at Emerson's request. I got into the back seat with Donna — it was so good to see her!

"Are you all right?" I asked her, meaning *Are we safe with them?*

"Yeah, they're cool," she said. "They're helping us."

The man said hi to me and handed me an oversized sweatshirt and a pair of flip-flops. I immediately put on the sweatshirt, and then Donna and I hugged and didn't let go of each other. It was about ten o'clock, and we were all getting hungry. Then Donna had the chutzpah to ask them if they could get us some pot. I couldn't believe it. I could tell it made them feel uncomfortable, but they said they could probably score some after we had lunch.

They did manage to score some weed after lunch, and we went back to their place and got high. Donna and I spent the night there. Emerson called the next morning, having just gotten off the phone with Mom. Jacqui had called the night before and told her about my escape. She told Mom that a sixteen-year-old girl at the house who had grown attached to Donna and me had also run away. Jacqui was convinced that the girl was with us, and she'd reported it to the police. Since Donna and I were now both eighteen, the authorities considered the matter a kidnapping of a minor. According to Jacqui, an all-points bulletin for Donna and me would go into effect at midnight if we didn't return. It seemed just like something Jacqui would do to get Donna and me to turn ourselves in. Mom and Emerson agreed that it was probably true, and that Donna and I had better get out of the state by midnight.

The rest of the day was a frantic rush, as we tried to get enough money for two airline tickets to Chicago. Mom refused to help us at first; she thought I should have stayed at Jacqui's. But when Emerson told her how I'd been tied naked to a dresser and whipped bloody with a willow branch, she relented and wired the money for the tickets. Donna and I caught a red-eye flight out of San Francisco International Airport to Chicago, just in time to beat the police APB.

A few months after I left Jacqui's, one of the kids under her care died. It was John Hartwell. Apparently, John had been acting out, so the family members in charge subdued him, tied him up, gagged him, and put him in the bathtub the way we'd done with Timothy. Apparently, instead of filling the tub with ice and water, someone decided to turn on the hot water instead. They held him down while the tub filled up with scalding water. They pulled him out when they noticed his skin peeling off, but it was too late. By the time they got John to the hospital, he was burned over his entire body. He died a few days later.

The authorities stepped in, and there was an investigation. The house was shut down, and people started getting prosecuted. Some of the schizophrenics were sent back to their respective hospitals; others were turned out onto the street. Some of them were temporarily taken in by neighbors who had come to know them. But many were left on their own. Some later committed suicide.

I never saw Jacqui again. She left the country and ended up in Bangalore, India, where she continued her unorthodox work with schizophrenics. She returned to America in 1985, in poor health, and died in California in 2002 of multiple sclerosis.

Turning Around

*M*y mother picked us up at O'Hare International Airport. Her face was drawn, and she looked grim. She moved the way she did at the hospital after my suicide attempt. As we hugged I could sense her anguish. It was obvious she loved me, but I could feel the heartbreak I was for her. Once again, my relationship with her had permanently changed. We walked in awkward silence to her car in the short-term parking area. Before turning on the ignition, she looked over at Donna and me and said, "I love you both dearly, but you're eighteen now and so my obligation to provide for you is over. If you come home with me, I want you out by the first of the month. I need a drop-dead date that I can count on for you to leave."

"We'll try," I told her, "but that's less than two weeks from now; we may need a month to get things together."

"I know you're still smoking pot," she said. *Jacqui must have told her.* "You'll have to keep all of your drugs in the bathroom next to the toilet."

For quick disposal in a bust, I thought. I agreed. That she was willing to let me have weed in the house told me she didn't feel she could stop me anyway and was disconnecting from me in a significantly new way. To be on my own and move out in a month, I'd have to do some serious dealing. I knew leaving Jacqui's meant I was going to have to go back to dealing drugs. Now, being over eighteen, I would no longer go to Charlietown if I got busted; I would go to prison. I'd have to get out of selling retail and deal exclusively at the wholesale level, no less than pounds at a time, in order to make enough money — and to control the number and quality of my contacts. Now, just carrying a knife probably wouldn't be enough. It also meant that I'd have more dope than I could flush down the toilet in a bust. I'd keep an ounce of weed in the downstairs toilet for show and bury the rest in a camouflaged water-proofed pit in a vacant lot behind our house. I hated lying to my mother, but I didn't feel as if I had any choice.

Donna and I moved into my room, where I found my old balance-beam scale and got busy locating our old drug contacts. It wasn't easy. Some were in jail, some had disappeared, a few friends had gone away to college, and even more had died from drug-related causes. When I did locate several contacts still doing business, another problem arose: I'd disappeared for nine months without a word, and suddenly I was back. That was highly suspicious in the drug world. It wasn't uncommon for dealers to get busted and turn narc. They'd disappear and reappear to buy dope from former contacts, then turn them in and testify against them.

I'd disappeared for nine months; now I was back urgently trying to score dope. I told my contacts that I'd gone to California but then decided to move back home. They were wary. That was when Donna told me about Steve, a guy she'd met in the mental hospital when she'd gone there to get clean. She wasn't sure why he'd been there. I didn't remember if she'd mentioned him before or not. So Donna called Steve, who told her he had pounds of good weed to sell. She explained our situation, and he agreed to sell to us. He also had a batch of black beauties, potent truck-driver speed. I didn't like the idea of selling speed, but it was part of the deal. I was willing to do just about anything for some fast cash.

We were off and running. The private phone in Neil's room was my business line. I immediately called all of my old clients and told them I was back in town and was about to score some really good pot, but I needed the money upfront. I'd always been a reliable source, so I was hoping they would trust me. A bunch of people said okay and fronted me their money. Donna and I got in the Chevy Vega she'd recently inherited from her dead grandmother and drove around to pick up the money. Then we drove to Steve's house with enough cash to buy two pounds and a hundred black beauties. Steve fronted us another third of a pound; then we went home and broke down each pound of weed into one-ounce baggies. I shorted each ounce, which I justified to myself as the only time I'd do that, and then we made deliveries to all of my clients.

But I kept wondering about Steve. Why hadn't Donna told me about him before? Why was he fronting us a third of a pound? He seemed nice enough, but it wasn't like he had money to spare. He was nineteen and living in his parents' basement with his pregnant wife. Why was he doing Donna favors? I asked Donna and she assured me there was nothing between them. Jacqui had said I was paranoid, but she also had said that Donna was an amoral, undetectable liar with a character disorder. That echoed in my head now. Still, we needed the money, and I couldn't afford to turn down help on an uncertain combination of principles and paranoia.

Less than a week later, Donna and I had enough cash for a deposit on an apartment in nearby Brandywine. We continued dealing and saving money, and soon moved into our new place. We'd made it. We had moved out by the first of the month, as my mother had demanded. It had been awkward with my mom, and we were all glad to part. I took most of the things from my room — my chair, couch, desk, stereo, and records. We got other essential household items from friends and Goodwill.

It was all very exciting. We were in our own place, living as a couple. I continued dealing weed while Donna got a job as a waitress at a high-end steak house. A few months later, she became a cocktail waitress at the bar of the same restaurant and started making even better money. We were fully supporting ourselves. We opened a checking account. In some ways, Donna was the brains of our partnership — the functional one who could read and spell to write the checks to pay bills. I was the engine, the driving will — the one who could manage the budget and make the deals. We both needed each other, and completed each other. Together, we almost added up to one person who could function in the face of all the practical, emotional, and energetic demands of life.

Words like *dyslexic*, *schizophrenic*, and *character disorder* had always haunted us. *Symbiotic* was another word that the experts and professionals applied to us. Today they would say we were *codependent*. We were bad for each other, they told us, but I was confused. We needed each other and depended on each other, but isn't that true to some degree in every relationship? Yes, we had strong dependencies, but we both had extreme disabilities, so what could they expect? They were saying we had an unhealthy relationship. Compared to what? What did they think our life should look like? Considering our disabilities, I felt that we were making healthy compromises in order to survive.

Most of the time our relationship was mutual and strong; Donna was lucid, and we were able to talk about everything, including the best way to help her with her delusional episodes. We were real partners in this. But leaving Donna alone while I went to work with Jacqui had damaged our relationship. We had been trying to be everything for each other, which proved impossible. She resented that I'd left her alone, and her trust in me had started to break down. If I did it once, I could do it again. And on my side, Jacqui had injected gnawing questions about Donna's motives.

Shortly after we moved, my mother learned of a new school for "exceptional children," meaning kids with autism and learning disabilities who couldn't function in public schools. The teachers were specially trained, and the curriculum was customized for each individual. They thought they could help me with more than just reading, including with my attention deficit problems, my biggest liability in day-to-day functioning. They could even help me with memorization. They expressed reservations about me being older than the other kids, but because I was far below the eighth-grade level academically, they decided to give me a chance. I could get the benefit of their specialist and improve my reading skills. Reading was more important than ever to me now that I had to support myself in the world. I'd be in class with kids much younger than I was, but I could receive a high school diploma.

The school was sixty miles away. I took a short yellow bus there and back each day with a bunch of kids who ranged from first-graders through eighth-graders. It was humiliating but not unfamiliar. I'd given up my personal preferences and my hold on trying to look good so many times before, just on the promise that something could help me. I dealt weed at night and on weekends. I worked hard and made progress, but it all fell apart after a few months. Someone broke into the school medicine cabinet and stole all the meds. I didn't do it, but everyone assumed I did so they kicked me out.

— 🧍 —

My friends had witnessed Donna's wild emotional swings and personality changes, and they thought she was manipulating me. I'd resisted that point of view because I felt they didn't understand how confused she got. It seemed to me that I was the only one who could see her struggling to incorporate the distinct personalities that were living inside of her.

After Jacqui's, I began to wonder if I was enabling Donna's extreme behavior. I felt the need to guard against her dependency on my willingness to help her. I decided to try to use what I'd learned at the house that had been effective with the schizophrenics there. I thought if I temporarily put more focus on demanding that she learn to distinguish reality from delusion, and to take responsibility for her emotional state, that she might have a breakthrough. This would free me from that responsibility so we could have a healthy relationship. As I said before, I loved Donna and wanted to be her boyfriend, not her therapist. I knew she had to find her own way to distinguish reality without me.

I was already less willing to see her confusion, and her inability to remember hitting me in her rages, as a part of an illness that she couldn't control. Now I wanted her to take responsibility, and I even questioned her honesty. I'd seen people sicker than she was have to manage this at Jacqui's. But it was devastating to

Donna and intensified the cycle of mistrust between us.

The mistrust was undermining much of the progress Donna had made in incorporating her divergent emotions and separate personalities. Her fears were taking over, and she felt utterly incapable of stopping her outbursts. The more I fought against it, the worse things got. We felt that we were fighting for her sanity and losing, in a cycle that was only getting worse. If it didn't change it could only lead to disaster, and we both knew it. It was like watching a train wreck in slow motion.

Donna's genuine fears of abandonment had frequently led to fits of unreasonable jealousy. Now, with my insistence that her fits had to stop, she became more suspicious and jealous than ever. I'd always been confident in my ability to handle her physically, but now I was starting to wonder. One morning I woke up with her on my back, screaming at me, hitting me on the head, and pulling my hair. She accused me of not really wanting to be with her and of desiring other women. She was having more frequent episodes of confusion, and I was seeing a lot more of this mistrustful, angry personality.

One night, while she was reheating a spaghetti dinner in a cast-iron skillet, she started in again with her accusations about how I'd looked at a girl walking down the street. If it was true, I was unaware of it. I sat at the table in front of an empty plate, feeling frustrated and overwhelmed. I knew something was coming. She'd had a migraine a few hours before, and that often preceded one of her episodes. We had smoked a joint, but it wasn't helping. The jealousy mood was coming, and I was unsure how intense it might get. In the past I would normally hold her and rock her, trying to calm her down and stave off a full-blown delusional episode with voices. But now I was determined to get her to take responsibility, so I insisted, "I love you. I may have looked at a girl, but I wasn't 'looking' at a girl. Everything's okay. Don't lose yourself in this fear. It's not true."

"I saw you looking at her!" screamed Donna.

I replied, "Donna, cut it out! You're just being paranoid. You've got to get it together."

Donna suddenly got very quiet. She seemed to be trying to control her paranoia. The spaghetti was ready; she walked over to me with the skillet. I thought she was going to ladle some spaghetti onto my plate. Instead, she dumped the sizzling contents onto my lap.

I jumped up with a yelp. I tried to brush the hot mess off my lap and burned my fingers. Suddenly I felt a hard crack across my nose and forehead. Donna had hit me with the skillet. Then she dropped it on the floor and began punching me.

Instinctively, I grabbed her, pinned her arms at her sides, pushed her back against the wall, and lifted her off the floor. It was the technique I'd learned at Jacqui Schiff's. Now she had no leverage to hurt me or get away. I held her there while she screamed in my face. I flashed back to the woman in the psychiatric hospital who used to beat up her husband, and how I'd thought that guy must have been weak and stupid to be in a relationship with such a woman. Now I understood. I had to get out of there. I dropped Donna and ran for the front door. She ran after me, screaming, "No! Don't leave me! David, don't leave me!"

She grabbed me before I could open the door. I whirled around and shoved her back as hard as I could. She fell on the floor, and I ran out of the apartment, down the hallway, and out of the building. I hit the street and kept on running. Then I heard Donna screaming behind me, coming after me. Then the screaming stopped. A minute later I heard a car approaching from behind. I glanced back and saw Donna's Chevy Vega rapidly approaching. I ran off the road and onto the sidewalk. Then I heard the loud thump of tires going over the curb. I looked back again. She was right behind me on the sidewalk. I veered right and scrambled up a six-foot chainlink fence in front of an empty lot. Donna veered after me and slammed into the fence. The impact knocked me off the fence, and I fell onto the hood of the Chevy. She put the car in reverse and started backing up. I scrambled off the hood with a whole new level of motivation, climbed to the top of the fence, and jumped down on the other side. I heard the Chevy's engine gun, and I took off running as fast as I could. The Chevy plowed into the fence again, but I didn't look back.

— 🤖 —

I walked around the neighborhood, rethinking everything I was doing. I knew Donna would have to come to a crisis before she could take responsibility for distinguishing her own reality. I'd seen it over and over at Jacqui's. But I didn't have the circumstances to keep us safe. Besides, if I'd thought it might have been inappropriate as her boyfriend to nurture her, it was far more inappropriate to discipline her like a parent. So I didn't know what to do. I gave her an hour to calm down and went back to the apartment, hoping she would no longer be delusional and we could talk it over.

The incident scared us both. We talked most of the night and came to an agreement: No more violent outbursts or I was leaving. The violence stopped after that, but things continued to degenerate in our relationship. We argued, got stoned, and had sex. We believed Jacqui's poisonous words, and we grew increasingly estranged from each other. Mistrust was weaving its way through all aspects of our lives.

Not long after the Chevy incident, Donna suggested that we needed to live in a house instead of an apartment, for greater privacy and security. Now that we were dealing wholesale, we had to be more careful than ever. It was only a matter of time before the noise from our fights and the smoke from our dope wafting through the walls of our apartment would get us in trouble — maybe busted, or at least evicted. Donna suggested that we could save money by getting a house with Steve and his wife, Chia. It says a lot about my confused state at the time that I'd even consider this idea, much less agree to it.

We looked around and found a nice four-bedroom house. Our share of the rent was less than we'd been paying for our one-bedroom apartment. Almost immediately I knew it was a mistake.

I'd periodically been wondering if Donna was having an affair. This hadn't come up for me before. It seemed as if her jealousy was triggering jealousy in me. If she was having an affair, I thought it might be with someone at the restaurant where she was cocktail-waitressing. But as I thought about it, I kept coming back to wondering whether it might be Steve. I also began to wonder if there was something else causing Donna's episodes: Was she doing speed? Some other drug?

We'd only been living in the house for a month when Chia moved out. We weren't there at the time and didn't know the details of why she left. A few days later she called the house and I answered. She told me that Steve had beaten her and kicked her out of the house. She also told me that he'd been in the psychiatric hospital because he'd pulled a knife and threatened his father — and that he'd given Donna speed when she was in the hospital to get clean. I blew up. I couldn't believe Donna hadn't told me. To my knowledge she'd never lied to me before, even through omission.

It terrified me that she might get back on speed. It would make our relationship impossible and eventually destroy her. It was not only important that she not lie to me about speed, but also that she not omit anything. The omission made me question how much involvement she'd had with Steve, and whether I could believe what she would say about that. It made me incredibly jealous that she would have this secret with Steve.

As I mulled it over in my head, I made it even worse. Bad enough that Steve had played me for a sucker, but for Donna to have conspired with him hurt me deeply. Furious, I confronted Donna. She claimed that she'd told me, and that there was nothing between her and Steve. I didn't believe her. But things were so painful between us I almost didn't care. I insisted we both leave the house immediately. I didn't want her living with someone who gave her speed. But she didn't want to leave.

I didn't understand how terrified Donna was that I'd leave her again, the way I'd done when I went to live with Jacqui Schiff. From her point of view, Steve was the only person in her life, besides me, who seemed to care for her. For Donna, reaching out to Steve was a survival mechanism. I started yelling, insisting we had to move out. She ran into our bedroom and locked the door. The argument ended when I put my fist through the door, injured my hand, and walked out. I was done.

I decided that I'd come back later to get my stuff. I was relieved to get away. Then it hit me. If I couldn't make it work with Donna, who would have me? Tears streamed down my face. I'd been the most caring and thoughtful and the best person I knew how to be, yet she still didn't want to be with me. Now I wondered how I'd function without her. How would I pay bills? Who would help me remember things? Who else but Donna would ever want to be with someone like me? Feelings of doom descended on me.

I decided to go to my mom's house. I knew she wouldn't want me there, but I had no place else to go. I was hoping Donna might have called to tell me she'd changed her mind. When I got home, Mom was asleep. On the weekends she was still in the habit of staying up late drinking and getting up around noon. I crashed on my old bed in my old room and slept for most of the day. When my mother got up, I told her that Donna and I had broken up and asked if I could stay at home for a few days to get things together. At first she refused, but she finally relented on the condition of no weed and the edict that Donna could not come over.

That evening, I returned to the rented house to pick up my dope and my clothes. When I got there all the lights were off. Donna and Steve were either out or had gone to sleep early. I was disappointed because I'd hoped to talk to Donna. I still had my key. As I opened the front door, I heard Steve yelp, "What're *you* doing here?"

"You're not supposed to be here," Donna echoed.

It was too dark to see, but from their voices I could tell they were on the couch in the living room. Eric Clapton was singing "Layla," a song about a guy who was in love with his best friend's girl. The smell of weed filled the air. I felt sick. I didn't say a word.

I walked past them, through the living room, and upstairs to the bedroom. I flipped on the light and saw a beautiful long dress I'd recently bought for Donna lying across the bed. I'd always believed there was a place in Donna's heart that was true, faithful, and always open to me. Finding her on the couch in the dark with Steve and seeing the dress was unbearable. How could she be with him after all we'd been to each other? We were more than just a couple in love; we had the bond of comrades in war, and now I just found out that my partner had joined the enemy. I had to get out of there.

I put my stash—several pounds of pot—into a duffel bag. I packed some clothes with the pot, then added my stuff from the bathroom as well. I'd have to make another trip to pick up the rest. Fighting back tears, I gave the room a last look and turned out the light. Then I went down the stairs, through the living room, and out the front door without saying a word or looking in their direction. Donna didn't say anything either. After more than four years together, I was devastated that she let me leave without a word.

I needed cash right away, so on the way home I stopped at a friend's house and negotiated a deal to sell him the rest of my pot. The next day I took my mother's extra car in for a tune-up. It needed it, and I hoped she would let me have it for a good price.

That night Donna called. I asked her, "What do you want?"

She said she'd left Steve's house and was at a payphone and needed to talk. I told her I'd meet her outside my mother's house, but she couldn't come in. As I waited for her, I wondered what she wanted to talk about, trying not to get my hopes up.

I was feeling a little more confidence now. She was coming to me. I noticed that when I felt as if she was leaving me I couldn't let go of her, but now that she was coming to me I felt strong enough to break up. When I left the house and met her in the drive, I asked again, "What do you want?"

"I just want to talk. I need to explain," she replied.

Her coming to me was just what I needed. I felt like I could finally be free of her. I couldn't think of anything that she could say that would excuse what I saw and how I felt. She began to explain. "I don't have any feelings for Steve —"

"Bullshit," I interrupted.

Donna insisted, but I didn't believe her. I told her that I wasn't interested in getting back together and that I wasn't going through this again.

She dropped her head in tears. Then, raising her head, still weeping, and reaching to put her arms around me, she continued. "I'm sorry; please forgive me. I'll wait as long as I have to," she pleaded. "I'll do whatever I have to do. I know how screwed up I am. I know I really blew it. You aren't like anyone else I've ever known. You've always been honest and good to me and been there for me no matter how full of shit I am or how crazy I get. I don't know what I'd do without you. I could never be with Steve. I could never love him or feel safe with him. I didn't realize it before, but you were right. He's a bad person."

I reminded myself that she was a liar, but I couldn't help asking, "Why can't you feel safe with him?"

"He's a jerk," she said. Then she started to cry. "He made me have sex with him."

Rage welled up in me.

"I'll fucking kill him! I'll fucking kill him! He's a fucking dead man! I'll rip his fucking heart out! God damn that asshole!"

I was beside myself. Then doubt crept in. Jacqui had said Donna would say anything, tell any lie, to get her way and to survive. And she needed me to survive.

"Donna, you need to tell me the truth. If he really did rape you, I may really kill him. I need the absolute truth. Did he really rape you?"

She shrugged and said, "I don't know."

"What do you mean you don't know? Was it rape or not?"

"Yeah."

"Are you sure?"

"Yeah."

"What did he do? Did he push you down? Did he hold you down?"

"No."

"Did he threaten you? Did he hurt you?"

"No. He got in my bed. I said no, but he climbed on top of me and pulled up my nightgown. I said no again, but he had sex with me anyway."

"So he forced you to have sex with him when you didn't want him to?"

"Yes."

She was hesitant as she spoke, cowering as if I might hurt her. I resented this, because she'd always said she trusted that I would never hurt her.

"Well, I guess that's it. I'll take care of it," I said.

I understood fight-or-flight, but I didn't understand or appreciate what the fear of rape and dominance can cause a woman to do.

I didn't know what I was going to do; it was a bewildering mess. I'd been suspicious of Steve's motives for a while, but Donna had said I was being paranoid. Now I knew I was right. I'd fronted Steve two pounds of pot; I'd done this before, but this time he was stalling in paying me back. I knew he'd been watching how I operated, who my contacts were, and also the problems Donna and I were having. This was his move on Donna and on my business. He wanted it all.

We both understood the rules of the world we lived in. It was predatory and highly territorial. You had to watch your back at all times, and above all you had to protect your street credibility. Your life depended on it. Things could escalate and get violent very quickly if people thought they could get over on you. Steve was highly competitive and hungry to prove himself. I'd seen his frustration once when I avoided a confrontation in a deal that went haywire. He saw it as a sign of weakness. We both knew his move on Donna alone required a violent response. Also his move on my business, independent of Donna, was a challenge I couldn't afford to let slide. I had to do something.

Donna knew that I thought she'd slept with Steve, and she figured the only chance she had of me taking her back was if it was rape. Now she was back with the ultimate victim story, looking for me to take care of her again — just when I was feeling strong enough to let her go.

I told Donna she had to leave before Mom got up or she'd kick me out. I didn't know where she would go, but I had other things to deal with. She'd handed me a bigger problem. I was back into taking care of her. How did this happen?

After Donna left, my mind was racing, trying to sort things out. What really happened between Steve and Donna? What was I going to do? Everything was so fucked up. If Steve had raped Donna, he deserved to die. I wanted to kill him even if he hadn't. But what if he hadn't raped her? I had to find out what really happened. I felt bad for not believing Donna, in case she was telling the truth. I decided to go see Steve. Maybe I'd be able to tell by the look on his face when he saw me. As I considered which knife to take, I asked myself, *Why am I doing this? Is it because of the dope or because of Donna?* I realized that it didn't matter; whether it was only for the weed or only for the rape, I would still have to do something.

I got up and drove to Steve's house and went through the side door into the kitchen. Steve, his brother, and two friends were standing around the kitchen table, piled high with stolen steaks wrapped in butcher paper. *A bunch of fucking thieves,* I thought to myself. Steve looked up as I came in. He was shocked to see me. It wasn't necessarily the look of a rapist — maybe just the look of a guy suddenly confronted by another guy whose girl he'd fucked. I wanted him off-guard. I didn't start with asking about Donna.

"I need the money you owe me for the two pounds I fronted you," I said.

"Bullshit!" he said. "You both left me with this house to pay for. I don't owe you anything. In fact, you owe me money for your and Donna's share."

"I owe you money, Steve? After you raped Donna?"

"Bullshit! I didn't rape her! She was as into it as I was!"

I looked in his face. He seemed startled but defiant, as if he believed what he was saying. But I wasn't about to give him the benefit of the doubt. This might be my best chance. First I needed to provoke him and get him to come after me. If he did, I'd hurt him. Bad. Maybe I'd kill him. It would be self-defense. I checked inside myself to see if I still had the rage living in me that I would need to do what I needed to do. I looked at him with total contempt, as if he were a sewer rat.

"You're a fucking liar, Steve. You rapist piece of shit."

"I didn't rape her! She's lying! I don't know why, but she's lying!"

"Okay, then, was she passive during sex or did she do anything to make you think she was into it?"

That stopped him in his tracks as he stuttered, "Yeah, she put her arms around me and kept telling me how much she loved me."

It stung me to hear this, but it didn't sound right to me.

"That isn't how she does things. That proves it. You're an asshole rapist, and you know it." I stood there looking at him, but he wasn't coming after me. I waited a few moments longer. He stayed right where he was.

Then, as I was urging him on in my mind, I heard myself say in a whisper just loud enough for everyone to hear, "Come on, do it, motherfucker. This is your best chance. You know I'll be coming for you."

"You better watch your back, asshole!" Steve yelled at me. "I'll burn down your mother's house!"

That was just the kind of thing Steve would say. And he would do it. The idea of getting a gun flashed through my mind. It was either him or me—at least that's how it felt in the moment. "I'm going to kill you, Steve," I said. He moved just a little. He looked at me but didn't say a word. If I couldn't settle this now, somehow, I'd always have to watch my back. I growled in disgust, "You chickenshit! You worthless peace of shit!" I had to get him to come at me. He just stood there like a gunslinger with his arms at his side, but with no weapon. He looked as if he wanted to kill me as much as I wanted to kill him, but he just wouldn't move. Desperately wanting him to make a move so I could retaliate, I turned my back and slowly walked out the door, mumbling, "You backstabbing little wuss! You fucking coward!

You'll take advantage of Donna, but with me you're too scared to even move." I left the house, but he never came after me.

There was no way to find out what really happened between him and Donna. I'd probably never know, but I was furious that either by rape or by consent, Steve had fucked the girl I loved.

My gut told me the truth probably lay somewhere between consent and rape. Maybe she gave Steve mixed signals. The first night I met Donna, she'd given me very mixed signals; she'd undressed and gotten in bed with me and then said, "No...don't." A lot of guys might have thought she was being coy. If I'd ignored her feeble protests, she probably would have given in and had sex with me. Would it have been rape? Maybe. Maybe Steve thought she was being coy. Maybe Donna didn't say no convincingly and back it up. Or maybe I was a sucker because I wanted to believe her when, in fact, she'd slept with him because she wanted to, but then later regretted it and wanted to come back to me. *Fuck!*

All this mattered to me, but the bottom line was that I couldn't leave her on her own. She was much stronger than when I met her, but her judgment wasn't good enough to survive in the world. At the time I'd arranged for her to leave her family, I knew that I was taking on more than just a girlfriend. My mother told me I had better know that even if our relationship fell apart we would still be responsible for her. Now she was alone again, scared, and looking for me to take care of her. I didn't have it in me not to help strangers when I saw fear in their eyes, so how could I not help someone I truly cared about? It was like leaving someone in the forest who didn't know the way out — someone who, as much as it pissed me off, would consistently pick out the wolves when she reached out for help. Could I leave her there, pleading for my help, when I knew the wolves would eat her alive?

I stopped for a moment; I wondered how much of this was my fault. I'd been pushing her to take responsibility for her illness, and maybe it was too much for her. Then my mind would flash back to the slinky dress on the bed. I guess it didn't go the way she'd hoped. Maybe I should leave her to suffer her own consequences. She'd gotten herself into this. She'd kicked me out and stayed with a creep who had given her speed in rehab, who had beaten up and kicked out his pregnant wife, and then moved in on Donna when our relationship was falling apart.

I'd lost trust in Donna, and it felt as if I'd lost everything. The rage I felt gave me energy and a sense of purpose; my mind raced out of control with fantasies of killing Steve. I'd go to see him and provoke him again, and not stop until he attacked me. I'd have my knife ready in my pocket. When he came at me, I'd pull it out, flick it open, slide it into his belly, draw it up inside him, and twist. Maybe I'd grab his throat with both hands, squeeze, and watch his face change colors and swell up like my dad's. Either way, I'd look right into his eyes and watch the life drain out of him. I'd give him what he deserved.

I knew I wasn't a sociopath. I didn't prey on weak people, and I didn't enjoy hurting people. Yet I often found myself in extreme circumstances, doing things I didn't want to do, things that went against my better nature but that I thought I had to do. Now I was contemplating the murder of Steve, an act that would move me to the next level of hell. I felt trapped. I'd already threatened to kill Steve, and he'd threatened to burn down my mom's house. We were both capable of carrying out our threats. Something was going to happen; I didn't know when, where, or how. I felt that I had to act before he did. He probably felt the same. If I killed Steve, I would cross a line I'd never crossed before. It would change me. It would damage my soul. Was this my conscience speaking from the depths of my being, beneath the volcano of emotions churning inside me, or was I just trying to talk myself out of it because I was a coward?

There was a fundamental, life-changing argument going on inside of me. Part of me believed that killing Steve would give me some kind of control over my life. And part of me knew that killing Steve would be an ultimate loss of control and an ultimate surrender to fear. On the outside it seemed to me that I had to kill him to not appear weak and become a victim. He had raped Donna, or fucked her, and he'd stolen my dope. Any one of those things required retribution. To not act under these circumstances was to be a coward, a victim, not a man. It was to lose control.

I had chosen to be in this life and play by these rules. The "game" was about controlling life through controlling fear. But life wasn't worth living on these terms, because I didn't want to be the kind of person I would need to be to survive. I had to grow up for real and put away these childish and destructive rules.

I heard a voice deep inside me say, *It's your fear that's in control.* I realized Jacqui was right — in fear, the logic of overcoming fear is to become the thing to be feared. But in trying to conquer fear in this way, you become like the thing you're afraid of, which is also the thing you hate. The thing you hate and fear outside now becomes a part of who you are inside. And this increases the necessity of being and becoming more like this over time. So this strategy for conquering fear doesn't really work; it only allows fear to define and rule your life. And in a mysterious way, it brings the violence to you.

This was a turnaround for me; the kind of behavior I had

always thought to be strength and control, I now saw as an expression of weakness and lack of power. My child-born habit of
turning my fear into rage had gotten me this far, but I realized
it would get me no further. It was no longer a viable solution;
it was the problem. To live on this new basis would require
a fundamental change of my personality and character. I wasn't
sure if I could change in this way, but I knew I had to.

I was still feeling tremendous pressure to do this thing
I didn't want to do — kill Steve. I knew that doing this would not
give me back control of my life. Life always had control of me;
it was always making me do things I didn't want to do. And it
always would. But I had a choice. I didn't have to become someone I didn't want to be.

The truth couldn't be a choice between either running from
my fears or trying to conquer them in this misguided way. To live
this way would be to live in the insanity of a world based on fear.

—— ✦ ——

When I returned, Donna was waiting for me in the driveway.
She pleaded desperately with me to take her back. The thought
that she might lie about being raped so I would take her back —
knowing that I might commit murder on her word — shocked
me. When Donna and I first met, I'd thought I could save her,
and maybe in the process save myself. Mom had told me at the
time that you couldn't save people; you can only help them to
help themselves. Now I understood. If they're going down, you
can't stop them; if you try, they'll take you down with them.
I needed time. Not knowing what else to do, I snuck her into my
bedroom, letting her know it didn't mean we were back together.

Overnight something inside me broke. I found my sense

of being—who I was deep inside—and that part of me never wanted to kill anyone. This wasn't small; if I weren't going to resort to violence anymore, I would have to change my whole approach to life. I felt that this would leave me vulnerable in ways I'd always thought of as weak and didn't respect. But if I didn't do something about Steve, neither Donna nor I would be safe in Chicago and we'd have to leave.

As big as this was, I would have to make an even bigger change. I would have to give up the personality I'd created when I was seven. I had decided then that I would have to be prepared to kill myself, and I'd hidden screwdrivers all around the house for fear that I would need to kill Emerson in self-defense. There was never a time when I hadn't felt that I might have to kill either myself or someone else if that's what it took to stay out of an institution and to survive. Now I'd have to give up my childish ways.

After considering all that Donna did or didn't do, what Steve did or didn't do, I finally decided that none of it mattered. What mattered is what I was willing to do. Was I willing to kill? No. Not anymore. It had nothing to do with Steve; I just came to the point where I wasn't willing to live a life that would require something as horrendous as murder from me.

Deep down I didn't believe I could survive as I was. I'd seen myself as stupid, broken, and dysfunctional for too long. I'd seen myself through the world's narrow, judgmental eyes. I could never meet its minimum requirements for basic functioning, for belonging and fitting in. Others saw me as lazy. I knew I wasn't lazy. I'd worked harder than anyone I knew, but I'd never gotten the results I needed. The messages of society—never give up; be a fighter; where there's a will, there's a way—hadn't served me. I'd look at people and think, *Everyone else seems to know a secret — the secret of who and what they are — but I can't identify who or what I am.* I realized that it wasn't about becoming more than I was; it was about accepting that *who I am* is enough.

I wondered to what degree the life I was living and the world I was living in were of my own making — a result of what I believed the nature of the world to be. My mind seemed to be an illusionist, promising to be the source of truth, and then just leading me in circles. From the point of view of my mind, I would be a fool not to be afraid.

It also seemed important for me to decide if the world was simply a bad place or not. If it was just a machine of death, then it didn't matter what I did — I'd made friends with death anyway. But if it wasn't, then it would matter what my actions were, and if I hurt someone or killed someone, then I'd suffer the consequences of those actions. I used to scare myself with my own thoughts, spinning worst-case scenarios in my mind, but when I stopped and looked deeply into any thought, I couldn't find any substance that was absolutely true, no future that was absolutely certain. If I wanted absolute truth, I was left only with what was in the moment. It wasn't about believing in one thing more than another; it was just about being completely present and fully aware in that moment.

I remembered when I was in the hospital. I was locked up in one of the worst situations I'd ever been in, with no vision for my future. It was what I'd been afraid of all my life. Yet I had a moment when I found myself feeling ecstatic. I felt connected to everything. I was at One, and at peace with existence itself. It wasn't just the relief and freedom from the burdens of existence that made me feel ecstatic; I experienced an ecstatic gratitude for being Awareness itself. Awareness was my connection to existence, to the Infinite, not my mind. Even life and death couldn't threaten it. There was nothing else I had to do — or be. That was enough. My willingness to be just Awareness was what made me free. Trying to think my way through life wasn't working for me. I couldn't find any security or truth in my mind or in the future.

If I wanted to live by the truth, I had to live in the moment. I came up with a motto for myself: *I'll do my very best in this moment, no more and no less, and let the future take care of itself.* I only needed to concern myself with the present moment. *Am I doing the best I can in this moment?* Just the way it was in the snow tunnel. My mind told me that I needed to know what to do about the future, but it was believing my mind that was causing my fear and panic. How things turned out was none of my business, because the future was a mystery to me as it was for everyone else.

I'll do my very best in this moment, no more and no less, and let the future take care of itself. This phrase reminded me that my mind was a liar. It seemed that my mind could figure it all out, but in fact most of my thoughts were born out of fear and only generated more fear. I couldn't stop the thoughts, but I could stop believing in them. Just the way Jacqui had taught the schizophrenics to do. When I thought that I had to learn how to read or things wouldn't turn out well for me, that was a thought that seemed true on the surface, but there was no way of knowing if it was true or not. When I believed it, I felt fear, and it only undermined me. Even believing that everything would be okay in the future was an illusion. All I really had was the present moment, without regrets about the past or clinging to hopes for the future.

Releasing the illusion of control was a profound relief. From now on, how I lived in the present moment was everything. I could no longer afford the luxury of taking things personally, of wasting time feeling bad or good about what I did or didn't do. My life would be an adventure now, one where I was no longer thinking I was in charge. I was more a curious observer, watching my life unfold as it would. A huge weight was lifted from my shoulders. My only responsibility was to do my best in the present moment, and let the future take care of itself.

When I got up that afternoon, Mom was waiting for me. As soon as I opened the front door, she handed me the keys to Dad's abandoned house and told me she'd call the police if I didn't get all of my stuff out immediately.

Now neither Donna nor I had anywhere to go but this abandoned house. I told her that she could come with me for now, but that she would have to quit all drugs and that it didn't mean we were back together. I'd decided that I wasn't going to force her to become responsible to see reality. What the hell was reality anyway? It was destroying us. I understood Donna was stuck and I'd help her as much as I could. She knew better than I did that she couldn't manage her life independently. Even with that, I wasn't sure she would agree to my terms. She did agree, saying she was very sorry and she would come with me anywhere as long as I'd let her. It broke my heart. I didn't see how I could be her boyfriend anymore, but I loved her, and I wasn't going to leave her unprotected.

Inkling

*D*onna waited in the car while I packed my clothes, some toiletries, two sleeping bags, and some camping gear into the back seat. Then we headed for the rundown apartment my dad hadn't lived to fix up. On our way to the vacant apartment, we stopped at a store and bought some cleaning supplies, some water, some hamburger and Hamburger Helper, and a small canister of propane gas for the camp stove.

The apartment was in bad condition and in a bad neighborhood in one of the worst black slums in Chicago. The Black Panthers had been in a famous shootout with the Chicago police a few blocks away. The entrance to the building was in the back. We chose the upper apartment and quickly went upstairs. The door had three locks — a padlock, a deadbolt, and the lock on the knob — and opened into a small kitchen with badly torn linoleum floors and no fixtures of any kind. There was no water or electricity. In the dry toilet was a crap someone had taken long ago. At least the windows weren't broken, and the roof didn't seem to be leaking, so we were protected from the wind and rain.

We stood in the kitchen for a moment taking it in. I couldn't help but wonder if this apartment was what my life was going to be like now that I was no longer selling drugs. Whatever life had in store for me now, I couldn't turn back. This was my test. Would life accept me the way I am? And if so, was this what it was going to look like? We cleaned up the apartment the best we could. We set up in the living room and laid our sleeping bags on the floor; then I set the camping stove up in the kitchen, cracked a window for ventilation, lit the burner, and started heating some water in an aluminum pan. We put the hamburger and Hamburger Helper into the pan and cooked it. But as we were eating it, I noticed a piece of fur in my food. It had to be rat fur. We both ran out to the back and started spitting over the banister. I felt nauseated every time I thought about it. I was more repulsed than sick. We went to bed in our sleeping bags without dinner.

We set out the next day to look for work. Donna searched the want ads for jobs, and after a few bad starts she tried for a job at an envelope factory, working the graveyard shift. We drove out to Addison, and she went in for her interview. There was a recession at the time so there weren't many jobs, but Donna could win over almost anyone. She came out to the car about forty minutes later. She'd gotten the job, and they had more openings so I went in to see if I could qualify for any of them. I lied and didn't tell them I was a high school dropout who couldn't read or write. I figured they'd find out eventually. They had a number of openings, but the only one I qualified for was the same one Donna had gotten. He told me they'd never hired a male for this position before, but I could have it if I wanted it. I was glad to have a job. For the next two weeks we worked the graveyard shift. At the end of each shift we washed ourselves the best we could in the factory bathrooms and returned to the abandoned apartment to sleep.

One morning, a few hours after coming home from work, Donna and I were awakened from a dead sleep by a loud tapping on the window. I got up and looked out the window to see two angry black women in their forties and three young boys standing in the middle of the street. They looked nervous and threatening — a bad combination. They'd been throwing pebbles at our second-story window to get our attention. They signaled me to open the window. As soon as I did, one woman started yelling, "You can't stay here! Ya hear? You have to leave now! Today!"

"We don't want your kind here dealing drugs to our kids!" shouted the other woman. "We see you leaving at night! We know what you're up to! You'd better get out if you know what's good for you!"

I tried to tell them we weren't selling drugs to their kids, but they would have none of it. I was more afraid of them, and the surrounding community, than of Steve.

Donna was terrified. Everything that had happened since Donna kicked me out, down to the rat fur in the food and this Unwelcoming Committee, felt like Chicago telling me to pack up and get the hell out. I was afraid to stay even one more night. Neighborhood vigilantes breaking in while we were sleeping seemed entirely possible.

I decided to leave the next day for California. With what we were owed at work, plus what we'd already saved, there was almost a thousand dollars. I planned to get my check that night, quit my job, cash my check in the morning, and head for California. When I told Donna, she asked if she could go with me. I said it was up to her, but no drugs.

We went to work that night, picked up our last paychecks, then snuck into my mother's house to sleep. I planned to be gone before she woke up. When we got up early the next morning, I went out to the car and found that all four tires had been slashed. It had to be Steve. At least he hadn't burned the house down. Now I just wanted to get out of there. Chicago had really kicked my ass.

I went back in, woke up Mom, and told her what had happened. Knowing it meant we would be leaving, she let me use her AAA card to have the car towed to an auto shop. I had enough cash on hand to buy four new tires. I had the mechanic check the gas tank for sugar, a popular form of sabotage that ruined an engine. Thank god, no sugar was detected. When the car was ready, Donna and I drove to the bank and cashed our checks.

When we came home several hours later, Mom told me that the police had come looking for me with a warrant for my arrest. She felt that she hadn't lied when she told them I didn't live there anymore. I wasn't sure what the warrant was about, and I didn't want to chance what it would take to find out. The APB out on Donna and me for kidnapping the girl from the Schiff house in California had been dropped months ago. As soon as the girl was found, she testified that we'd had nothing to do with her running away. Donna and I couldn't help but see the irony that just a few months ago we were escaping California with an APB out on us and now we were escaping Chicago with a warrant out for me and going back to California. I figured Steve had slashed my tires to keep me there, then anonymously turned me into the cops for dealing, hoping they'd come and arrest me. Later I would find out that the landlord of the house where we'd shared a lease had filed a complaint against Donna and me. Steve was still living there. He told the landlord that we'd damaged the house and defaulted on the rent. The only damage we did to the house was the door I had put my fist through during the argument with Donna, but he was right about us jumping the rent. I rationalized that the two pounds of weed and having sex with my girlfriend more than covered our share.

— ⚛ —

We had recorded a dozen records onto tape for entertainment and had bought a tent made specifically to fit over the open hatchback of the Chevy Vega. We also had camping gear, so we were all set.

We were excited about the possibilities for our new life. Maybe I could love and trust Donna again, and find some kind of happiness in a quiet life. Maybe, if we worked really hard at it, we could continue to stay away from drugs. If nothing else, we were on a road trip far from home, far from Chicago, and far from Steve and the warrant for my arrest.

On the long drive from Chicago to San Francisco, I made a series of firm decisions: I would never hurt anyone ever again, unless it was absolutely necessary to protect myself or someone else. When I got to California I'd stop using and selling dope. And I'd stop hanging out with the kind of company I'd grown accustomed to these past few years. I'd find a legal way to make money. I'd get a straight job, maybe picking fruit. I'd live a quiet life. And I'd begin to learn how to live on a spiritual basis. I knew I'd have to struggle, but I had struggled my whole life. I knew that by making these decisions, and by living with them as my base, I might not survive, but it was the only way to get back my self-respect, and recover my soul. I committed to live by the motto I'd made for myself: *I'm going to do my best, no more and no less. And that will be good enough.* I would repeat that motto to myself thousands of times in the coming years.

Donna and I shared these things on the drive, and by the time we got to California we were both excited about the possibilities for our new life. I didn't know if we would stay together. I wasn't pinning any hopes on that. I'd been disappointed too many times before, pinning my hopes on survival fantasies that never panned out.

I knew there were no guarantees. Even if I did my best, I might never succeed. I might never learn how to learn. I might never get a high school diploma, or have a satisfying career. I might always be poor. I might never find workable solutions to the practical dilemmas of my life. But now I knew that all that didn't matter; it wasn't the point. The point was deeper than all the things I'd been chasing for so long — survival, acceptance, respect, money, education, and control and power over my life. The point was to be able to live at peace in my own skin — to be able to face myself in the mirror, and look anyone in the eye. The point was to contribute something of value to life instead of living in it as a war zone.

There was more to it than that, but I couldn't fully grasp what it was. It lay in the realm of spirituality, on a path I dimly intuited but had not yet traveled. I knew something different was happening inside of me now. I had started this trip running away from my old life. But now I was rushing into a new life, yet to be discovered, with a hope and clarity I'd never felt before. I couldn't know the future, or base my actions on a particular outcome. How things would turn out in the end was not a relevant factor now, because the future was a mystery. From now on, how I lived was everything.

Hope and Fear

*W*e stayed at camping grounds and bought bags of potatoes, our staple while on the road. The occasional fast-food restaurant had become our special dinner out. By the time we arrived in California a week later, we were running low on money and ready for a break from the road.

Northern California was too expensive, so we decided to continue on to Southern California. We arrived in Los Angeles and found a campground near Disneyland. Even though we were very low on money, we decided to go to Disneyland. As tacky as it was, we decided to forget that Disneyland was just a façade, imagining instead that we could live there forever. The cheerfulness of the tourists and the generally happy vibe rubbed off on us. This new beginning was a dramatic contrast to the life we were fleeing from, and we were the happiest we'd been in a very long time.

We found a small one-room house for seventy-five dollars a month. We'd be living among migrant workers. We'd never imagined we could get a place that cheap, let alone a clean house with electricity and running water. It seemed things were starting to go our way.

The first night in our new home, Donna looked through

the want ads for potential jobs. On the way out to look for work the next day, we found an amazingly clean sofa bed left at the curb next door. Without a word, we looked at each other, got out of the car, and dragged it to our house. Later that day I got hired for a paper route.

Every morning we'd pick up the papers, fold them, and load them into the Vega. I drove and threw papers while Donna guided us to the next house. Although it wasn't much money, we made enough. Still, I felt I was holding Donna back. How long would she want to be with someone who wasn't pulling his weight and most likely never could?

Since we were working from two until seven in the morning, we signed up for classes at the local junior college. Donna took English and social science classes; I took algebra, geometry, and a remedial reading class. As long as I was under twenty-one and in school, I qualified for almost two hundred dollars a month from my dad's Social Security due to his military service. Our lives became calm and manageable. We couldn't go out to nice restaurants the way we used to, but we could go to McDonald's or walk to Walgreens for an ice cream every few weeks.

After a grueling first semester, I got my grades. I thought I'd done pretty well in my math classes, but I was afraid to get my hopes up. In the past I'd thought I'd done well on a test or in a class only to find out I'd failed or gotten a D. When our grades came in the mail, Donna opened the letter and read it to me. First she read, "Remedial Reading: Pass."

"Okay," I said, "but I knew I'd pass that because all I had to do was show up."

Then Donna got excited. "David, you got a B in algebra — and an A in geometry!"

I was in shock. "Donna, are you sure?" I asked.

"Yes, it's true!"

"I've never gotten grades that good before, and this is college!"

I looked up at her. "You know, Donna, I like math. Do you think maybe I could forget about reading and just do math?"

"I don't know, hon — maybe?"

I had some hope. This was the best my life had been for as long as I could remember.

Then one day Donna came home with a bag of pot. She told me about an old Hell's Angels guy she'd met in one of her classes who was cool and had this really good weed at a cheap price, and she just had to get it. *Here we go again,* I thought.

The Teaching

9'd lost track of my brother Emerson. We'd grown closer over the course of the Jacqui Schiff nightmare, especially when he helped me escape. Emerson had been traveling and heard about our return to California. We had no phone, but we got a letter from him telling us he'd be stopping by. During his visit he told us about an American spiritual teacher named Franklin Jones, who had adopted the curious name of Bubba Free John. Emerson had read a great deal of spiritual literature, and I valued his opinion. He felt that this guy was the real deal and the best spiritual teacher in the United States.

Coming from a Western culture, I found the idea of a guru strange. This was before stories about cults began to circulate. At that time there was a strong countercultural movement among the youth in the United States. One of the significant influences in the counterculture was the introduction of Eastern spirituality. The Beatles sparked a lot of public attention when they got involved with the Maharishi in the late 1960s. For most people in America, that was the first time they'd heard the word *guru*. I remembered being fascinated by the boy I'd met at camp who was practicing a mantra. That had been my first glimpse of any sort of Eastern spiritual practice, and I never forgot it.

I began to study Eastern teachings, especially the Indian Vedanta tradition, and some Buddhism. I couldn't read the books, but I listened to audiotapes and went to lectures and discussion groups. These spiritual traditions had a completely different take on life than Western religion did. They were much more focused on the transformation of the individual through meditation, yoga, and a deep investigation of the nature of the mind. The goal was not to get into heaven, to be forgiven for your sins, or to be saved. The goal was to realize the true nature of your own being, and to be liberated from suffering. However, I found the teachings difficult to apply to our time and place, and I began wanting a living teacher. Although Bubba Free John was an American, he had been a student of Baba Muktananda, an Indian yogi who was from the Siddha Yoga tradition. Bubba visited ashrams and holy sites in India during the course of his spiritual journey, and was steeped both in the yogic tradition and in the Vedanta school, an esoteric branch of Hinduism. There were many spiritual organizations and self-actualization techniques that were coming onto the scene at that time. There were also large communes where young people were trying to live collectively, with a different set of values than their parents and the "establishment." Having grown up in the co-op, I found this appealed to me.

More important, the solutions the conventional world was offering to me weren't working. Psychologists and therapists had failed me, and no expert or authority had ever helped me find a workable solution. None of them even seemed to be happy.

Years before, the priest I'd talked with had told me that there were two parallel paths in the search for happiness and meaning.

The first path was a practical path of success in the world. That path was closed to me. The second path was a path of spirituality, and he'd said that was the only path to true happiness. That is what Bubba Free John's teaching was about. It was about how to be happy, how to be free of suffering, how to see through the illusions of the conditional world and realize the divine nature of your own being. More than anything, I wanted to find meaning in life, to know what it was to be happy. Bubba Free John seemed to be happy, he seemed to be free, and he was inviting people to take up a true spiritual practice in relationship to him as a realized teacher. This was not a religion about somebody who died two thousand years ago; this was an opportunity for a living relationship with an enlightened being. Or so I hoped.

Bubba Free John had only published one book at that time—his autobiography, *The Knee of Listening*. There was a picture of him on the cover. He looked young, in his early thirties, with a broad, open face and large, wide-set eyes. He wore a tailored shirt with no collar, and held up his hand in a clenched fist. This was his gesture for the activity of the ego, the "self-contraction," the clench of your own being that creates the separate self-sense at the root of all suffering. That separate self-sense was the root of attachment and desire that caused us to continually grasp for external objects, conditions, and others as if they could bring ultimate fulfillment. But all such grasping and all such seeking were just more clenching of the fist that reinforced the sense of separation, the identification with an illusory "I." But, understanding this, you could begin to open your hand—to surrender, release the contraction, and awaken as the true Self, the Heart. Bubba described his attainment of enlightenment—in 1972 at the Vedanta Temple in Los Angeles—in *The Knee of Listening*.

And in 1973 he began his teaching work. His second book, *The Method of the Siddhas*, was due to come out in just a few weeks.

Over the next couple of months, Donna began reading to me from these books. I was immediately taken by Bubba's description of real spiritual practice, which he called Radical Understanding. His fundamental assertion was that conventional life is suffering, and that we cannot find ultimate fulfillment from any experience — not even spiritual experience. But there is a prior condition that is untouched by experience, that is not a result of or dependent on any experience. That prior condition is our true nature. It is a transcendent reality that's always already happy and free. He called it the Heart — not the physical heart, or the heart in the emotional, romantic sense, but the heart of reality, of the true Self. The Heart exists prior to ego, prior even to our birth, prior to all manifestation. It is the substratum of all existence. According to Bubba, seeking happiness as a goal to be attained at some point in the future was an activity of ego that only took you further away from the already-perfect condition of the present moment and your prior transcendental nature.

The more I studied Bubba's teaching, the more impressed I was. He seemed to express my deepest intuitions — what I'd been feeling but could never put into words. His teaching was not some New Age spiritual philosophy of magical thinking. It was grounded in the reality that experience is unavoidable suffering. It spoke powerfully to me — who had known suffering at every turn, who had failed at every attempt to succeed in life, who felt continually boxed in, caught in a trap with no way out. My failed confrontation with life had finally led me to the conclusion that all I could do was be as present in the moment as I could, do the best I could, and let the future take care of itself.

I'd always assumed that my predicament was caused by my disabilities. But Bubba's teaching showed me that everyone was suffering his or her version of the same condition of separation from reality. What was true for me was true for everyone, no matter how successful they appeared to be in life. It was the universal condition. I didn't need to be convinced that life was suffering. But Bubba's teaching took my epiphany that all I could do was be completely present in the moment to the ultimate spiritual level.

At that time, Bubba had a spiritual bookstore on Melrose Avenue called Dawn Horse Bookstore. It was the point of entry for anyone interested in his teaching. It also served as the meeting place for his current students, who numbered about sixty at the time. Donna seemed to be interested in Bubba, too, but panicked when I told her I wanted to join. I was going to do it whether she was coming or not. She reluctantly decided to join, and in November 1973 we formally became students.

Donna and I were only nineteen and among the youngest in the group, which included people from a wide variety of backgrounds — hippies, dope fiends, ex-New York gangsters, middle-aged housewives, and even Harvard scholars. All kinds of people were showing up from all over the world. But the one thing that struck me most was that they were all very smart.

To meet Bubba, we first had to fulfill the student conditions, which were the prerequisites for becoming his students. At the time, I thought I'd be taking up a quiet, meditative, contemplative life. For the first few months, we adapted to a vegetarian diet, did yoga every day, read Bubba's teachings, and attended a regular study group at the bookstore. I had problems with it right away. I felt agitated while meditating, sometimes finding myself suddenly jumping up, and a vegetarian diet left me craving. But shortly after we became students, the neat and tidy routine of yoga, meditation, and vegetarian diet relaxed. Around Christmas, Bubba threw a party with all of his students. Donna and I couldn't attend because we were still only preliminary students adapting to the diet and other regular practices.

The party, we were later told, was an ecstatic celebration. Bubba gave a talk about how spiritual enlightenment had nothing to do with good behavior, a pure diet, or obedience to his teaching. It was about throwing yourself to infinity, becoming ecstatic for no reason, and surrendering to the Divine with every fiber of your being. The first party was the beginning of a celebration that would last for eight months. Bubba used these parties as occasions to give marathon talks on "the process" of spiritual realization, to break people out of their conventional thinking, to give them a taste of what it was like to be truly liberated. Much of his teaching, and the content of his books, came from the talks he gave in these gatherings.

One of Bubba's main objectives was to create a spiritual community in which students could live his radical teaching together, breaking what he called "the cult of Narcissus." The average person, he said, was like Narcissus in the Greek myth, eternally distracted by the reflection of his own image and therefore cut off from all relationship. The habit of Narcissus was the activity of ego itself—the root and epitome of all suffering. Narcissus meditating on his own image in a pond represented our unconscious meditation on an illusory self, and a complete forgetting of our true Self. This separative activity was duplicated in the structures of conventional culture and politics, resulting in a society that reinforced and trapped others in the illusion of separative existence:

> The cult of this world is based on the principle of Narcissus, of separated and separative existence, and the search for changes of state, for happiness.
>
> There is not now, nor has there ever been, nor will there ever be an individual being. There is no such thing. All of the cultic ways are strategic searches to satisfy individuals by providing them with various kinds of fulfillment, or inner harmony, or vision, or blissfulness, or salvation, or liberation, or whatever. But the truth is that there is no such one to be fulfilled; literally, there is no such one. The principle of spiritual Community is that there is already no such person, no such separate one, no such dilemma.*

The underlying premise that there is, in actuality, no separate self, was a radical principle. But this didn't mean there aren't individual people with individual bodies and personal perspectives and experiences. It meant there isn't an independent, self-contained entity living inside each body who's separate from everyone and everything else. The "I" or "me" we believe ourselves to be, who seems separate from everything that is "not I" or "not me," was an illusion we each create unconsciously from moment to moment, as a kind of meditation, like that of Narcissus gazing at his image in the pond. This radical idea is the basis and the realization in many Eastern spiritual traditions, especially Buddhism and Advaita Vedanta. The ego, the separate "me" trapped inside a body, isn't real. Who we are in reality has no independent existence.

According to Bubba, the path to realization required a kind of

---

* Bubba Free John, *Garbage and the Goddess* (Clearlake: Dawn Horse Press, 1974), p. 5.

ego death, a death of the illusory self that distorts our natural perception of reality and prevents us from knowing our true nature.

Goodbye, Devi

$\mathcal{S}$oon after the parties began, Bubba decided to close down the Los Angeles center and move the whole community to Northern California. In January 1974, the Communion, as it was known, made the down payment on a dilapidated hot springs resort in Lake County. It would become a spiritual sanctuary and afford Bubba the privacy he needed to do his work, as well as a place where his students could live out this radical experiment. He named the property Persimmon.

After Bubba left for Northern California, Donna and I moved into his vacated house in Laurel Canyon so we could help load the van with his belongings. His waterbed was the last thing to be packed, so Donna and I slept on it overnight. Although we had both slept on waterbeds comfortably many times before, we both felt nauseous that night, throwing up all night long. We were unsure if we would have the stamina to help load the van the next day. The next morning we felt fine, and when the other students showed up to finish loading the van we explained to them what had happened. They all laughed and told us about the *shakti*, the name for the powerful energy transmitted by an enlightened spiritual teacher. Apparently it was common for people to get sick after experiencing it for the first time. I smiled politely, and thought it would be amazing if such a thing were true, but I wasn't able to believe their explanation.

By the end of February, the first wave of people had gone up to San Francisco to find apartments and look for work. In March, we arrived and moved into an apartment filled with other students. The focus of everyone's attention was always on Bubba, and what was going on at "the land," as they called it. A core group of people was living on the property with Bubba and his household, trying to refurbish the decrepit buildings. Emerson was already living up there, working as an editor on Bubba's next book. It had been four months, and we still hadn't met Bubba.

Finally the day came. It was Saturday, March 23. We were invited to Persimmon to meet Bubba. Excited out of our minds, we packed the Chevy Vega with as many people as it would hold and headed up to the land to join the party.

It was a two-hour drive from San Francisco to Lake County and the top of Cobb Mountain, where Persimmon was located. It was drizzling when we got there, as it had been for several days. We walked down from the parking lot to the main dining room, located next to a large kitchen. The old resort had been built around a natural hot springs. The property had an assortment of cabins, a small two-story hotel with individual rooms, and a family-style dining room. There was an outdoor Olympic-sized swimming pool, stables, and an outdoor pavilion, which must have been the site for many dances and social events over the decades. There was also a bathhouse, which contained a medium-sized soaking pool and half a dozen individual rooms with sunken tubs. All of it was in disrepair, and many of the buildings were condemned.

As we walked down the drive, we could hear music and laughter coming from the dining room. Fifty or sixty students were there, waiting for Bubba. He lived in a small house located a short distance from the dining room, in close proximity to the main buildings at the center of the property. The dining room was filled with a random collection of old couches and chairs. Right away I noticed a single upholstered divan sitting on a small dais, slightly elevated off the floor. I figured it must be for Bubba. Everyone was gathered to watch a movie, waiting for Bubba to arrive.

I'd seen many pictures of Bubba, and I was curious what he would look like in person. About an hour later, his laughter announced his arrival. He was not very tall, maybe five feet nine, but he had a large head, a big round belly, and a presence that made him seem much larger than his physical size. He was wearing a plaid shirt and a knit beanie on his head. Everything about him seemed round and whole. He never stopped laughing and joking. He was fascinating to me, but I also had my antennae out, not wanting to be blindly swept up in something that I'd regret later. I'd met quite a few charismatic people before, and they all seemed to posses the ability to act with complete freedom and disregard for the rules of society and feelings of others. By offering to do you a favor, they made you feel special and invited you into a world that was more glamorous than your own. The next thing you knew, you were doing or allowing something you never would have before. So I was on alert to this possibility.

We never saw the movie that night because Bubba began to speak. He went on to give a talk that would change the lives of all those around him; it was called "The Saturday Night Massacre." It was the first time Bubba really laid out to his students what he expected of them in terms of their relationships, and how life in a real spiritual community — his spiritual community — would be radically different from life in the conventional world. He criticized the world as being a cult of Narcissus. He said it was the responsibility of his students to undo the cult as it appeared in their community. Among the various types of cultic attachment were conventional marriages, which he called the "cult of pairs." He criticized conventional marriages as having little to do with intimacy or real spiritual practice, and as mostly serving to reinforce the identification as a separate self, with two illusory selves mirroring each other.

I understood that I suffered from my attachments, and it made sense to me that if there was no separate self then there could be true freedom — the freedom to love beyond the limits of self-interest. It would be truly selfless love. I'd experienced something like that many times in my life, including when I first met Donna and saw the fear in her eyes. For me, this love seemed to come from a place that was prior to myself, prior to my personality — or Donna's personality. It was from someplace where we were already the same person, the same *beingness*. I could see that by loving all as one, with no separation, we could love without holding back, and there would be no conflict due to personal self-interest. But I wasn't sure how that played out in the world. If everyone was "the Divine" and ultimately without a separate self, then how do you choose your relationships? Do you just "love the one you're with"? I was confused.

It seemed impossible that people could live without acting out of self-interest, or stop seeking fulfillment through self-improvement. An egoic mind couldn't find its way beyond an egoic mind any more than a psychotic mind could find its way beyond a psychotic mind. It seemed to me that anyone who was truly serious about transcending the ego had to take on a teacher.

Bubba wasn't proposing a utopia, where everybody loved one another and nobody was ever unhappy. He was trying to create a community in which the enlightened, nonegoic state was the presumption, and each individual could have the best opportunity to discover that within himself or herself. Bubba's spiritual presence was so powerful and his freedom was so ecstatic that, maybe, with his agency, it could be possible for us to realize our own divine nature, too.

After his talk, Bubba returned to his house with his entourage, where they partied throughout the night. The rest of us stayed in the dining room and partied together, but the only thing anyone really cared about was getting invited over to the party at Bubba's house.

Donna and I spent the night in one of the cabins and woke up late the next day. By the middle of the afternoon, the party started up again in the dining room. Later that day, Bubba came over with some people from his party. He stood in the doorway, looking around and joking, asking the people who'd come over with him who they wanted to invite back to the party. A number of people were invited, and they seemed ready to leave. Then Bubba looked around and said, "Is that it?" He smiled when he saw Donna. "What do we have here?" he asked. Donna was invited over, and I watched with a knot in my stomach as she left with him and the others — back to his house.

The rest of us went on with our party, but all I could think about was Donna, and what she was doing. Late that night I went back to the cabin to go to sleep. Donna never returned.

Early the next morning, Bubba, his inner circle, and the rest of us all went to the bathhouse. I sat next to Donna in the large pool. But she was all over Bubba. I could tell they'd had sex, and I could tell that she didn't want to be with me. I sat around in the pool, intensely aware of how attached I was to Donna, even though I knew our relationship needed to change. Then Bubba started to talk, and what he said was confounding and disorienting from the moment he started. He began by praising Donna, saying that Donna was "the Devi." In Hindu mythology, the *Devi* is regarded as the manifestation of the cosmic female principle, the incarnation of the Divine Feminine in the world. Bubba was saying to everyone that Donna was literally a goddess! He kept saying, over and over, that Donna was the Devi. He said that they'd been together for countless lifetimes, and that she was destined to appear at this time — destined to be with him. This was not only staggering to me but to everybody there. Suddenly, from out of nowhere, Donna had arrived and was instantly recognized as a goddess! Not only that — she was now Bubba's main consort. She moved in with Bubba and had no contact with me after that.

I had to go back to work the next day. I'd found a temporary job reviewing computerized tax forms. I didn't need to read, just compare characters and numbers. I wasn't doing well at it, and now I'd missed a day, so naturally I was afraid that missing another day would put my job in jeopardy.

Devastated doesn't even begin to describe how I was feeling. I was in physical and emotional shock. As I drove home, I thought about how just a few weeks ago I was ready to leave Donna to study with this teacher; now she had left me to be with him. We both knew that our relationship hadn't been working and needed to change. But it had happened so fast. I was far more attached to Donna than I'd ever realized. Over the next few months, I recognized I would have to understand and accept the loss of her without ever having closure.

I had to reconsider why I'd joined in the first place. It seemed that Bubba just surrounded himself with people who could do him the most good. They had money, or they were good writers, or they were sexy and beautiful. I seemed to be right back where I'd started, in a world where people who were more successful, more beautiful, or simply more valuable to someone else's self-interest were rewarded. It was revulsion toward these qualities that had led me to consider a spiritual alternative in the first place. I kept asking myself if Bubba was really doing all this for the "sake of his students" as he claimed, or whether it was just how he wanted to live, and now he could play it out.

I wasn't sure what a true or healthy relationship was, and it made me feel profoundly alone. If Bubba's teachings were correct, it was my attachments I was suffering. When I looked into my own case, I knew it was true. And it wasn't just people I was attached to; it was also my ideas about what I should be doing and who I should be — my attachment to the hope of learning how to read, my attachment to the desire to be married and have a family. I was attached to everything I valued, and I suffered all of it. I wasn't even sure what it would look like to be free of attachments. Did it mean being free of concern for others, as Bubba seemed to be? Donna wasn't going to survive without the support of others. I'd seen all kinds of handicapped people, both mentally and physically. How could they not be attached to other people or not need other people? Maybe these people can never be free of attachments and can therefore never be happy. And was it true we keep coming back, lifetime after lifetime, as long as we have attachments to anything in this world? I couldn't survive without help. How could I not be attached to the people who helped me compensate for my disabilities? I didn't see how I could be free of attachment to other people without being free of needs. And I didn't see how I could be free of needs.

I realized that the thoughts of suicide I'd had all my life were really about the desire to be free of my needs, so that I wouldn't suffer rejection at the hands of the people I depended on. Because of my needs, I inevitably became a burden to them and was to be avoided, except out of pity. No matter how much they loved me, they would avoid me when they saw me coming. Even my mother, for as long as I can remember, had been trying to figure out a way to be free of me and free of my needs. I couldn't find self-respect when others found me to be a burden. And I would rather be dead than be a burden to the ones I loved.

That was when I realized that I was very different from everyone else I knew. I was only alive because of my mother's unyielding insistence that I join the world. I'd resisted it with my whole body because the simplest input—a light, a touch, a sound—was overwhelmingly painful. But because of my mother's constant connection to me, I was pulled into the world of others against my will. I'd left the safety of my small internal world, where I kept tight control on all sensory input. At that time, my mother was the thread of my connection to this world, and I felt lost without it. This set my extreme, baseline need for connection; yet that connection could always be broken and was not reliable, which threw me into a profound state of fear. I'd always felt stuck, and I'd vacillated between impossible options. I was unwilling to remain dependent on others my entire life, but independence, for me, had required dealing drugs and living in a violent world where I'd have to resort to violence. And I had decided I would rather be dead than live that way.

For most of my life I'd felt betrayed that I had finally come into this world of relationships, where I had limited control over input, and along with that a disability that made it impossible for me to function in this world. It was as if I'd stayed here solely at the urging of other people, knowing that I couldn't participate in their world, and then they said, "Well, you're on your own now." They didn't believe, or they refused to believe, that I was lacking the capacity to function like everyone else. I couldn't integrate ordinary sensory input. I was so overwhelmed with sensory overload that just being alive was terrifying. I couldn't look into someone's eyes without being overwhelmed by their emotions and the relational demand. And the worst thing of it all was that I was only here because *they* insisted that I be here.

I could see now that it was impossible to base freedom from attachment on not having any needs. Everyone has needs. But my disabilities created needs that made me extremely dependent on other people — and at the same time those needs isolated me from those same people. My disabilities were profound and at the same time invisible, so that people often didn't believe they existed. When I'd tell people that I couldn't read or remember names, they wouldn't believe me. They'd say, "There must be something you can do about that." But there wasn't anything I could do, and nobody would acknowledge it. Nobody wanted to go there. The more support I needed, the more people wanted to get away from me. I needed a deep and constant level of intimacy and communication with someone in order to function, but that intensity made people withdraw.

To have self-respect I needed to be of value, but at the time it seemed the only hope I had of ever having an equal relationship with someone was for that person to have disabilities and needs that were as bad as mine. Together we might bring enough value to each other to add up to one complete person. This was the chance I'd had with Donna, seemingly my only chance for self-respect. Of course, to psychologists and therapists we would appear to be two highly dysfunctional people in an unhealthy codependent relationship. That's what they always said.

My need for connection in order to function, and the way that my needs drove others away and isolated me, was so extreme and so painful that suicide had seemed the only solution to escape the cycle of suffering. Suicide would extinguish all my needs and the pain of not getting them met. But now I was being presented with another alternative, and that was to go through another kind of "suicide"—an ego death.

According to Bubba's teaching, the ego was not an entity; it was not an objective *thing*. It was an *activity*. The primary activity of the ego was contraction. That contraction occurs in the moment we identify with an illusory separate self, an "I." In the moment of experiencing that "I" as separate, we simultaneously realize a world of "others" out there. In the East they say, "Whenever there is an other, fear arises." It is true that there's an individual body and mind, but the contraction of consciousness into fear and body-identification creates an illusory "me," reinforcing the sense of separation. The Vedanta tradition refers to this as *identification, differentiation,* and *desire.*

Once we have identified with an illusory self—the ego—fear arises, and a sense of separation distorts our perception of reality. Then the grasping for external objects, the attachment to external conditions and others, and the search to attain security for this apparently separate self become continual pursuits, even the point of life. This habitual grasping, attachment, and seeking reinforce the core contraction, and the illusion of a separate self. And this cycle repeats itself in an endless loop, which is our suffering. Until we understand and awaken. But to the ego, this awakening is death.

I had once been willing to kill myself to be released of my needs and attachments. That had taken a kind of courage. Now, knowing this, it seemed to me it would be cowardly to commit suicide if I didn't at least try to live with my needs, whether they were met or not, and surrender in the midst of suffering and attachment while I was alive. This would require greater courage.

As an infant and a small child, I said no to experience. I chose to withdraw rather than suffer the overwhelming pain of stimuli I couldn't integrate or control. I chose contraction and denial of life and experience. Now, practicing the release of the ego was the radical opposite of that withdrawal. I was saying yes to life, and consenting to experience it fully. It wasn't a leap of faith. It was that I'd reached a point of exhaustion and utter brokenness, where I saw there was no other choice but to accept what I was, to stop struggling with things I couldn't control, to stop grasping for security. I wasn't giving up the will to survive; I was giving up the need to escape, the need to control, and the need to know. It would no longer be me living life. Life would be living me. I felt like I'd been holding on desperately to a root in the side of a cliff, terrified of letting go and falling. Finally, exhausted, I let go. And just as I feared, I was falling, but I was only falling. There was no bottom, and there was nothing to fear. Letting the future take care of itself was the best I could do. I had no strength left in me. Letting go was the beginning of freedom.

As I was coming to terms with these insights and applying them in my life as best I could, I was also dealing with the aftermath of my sudden loss of Donna to the guru whose teachings formed the basis of my new spiritual life and practice. I wondered what Bubba would do when he discovered her dramatic mood swings, her desperate emotional needs and attachments, her terrifying psychotic rages. People had always judged Donna for her failings and weaknesses — she was a drug addict, she was manipulative, she was promiscuous. How would Bubba deal with her?

What I learned as the months passed was that Bubba did not judge Donna. He wasn't afraid of her. He seemed to be trying to get her to accept all aspects of herself (the same thing I'd been trying to do, but he took it to the absolute limit). He saw beyond her failings, her weaknesses, her brokenness. He appreciated and even glorified each broken piece of her, holding her in a state of wholeness and perfection, which he saw as her true nature. He held her as a goddess. I'd never seen anyone else do this before. Maybe this was the love of an awakened Heart. Maybe this love would put Donna back together. If Bubba could do that, then I was happy for Donna, and incredibly grateful to him. If Bubba could make Donna whole, then maybe he was for real.

Moving On

*T*here was much more going on during this period than parties. A spiritual force was turned loose in our community, unlike anything any of us had ever experienced. The energy transmitted by Bubba sent people into rapturous states of absorption, and triggered dramatic internal experiences and higher states of consciousness. This spiritual transmission had its roots in the ancient Indian tradition of *kundalini yoga*. The source of the *kundalini* was the *shakti*, the primal life energy that animates all living beings. The kundalini was said to lie dormant at the base of the spine, like a sleeping serpent. Awakened by the initiatory touch of a spiritual master, it rose up the spine, opening various energy centers in the body, culminating in the opening of the center at the top of the head. This resulted in illumination, a merging with the Infinite, an awakening as the true Self. Bubba's own gurus were adepts of this yoga who had awakened in him the powerful shakti that he now transmitted to his students.

When Bubba sat in formal meditation with everyone, his face contorted as he channeled this force. People sitting with him were often overwhelmed with yogic energy. Some shook uncontrollably, and others wailed, as waves of shakti poured through them. Donna, extremely sensitive to this spiritual force, would go into ecstatic swoons, shaking as the force of the shakti moved through her. I had seen her take drugs and act out wildly in the past; she was the most extreme person I'd ever met, and now she was throwing herself into her relationship with Bubba as if it were a drug.

Meanwhile, I was not having any of these experiences. I figured those who seemed to be having them were putting it on. Or, maybe I just wasn't a spiritual type. Then, one day, I experienced the shakti. We had all been sitting in a large meditation hall between the kitchen and the main house. Bubba had just left. And I began to feel a "buzz" as if I'd taken LSD. A powerful energy began to fill me. Colors got richer and brighter, and the room began to shimmer. Everything was suddenly alive. There was no future or past. There was only the present moment, in which I was part of everything. The peace of this was profound and primordial. It was a consciousness that existed prior to my human personality, and long before my birth. It seemed to precede the first appearance of humanity, continued up to this very moment, and would exist into an endless future. It was more real and true than anything I'd ever experienced. And this consciousness was my own nature and the source of my being.

In this state, I perceived my thoughts as passing illusions, not to be believed. I saw how my thoughts and fears, my desire to control my life and survive, controlled me, possessed me, and created the very sense of me. And this was my *dis-ease*. I was filled with profound appreciation and gratitude.

In the hospital after my attempted suicide at fourteen, I'd experienced this prior condition as an inner source that was awake and alive in me. This was the source of all the love and connectedness I'd ever felt in my life. I knew I was being sustained by a force that flowed through me now from an infinite source. I always had been. And I knew, for my life to ever work out, I had to trust completely in the reality of that source. In Bubba's terms, I had "understood." This experience was a turning point. And this experience and the understandings it communicated were reinforced many times over in formal meditation with Bubba. What I felt in his presence was a magnification and a confirmation of my own Self, my true nature and being. The point was not to discover what was true about him, but to realize what was true about me.

My family and old friends couldn't understand what I was committed to, and were afraid for me. Even the few who did understand didn't believe that Bubba had the answers. The choice I was making was impossible to explain to anyone who wasn't there, who hadn't seen and felt what I had in his presence. I knew that following a false teacher would be more damaging than continuing on my own ego-based path. I also knew, at least intellectually, that Bubba's teaching was true, and what I'd experienced in meditation absolutely confirmed my deepest intuition about the nature of my own being. I realized that it wasn't about following Bubba, or trusting anyone else, for that matter. It was about trusting the thread of my own intuition, and following my own path. Right now, I felt that I needed a teacher; if that changed in the future, then I'd move on.

As word got out about the extraordinary events taking place in Bubba's company, hundreds of people started showing up. The Free John community was not the only spiritual community trying to live out a radical experiment at that time. In Boulder, Colorado, Chogyam Trungpa, a Tibetan Rinpoche, was also forming a community around his lineage of Tibetan Buddhism. He was well known for his drunken parties and wild, unconventional behavior. In India, Bhagwan Rajneesh had thousands of Western followers, and he would later bring his community to the United States. Bubba's teacher, Swami Muktananda, was opening Siddha Yoga ashrams here, and the Maharishi was spreading Transcendental Meditation far and wide, introducing meditation to mainstream America.

In San Francisco, the community of Bubba's ordinary students was beginning an experiment in cooperative living. A community organization was formed, called the Free Community Order. We became spiritual renunciates. We all moved into large apartment buildings, where we shared a common kitchen and a common meditation hall. One three-bedroom apartment would house six or more students. There were several households like this.

Meanwhile, I continued to flounder from one job to another, always hoping just to collect as many paychecks as possible before I got fired. One time I got hired for a job, but when the phone rang after the interview my new boss asked me to pick it up. He told me to be sure to take down the date and time. I didn't know the number of the month, or the spelling. He told me to get out. I'd lost the job only minutes after being hired. At one point, I had a job sewing up corpses after autopsies. That didn't work out. I also ran an ad in the newspaper for doing appliance repairs. I'd show up at a house, often without any idea what to do. With my knack for fixing things, it sometimes worked out, but sometimes it didn't.

I began taking classes at San Francisco City College. As long as I was in school I still had the Social Security support from my father. Because I didn't have a high school diploma, there was no way I could actually get a degree, so I just took classes I was interested in for the sake of learning. I took engineering classes and thermo-fluid dynamics. Calculus and physics were naturals for me, and I did very well in them. But all my efforts and studies seemed like hard labor that never amounted to anything, and I didn't know if any of it would ever be any use.

At that time, I related to the famous story about Milarepa, one of Tibet's greatest saints, and the relationship he had with his guru, Marpa. In exchange for the sacred teaching, Marpa instructed Milarepa to build a tower in honor of his son. Milarepa built the tower, only for Marpa to tell him to tear it down and demand that he build another one. This went on for years, with Milarepa building house after house, and Marpa telling him to tear each one down and build a new one. Eventually, Marpa gave Milarepa the teaching, and Milarepa went on to become enlightened.

Not that I went on to become enlightened like Milarepa, but it turned out to be an important time for me. Even with so much I was unable to learn, I was learning more than I knew. For the first time I was living a non-goal-oriented life. I grew in my understanding of what I could and couldn't learn. This helped me identify and avoid the things that I couldn't learn. Up to that point, I'd always been given things to learn that were supposed to be essential. But many of these things disrupted my ability to stay focused on what I *could* learn. I began to enjoy the experience of building momentum with my learning. I found that I learned more by pushing myself to my limits without violence to myself. I began to let kindness be the guide to my limits, always knowing that the farther I could go now, the farther I could go later on. I reminded myself often: *I will do my very best in this moment, no more and no less, and let the future take care of itself.* My best chance to succeed was to do the best I could without attachment to results. When I failed, I would use that in my spiritual practice to remind me to go inside and rediscover what it is to be happy, prior to my worldly circumstances. This gave me the strength to go on. Not a Rambo kind of strength that attacks and destroys its enemies, but a quiet kind of strength that allowed me to remain calm and clear in the midst of a crisis.

I committed myself to wasting no time. I spent no time with anything that didn't add to my learning or somehow build my chances for a career; I avoided anything that was detrimental to my health. Staying on task when I had no idea how my life could ever work out was like being buried in the snow as a kid, and not knowing how, or if, I could get out. I didn't spend time worrying if there would be enough air to breathe or enough room in the tunnel to dig my way out. I just made the best use of every nook and cranny, packing the snow around me as best I could in the moment, then putting my attention on the next handful of snow. If I did the best I could at each step, I'd get the best result. I might not survive, but living this way was my best chance. And when I was busy in this way, I wasn't suffering in those moments.

In addition to reminding myself to stay fully present in the moment and let the future take care of itself, I also had the deeper understanding from Bubba's teaching that we are "always already happy," prior to our conditional circumstances. It became important for me to locate that feeling of prior happiness in order to stay present in the moment. Working with the issue of releasing my attachments had prepared me to find this place of awareness and happiness, in moments.

Married, with Children

*O*ne of the primary responsibilities of Bubba's students was to communicate his teaching to others, and to create forms of access for new people who were approaching. Those who were serious about getting involved with Bubba went through a series of screening interviews conducted by students who'd been around for a while. I was conducting some of these preliminary interviews one night when a beautiful young woman showed up. Her name was Cathy. I continued to run into her at community functions during the week, and on the weekends we'd meet at the sanctuary and take walks together. Long story short, we fell in love and got married.

It was a relief to be in a relatively healthy relationship. Cathy and I were not dependent on each other, as Donna and I had been. We were both highly focused — I on school, and she on cooking for more than forty people. And we both had our meditation and other daily practices. Due to the structured life in the household, where meals were prepared and bills were paid, many of life's ordinary stresses were absent from our relationship. Many problems I'd previously thought to be psychological were actually practical. Just by living in a managed circumstance, the common relationship codependencies and emotional complications simply never arose.

I was constantly confronted by the paradox of Bubba and his teachings, which couldn't be understood by conventional standards. And I was always left with no certainty that he was who he said he was. Bubba's assertion that there is, in reality, no such thing as a separate individual self could easily be interpreted by the medical establishment as a form of mental illness. Yet this same realization has been spoken of by many spiritual teachers throughout history, particularly in the East. India is full of stories of saints and sages who acted in completely bizarre and antisocial ways. Jesus went into a temple, overturned the tables of the moneychangers, and drove them and all their livestock out with a whip. And St. Francis of Assisi talked to birds. What Western psychology defines as sanity is based in a consensus reality that isn't universally shared by all cultures in all times. And many enlightened beings would be diagnosed insane by current psychological standards. Even the most basic principle of Eastern teaching — that the personal, individual self is an illusion — is incomprehensible and unacceptable to most Westerners.

I can't say I ever came to like Bubba, partly because there was no way to get to know him. He was not a conventional person with conventional goals, and it wasn't possible to form a conventional friendship with him. There never seemed to be anyone "there." I never saw him exhibit compassion or generosity toward any individual; the only thing he seemed to care about was making his teaching point.

— 🙂 —

Soon after Cathy and I were married, we moved out of San

Francisco and over the Golden Gate Bridge to Marin County. We lived and worked with other students who were building a health-food store in Mill Valley. In May 1977, we had a baby — a beautiful, healthy boy. Fifteen months after that, my beautiful daughter was born. They were miracles. But now my greatest desire in my life had collided with my worst fear. I had children and a family. I knew in my body that this was a life changer. But I felt I didn't deserve them, and the weight of responsibility was crushing. The world now had access to hurt me in ways it never had before, and deeper than it had before, through my children. For the first time in my life, suicide was completely out of the question.

Shortly before my daughter was born, we'd moved to Sonoma County, where rent and living expenses were much cheaper. I had a family to support and needed to make something happen, but I still didn't have a clue what it was going to be or how I was going to do it. Fortunately, I was soon to get a break. But it started with a loss.

I'd known from the age of seven that it was up to me to take care of myself. Nobody knew how to help someone who couldn't read. I'd always held onto the hope that someday I would learn to read. Then I could get a high school diploma. With a high school diploma, I could get a job. But time after time I'd failed. Now I was married with two small children, and I still couldn't read, I still had no GED, and I still had no job. Time seemed to have run out. Finally, I had to accept the fact that I would never learn to read and would never get a high school diploma. It was devastating. I mourned it like a death in the family — the death of who I'd hoped to be, and the death of my hopes and dreams. I remembered as a kid staring at all the books on the shelves that filled our house, daydreaming about how I would read them someday, so I could be as smart as everyone else. Now I accepted that I'd never be able to read any of the books the rest of my family had devoured and talked about enthusiastically. It hurt down to my soul.

Yet giving up on trying to learn how to read opened up possibilities I couldn't have imagined previously. I set out with a new vision, on fire with an intention born of necessity and desperation. My two young kids depended on me. Determined to find work, or to at least get vocational training, I went to the California Department of Vocational Rehabilitation (CDVR) for help. I hoped that there was some way I could get around the problem of my lack of diploma — that my inability to read could be treated as a disability. I met with a counselor who asked me what I liked to do. I told him I loved electronics, and though I couldn't follow written directions, I could read schematics. The CDVR normally provided help for people with physical disabilities. They provided training for people with disabilities so they could get work. If they used wheelchairs, the CDVR assisted them with access problems. The jobs they offered were generally low-level assembly-line work.

My counselor had never dealt with someone who couldn't read before, but he recommended that I meet with the head of the electronics department at Santa Rosa Junior College (SRJC). If it seemed possible that I could actually get a job with a degree in digital electronics without being able to read, he would see what he could do to get me financial support.

I met with Mr. Bacon, the head of the electronics department, who took my interest in electronics seriously. He knew earning a living in electronics required knowledge and skill but didn't necessarily require a lot of reading, though I'd have to find a way to learn the course work. With Mr. Bacon's support, I was able to persuade the SRJC to waive their requirement of a high school diploma, so I could work toward an Associate Science degree in digital electronics. That took care of the GED problem. Now I had to find a way to learn without reading. The solution was to have all the course material recorded onto audiotape. The CDVR agreed to pay to have the material recorded, as long as the SRJC would supply a document stating their opinion that such materials would enable me to graduate and find work. It was the biggest break of my life; I was finally going to get the help I needed.

I'd always suspected that I might be smart, and wondered if I might have done well in school if it weren't for reading and writing. Now, by listening to the course materials, I excelled in school. Here, finally, was proof that I was school-smart, even if I couldn't read and write. The difference between believing I was smart and experiencing that I was smart was enormous. It had taken tremendous effort to change the policies of both the state rehab department and the junior college, but these changes opened the door for many individuals with disabilities who followed after me.

After completing the two-year program and getting my degree, I got my first job as a bench tech for an electronics company in San Carlos. On my first day I showed up early, feeling both excited and anxious. After giving the receptionist my name, I sat down and tried to calm my nerves before meeting my new boss. His name was José. He arrived a minute later and introduced himself. I guessed he was in his early thirties, and he seemed very nice. As he led me to my bench at the far end of the factory, he explained that the company was a division of GTE that contracted exclusively for the U.S. military. I would be working in the division that built microwave radios for land and satellite communications. We walked indoors for what seemed like six city blocks, through building after building. We finally got to my workbench in the far corner of a massive building. The bench was impressive, filled with racks of very expensive testing equipment. He explained that my job was tuning frequency modulating oscillators (FMOs) for microwave radio transceivers. I had over a million dollars of test equipment on my bench, and I had only limited lab experience with some of the most expensive equipment. Each FMO had to pass stress tests that included cycling each one between freezing cold and burning hot temperatures. Each transistor was made of silicon and pure gold.

José was extremely gentle; the only time I saw any sign of sternness was when he told me that each transistor cost over seventy-five dollars. He said that he'd started on this bench, that it was the toughest bench in the plant, and that I was starting here because I'd done so well with the technical questions in my interviews. He explained that new hires were all on probation for the first ninety days; after that I'd be considered permanent and all my benefits would kick in. He said I'd have the full ninety days, but at this bench he could tell by the first two weeks if a new tech was going to make the cut. I appreciated the confidence they had in me to put me on this bench, but I was concerned that this was becoming a setup to fail, and I badly needed this job.

Tuning the transistors was a highly intricate process; adjustments on any one parameter changed the readings on all the others. I had to adjust the frequency by moving the tuning conductor closer to the transistor deep inside the FMO, and at the same time adjust the voltage and power to exacting parameters. I felt as if I needed three pairs of hands and three pairs of eyes to track and compensate for the slightest adjustment. I worked intensely that first day, but every transistor I tried to tune popped; sometimes they popped without even touching the FMO. With every new attempt, I'd remember that my entire future and the security of my family was tied to whether or not I could adjust this transistor without it blowing up. Finally, late in the afternoon, with all my attention tightly focused on just the last few adjustments needed to get an FMO to the exact frequency…I got it. Then, to secure the adjustment, I laid a small amount of epoxy to the post of the power probe, just fractions of a centimeter from the transistor. I pulled my hand back, and it held. Just then, all my equipment gauges went to zero and the transistor blew! By the end of the day I was sitting at my bench still struggling to get even one transistor not to blow. My boss José told me, "Keep at it. It'll take practice."

Over the next two weeks I kept count of the blown transistors that were piling up next to my test equipment. All day I would watch that pile grow. I kept remembering all the jobs I'd gotten fired from and thinking that I was going to get fired again. As each transistor blew, I began to feel that old, horrifying darkness descend on me, that sense of doom. I was so habituated to it that I would find myself having thoughts about the inevitability of my failure. As another transistor blew, I'd think, *This predicament is just who I am. It will follow me forever, and it can never be different for me.* But I continually reminded myself, *Don't believe your mind; don't believe in the story. All I can do is the best I can do and let the future take care of itself.*

Even after two weeks and much improvement, I was still popping about fifty percent of the transistors. I would add them up at the end of each day, and at seventy-five dollars apiece I was costing the company far more than they were paying me.

As I went into my two-week review, I was ready for the inevitable. I was trembling with a mix of dread and resignation. I walked up to the chair by José's desk at the appointed time.

"Hi, José."

He was writing on some papers and didn't look up.

"Hi, David, have a seat." Right away I could tell José was being more formal than usual with me. Looking up at me with a polite smile, he said, "Okay, David, let's get to it."

I listened as he went down the evaluation list.

"Attendance: one hundred percent. On time: one hundred percent. Working as a team, you got a top score, which is very good. 'No delays on assembly line' isn't applicable to your position, but we all get measured on it. So, very good."

I kept thinking, *Yeah, but wait till he gets to the transistors.* I was seven years old again. I could almost hear the news in my head that I wasn't moving on to third grade. Finally, he got to "consistency of work, very good." I felt some relief. "Quality, very good." He looked up at me and asked, "Any questions?"

Was that it? He was done? He had given me all top ratings! I wanted to just get up and leave, but I had to ask, "What about all the transistors I've popped?"

"You're doing better than anyone else has on that bench," he said. "Other techs have popped more transistors than you and had fewer FMOs pass the stress tests with lower total productivity."

I couldn't believe it! I suddenly felt as if I had been crouching my whole life and now, for the first time, I was able to stand up straight and take a deep breath. A dark cloud that had always covered me lifted, and a blue sky, never visible before, appeared. As it appeared, I imagined horizons and possibilities I'd never allowed myself to imagine before. I had never experienced such relief and joy. For the first time in my life I was a real person with a real job. I could take care of myself and support a family. I had no special considerations; I was just like everyone else. For the first time in my life, who I was, was enough!

"Excuse me," I said.

I suddenly got up and turned away, afraid he would see my eyes tearing up or hear my voice crack. But I couldn't help it. Now, ringing in my head for the first time in my life, I heard, *I am enough! I am enough!*

Making a Difference

$\mathcal{F}$ or the next few years, I couldn't be stopped at work. I moved to better jobs and worked as many hours as I could get. I discovered that I had an uncanny knack for troubleshooting. By 1981 I was twenty-seven years old and making a six-figure income, owned two cars and a house in Marin County, California, and knew that very few people could do what I could do professionally. Within my first year out of school, I had paid more in taxes than the government had paid for reading my books onto tape. Several years later I was getting the top assignments in my field, and I was being given all the hours I could work. I often slept for a few hours in the office, got up, and went straight back to work.

I was the go-to guy. On one of my first high-profile projects, the president of Fireman's Fund and American Express (back then they were the same company and shared the same data center) informed me that while his system was down they were losing five million dollars every twenty minutes — on the insurance side alone. I knew this had to be true, because he screamed it at me only inches from my face, and his neck was bright red.

Some people might feel intimidated having the CEO of

a Fortune 500 company yelling in their face. But this was nothing compared to Chappy pinning me to a wall in front of an enraged Black Coalition, staring at me with bloodshot eyes, and saying, "I'm going to kill you, you little white piece of shit!" or to Yellow Shirt and Gold Chain trying to toss me down a tenth-floor stairwell. This CEO was a teddy bear by comparison. So, I sat down and calmly told him we could either talk about it then, or I could work on it and we could talk later. He walked out and personally stood guard outside the switch-room door to make sure I wasn't disturbed by anyone. After two intense hours, I got the system back up and running.

I realized that what would be too stressful for most people was an enjoyable challenge to me. I was able to remain calm and function at my best in a crisis. I'd arrive at an office where everybody was freaking out and nobody knew what to do. And I'd just get to work diagnosing the problem and figuring out what the hell to do. I never began from a place of knowing what to do to fix the problem. I always started from a place of total ignorance and not knowing what to do. But I was completely used to being ignorant, confused, and not knowing what to do, so it didn't bother me and I was able to remain perfectly calm. I developed my uncanny knack for solving problems by following my intuition. I was able to relate to and interact with a computer system as if it were a person. That's the best way I can say it. And I started hearing from my boss that I was leaving behind what he called "a wake of very impressed and happy customers."

My supervisor, a topnotch tech whose skills I respected, once insisted on going with me on a job, to learn about a new piece of equipment I was working on. But he left in the middle. Afterward, I heard he had told his boss, "I can't watch David work;

it's too nerve-racking. The way he works doesn't make sense to me. I don't know what he's doing, or why, or how he does it. But when he's done, everything always works."

When people who'd known me from the past told me how much I'd changed, and how I had accomplished so much now that I had finally "buckled down," I'd think, *Screw you! I was working harder when I was failing.* From my point of view, it was the world that had changed and given me a chance. I just kept reminding myself to be completely present in the moment and let the future take care of itself. It was only when I gave up the struggle to become more, to become better, and simply accepted the present moment, that the present worked out and the future took care of itself. Everyone else thought I had done something different to earn it. But I knew that what I'd been given was a gift.

— ❦ —

As time went on, Bubba's teaching seemed to get further away from his original path, which he called the Way of Radical Understanding. Insight into the self-contraction, and surrender into the prior freedom that was our true nature and condition, was being replaced by a demand for unquestioning devotion and obedience to the guru. Yet the average student had little or no contact with Bubba by this time. What had previously been exciting personal events with Bubba were now replaced by lectures from self-righteous students and endless courses of study — neither of which were of any use to me. Increasingly, people were expected to devote their time and donate money to the community and the formal organization. And people's "practice" seemed to be measured by how enthusiastic they were to do whatever they were told. What had started out as a radical experiment in living a truly spiritual life had calcified into a rigid and dogmatic organization that was becoming, it seemed to me, the letter without the spirit, emphasizing form over content.

After seven years of marriage, Cathy and I began to move in different directions in our lives. We agreed to divorce, but we remained good friends. The end of my formal involvement with Bubba and the community came in 1987. By this time I already had custody of my son, and soon afterward I gained custody of my daughter. Bubba had talked about how students can reach a point where they can no longer make proper use of their teacher. At the outset, I knew that it wasn't about following Bubba; it was about trusting the thread of my own intuition and following my own path. It was time to move on.

When I became Bubba's student, I did it with eyes open, choosing to enter into one of the most wonderful and terrible periods of my life, the adventure — and ordeal — of practicing the most stringent version of spiritual life imaginable. I knew at the time that it was a rare opportunity to be around a truly extraordinary individual. From my first encounter with Bubba, the truth of his teaching and the confirmation of the nature of my own being through his spiritual transmission have never left me. It truly was a rare opportunity. But what I needed to find now was in myself.

— ⚹ —

I began writing this book during a dark time in my life. I hoped that in the process I might discover something true and fundamental about my life and about myself. I worked on the book for several years. As I wrote, I found that nothing from the past was real now. It was all in the past. The only things that hold me to the past are the stories I still tell myself. When I began to write about these stories, I discovered that I had forgotten the events that caused me to create them in the first place. It was not the events or the people in the stories that I suffered from now; it was the stories themselves. As I wrote about these stories — and by seeing that they had little to do with me now — I could let go of them. This way the stories no longer had a hold on me.

When it came time to write about Donna, I found that my relationship to her served as a poignant archetype of this mistake. Even after I had long since put Donna behind me, the stories — and lessons — stayed with me and informed my way of thinking. These were stories I had told myself to make sense out of things I didn't understand about our relationship. Such as, why was Donna able to disregard me so utterly and easily after all we had been for each other? I concluded that her relationship to me had been based only on need and therefore must have had no substance — that when she could get her needs met more effectively by someone else, she could easily move on without looking back. I wasn't sure what relationship was, but whatever it was, I was sure it couldn't be based on need.

The story for me was that I loved her, but that we were very young and dysfunctional and incapable of a real or healthy relationship — and that she had great needs, depended on me in childish ways, and never could really love me. The biggest story I took away from this relationship was the story that my loving didn't have any value. In fact, the theme of my life has been a question: Does my loving matter? It has played out over and over, and was demonstrated in my relationship with Donna in a dramatic way. Even after thirty years I still didn't know if my loving made a difference in Donna's life.

For over twenty-five years, Donna had been living with Bubba
and a small community of students on an island sanctuary in Fiji.
By now, Bubba had changed his name to Adi Da Samraj. His students referred to him as Adi Da or Bhagavan, but to me he was
always Bubba. Over the years, I'd never been certain that he was a
genuinely Awakened being. He was an extraordinary person who
defied all conventional expectations. I can say without any doubt
that his teaching made a profound difference in my life, and that
his spiritual transmission confirmed my deepest intuition of my
true Self. I met many wonderful people and made many lifelong
friends in his company. On November 27, 2008, Bubba died
suddenly of a heart attack. I immediately thought about Donna.
What would she do now that he was gone? She had devoted her
entire adult life to him. What would her life be like without him?

I had been enjoying reconnecting with my old friends from
childhood and sending them rough drafts of this book, in hopes
that they could help with the accuracy of the events I was writing
about. I hadn't had any communication with Donna for decades,
and I had no expectation of getting her input. But then, out of
the blue, I received a message from her.

At the time of Bubba's death, my brother, Emerson, was in
Australia on business. He took advantage of the opportunity to
travel to the sanctuary in Fiji to pay his respects to Bubba and
share in the momentous occasion with his friends who were living there. When he returned home, he shared with me a conversation he'd had with Donna about our relationship.

She expressed to him her understanding of how our relationship had been structured around the sorrow of our individual
lives, and how my love and caring had helped her to find her
own strength and capacity for relationship and devotion. She

told Emerson how grateful she was to me for "saving her life." Most profoundly, she spoke of her ecstatic love and absolute, unwavering devotion to her guru, and her gratitude for what he had given to her over the past thirty-five years.

I was struck by how the sorrows we experienced were in a way universal.

When Donna first left me to be with Bubba, I was extremely confused. I had an incomplete comprehension of who he was, or what was going on around him. At the time, the only tangible measure I could rely on to make sense out of him was to observe what effect he would have on Donna. Hearing her message through Emerson, it struck me how at peace she is, and confirmed to me that she is still the wonderful heart I knew so long ago. This alone was the proof that I was right not to interfere, and a testament to Bubba's love for her.

When Donna and I were young, our individual disabilities were so extreme that neither one of us ever had a chance for a conventional life. Because of this, we were both forced to find a deeper meaning to life, pushed to consider the ultimate question of life itself. When I first met Donna, she was guarding a drinking fountain. Now she will be spending the rest of her life at Bubba's burial temple, performing a constant vigil and service to his continued presence in this world. This is something that only a very rare person could ever do, but Donna is that rare person.

In the past, I'd hoped that Bubba could make Donna whole by putting all of her broken pieces back together. After hearing her message, I knew that she was living from a very profound place, and I believe she has awakened to a reality beyond our conventional perception of separate and separative existence. I understand that some people in crisis have encountered the

Infinite and experienced the incomprehensible power of the Divine, and that such experiences can temporarily overwhelm and even shatter the ego. The conventional world tends to pathologize such experiences and use them as evidence of insanity, further alienating the person having the experience, which accounts for a number of people who end up in mental institutions. Bubba didn't make Donna whole by putting all her broken pieces back together. He didn't believe that there was any answer at the level of the individual personality or limited self. His teaching was to resort entirely to the prior, underlying condition of Awareness, where we all exist in an unconditional state of wholeness.

I knew that Donna had spent her life confronting and inspecting the limited aspects of herself that could be said to describe who she was and what her life was. Bubba helped her break through that process to realize the condition of consciousness, or Awareness, that supports all life and is the ultimate truth of who we are. I'm grateful for how the force of life itself drove me to confront and inspect all the limitations of my life and mind, breaking me down to find that this Awareness itself was all that was left. It's so amazing to me that two damaged kids continued to contemplate the ultimate issues of life, each coming to the point of complete frustration and despair in ever being able to fulfill the story of "me." We were not all the things life and experience seemed to say about us. We were both moved to realize the Heart, the pure Awareness of being prior to birth and all limited form. That had been the source of our connection from the very start. That is the source of love I have for my family. The Awakened Heart was the source of love itself.

The story that had stuck with me all these years was that our relationship had been built on unhealthy dependencies, and that my loving had no value. When I joined the community, I was told that our relationship was cultic and built on self-serving attachments. The world had always told me that I wasn't enough, and then Donna left me and didn't even want to see me. I kept asking myself: *If I can't find anything of value that I can do in this world, and if the most selfless love I'm capable of has no value, then what am I doing here?*

But now, after receiving the message from Donna, I saw that all my stories were just that — stories. They are fragments of reality that may be relatively true, seen out of context, but can only be rightly understood within a much larger picture. It's true that Donna and I were dysfunctional and childish, and in the world of the survival of the fittest, we had no right to survive. After believing for thirty years that my loving hadn't made a difference in Donna's life, I received her message saying that my loving not only had made a difference, but she felt that I had "saved" her life. I don't need to know the larger picture to know that living from the Heart has value, even though it can't always be seen reflected back in the fabric of life. Whether or not we have what it takes to survive in this world isn't our measure; in fact, it's our brokenness and our awareness of our mortality that give us depth and gratitude in our loving. We all have value as the Heart. This Heart needs no justification to exist. It simply is. Donna said it best in her conversation with Emerson: What does not perish is the Heart.

If I hadn't written this book, I might never have received the confirmation that I made a difference in Donna's life. Doing the most improbable thing in the world for me to do, which was to write a book, also turned out to be the perfect way to end Donna's and my story.

The Big Bang

*S*hortly after my divorce in 1982, I met my current wife, Ria. Right away I knew there was something special about her. Ria was beautiful, considerate, and very smart. She understood me and found my problems interesting, not problematic. She thought of me as her equal and seldom judged me. To her, everyone had strengths and weaknesses. I was newly separated, but I knew that I wanted a healthy long-term relationship. We began living together in 1983 and married shortly thereafter.

At that time, Ria was working as a clerk in a natural-foods store. I knew she needed a career that was worthy of her intelligence and her extraordinary capabilities. I was making good money at the time, so I told her I would support her in anything she wanted to do. One of my proudest accomplishments was supporting her through graduate school, which included postgraduate work at Stanford. For almost thirty years she has been a miraculous source of unconditional love for me.

With the assistance of my computers reading to me, I was able to enjoy great success in the telecom business for over twenty-seven years. I started my own telecommunications consulting business, making well into six figures. At that time the phone systems I worked on were room-sized mainframe computers. But gradually the systems shifted from hardware-based computers to software-driven servers. Troubleshooting was no longer required as the "black boxes," as we called them, were just thrown out and replaced. My business began to suffer as Nortel, the maker of the equipment I specialized in, and one of the largest telecommunication companies in the world, was pushed into bankruptcy. At the same time that the systems became software based and required onscreen reading to be able to work with them, email became the primary form of communication. In the past, I'd taken work home, where I could do it on my own time and use the specialized software I had that would scan written information and read it to me. With my wife's help on reports and documentation, I could get by. But once email became the primary form of documentation and communication, my skills fell short. At first I was worried but able to grow with the changes. It wasn't clear how serious this transition would be. Each step in the dissolution of my business took a bite out of me. By the end I wasn't handling it well; it felt as if the walls were closing in around me, and I began having panic attacks.

In 2001 I was hired by a major cell-phone company to be in charge of their landline phone systems. By this time, email had become the only allowable form of communication. Ironically, it was technology that had made it possible for me to work; now it was a new phase in technology that was ending my career. I'd done very well in the niche I had found, but now I was in a different world. I shared the company of many ordinary, non-disabled people who lost their livelihood at the same time, but I couldn't help feeling that the past was coming back to haunt me. It was then that I realized how significant this shift in technology was, and I began to watch my psyche disintegrate.

My wife was understanding of what I was going through, but she hadn't seen my childhood struggles; she had never seen me as the person I was becoming. Neither had my kids. I had tolerated so much shame as a kid that I couldn't bear for them to see me as that person, much less for them to have that person be their husband or father. I really believed that that person had vanished more than thirty years ago, never to come back. But once again, I felt that I had little value, and that there was no chance I could rebuild or have a future.

This came to a head for me as a deep, unyielding depression, a monster of darkness I couldn't find a way out of. At the level of my mind, the content of this depression was the repetitive stories I'd told myself over the years to explain my life circumstances, leaving me with the conclusion that I had no value. I lost hope that repeating these stories could ever improve me, or that this brokenness that had been my conditional identity could ever be fixed. I went for counseling, hoping that I could gain some self-understanding, or have the perfect insight that would solve all my problems. But that insight never came. I saw that each insight was like trying to reach a goal by cutting the distance in half. I could keep having insights and cutting the distance to the goal by half forever and never reach the goal, no matter how refined the insight.

It was at this point that I began to write, hoping to uncover some deeper meaning to my life, some answers to the questions that tortured me. Yet my hopes seemed to be pinned on do-ing something that was impossible for me to do: write a book. I couldn't read a book, much less write one. So, as I had done so many times before, I just kept trying not to get too attached to the result. But as I struggled to tell my experiences as truthfully as possible, I realized that no matter how deeply I dug into my past, or how perfect a job I did on the book, I could never capture who, or what, I truly am. The recognition that I couldn't be defined by my stories left me in a state of total hopelessness that I could ever resolve the story of "me."

When I was a kid I'd learned to face down fear, always trying to be stronger than my fear, trying to conquer it rather than letting it conquer me. Later, I'd realized that I was, in a more subtle way, still being controlled by fear and creating a life that was based on fear. At eighteen I'd realized that I had to be myself as I was in each moment, and not believe the stories in my head. Now, with my life falling apart, this wasn't enough to pull me out of the darkness. Nothing from the past could help me now. No insight or realization from before could do the trick. No spiritual teaching and no amount of spiritual energy transmitted by a guru were going to make any difference. This was a new moment. I didn't know where the answer would come from. And then one night I had a dream.

I was standing alone, feeling small and limited, feeling very much myself. Suddenly, I was moving very fast through space. I was losing my sense of identity with my body. I was becoming less dense, lighter, and then transparent, with a tail like a meteor racing through space. Leaving the Earth, flying past all the planets in the solar system, I realized I wasn't just passing through space but I was going back in time. The planets and objects in space started to break up, and then became balls of gas. All matter was coming together to a single point. I thought it must be the source of the Big Bang. All matter, including the matter from my body, consolidated into a single point and disappeared as if into another dimension. Then there was nothing but vast and deep emptiness. There was no time, no separation, just an infinite spacious Awareness.

Suddenly, out of the silence and emptiness there was an explosion. Out of nothingness, matter appeared and expanded — the opposite of what had just happened. Gases and solid material began condensing and forming into galaxies and then planets. I became aware that time was moving forward. As everything took its present form, I also took form as myself. But this time, the Awareness and depth of the emptiness that I once was stayed with me.

As my body formed, this ecstatic Awareness remained. It flowed in waves through all my senses, then out into the space surrounding me and into the infinite. I was one with the infinite, riding the waves of ecstatic energy. But suddenly I had the thought that I was a limited form, separate and vulnerable to all this sensory stimulation. It was overwhelming. This limited form became fixed in space and began to collide with the waves of energy I had previously been riding.

As soon as I had the thought that I was limited and identified as this form, I could see the logic of protecting myself. If I were just this small separate entity, then I would have to control my experience and shut down my senses. The sensory stimulus was too much. The Big Bang seemed like the primal trauma, separating everything from its source. Everything that arose out of it, all limited forms, including myself, were the offspring of that original trauma — the trauma of separation from one another and the source. And yet it seemed that all form, in its essence, possessed an urge to return to its prior state of wholeness. As a limited form, separate from all others, I was left with only the craving for that oneness. I was now in exile. From this point of view, I couldn't help but make limited form into a kind of god, and give it the power to define my reality and to reflect to me the meaning of who and what I am. Feeling dependent on my limited form to survive in a world that was made up of other limited forms, the resulting fear and suffering became intolerable, and I no longer wanted to exist.

Then I could see myself as a young boy, telling my mother that I didn't want to be alive. I understood why I wanted to commit suicide. It wasn't death I wanted; it was freedom from the suffering and the isolation of limited form. I had misinterpreted my true condition. I was believing in the optical illusion of embodiment as form. I had traded my sense of wholeness in spacious Awareness for what my body, my limited form, was telling me. All my senses told me I was this body. Others with bodies acted as if I were separate from them. So I let the limitations of form define what I am.

But what or who am I that was aware of all this? It wasn't my body, or my mind, because I was aware that I was observing both my body and my thoughts. This meant they were not "me." I was just that observing itself — Awareness — not separate as an observer, but resting as the "observingness" itself. As soon as I identified as "observingness," I was whole, and all suffering was released. Nothing born from the Big Bang could hurt me. I was no longer in conflict with reality, at war with existence. I was prior to form and limitation. I couldn't die because I'd never been born. I understood that life and death are not opposites. The opposite of death is birth, not life. Life is there before birth and after death. It's impersonal. I saw that the experiences resulting from the Big Bang did not define me or limit me. That was believing in the illusion. Experiences were to be fully lived and not avoided or controlled. They didn't limit or define who I truly was. This Awareness needed no protection.

Just then, I woke up. I rarely remember my dreams, but this one was particularly vivid. It stuck with me, and it has become a metaphor for a new understanding of my true nature and a new perspective from which I view experience.

I can't say I'm living this experience fully, but it has changed me. This marked the end of my spiritual search and the beginning of a true spiritual practice. In a way it changed nothing, and yet it changed my relationship to everything. Suffering became a grace. Not that I would choose it, or not act to remove the source of it from my life, but now I found it useful. Knowing that all identification with form is created by thoughts, and that the suffering that results from identifying and believing the thoughts is its own creation, I'm reminded that it isn't real, and returned to the Awareness that is the truth of who I am. Mysteriously, I was still moved to continue writing this book, but now, instead of being a story about me, it turned into a story about the failure of the sense of me suffering the illusion of a "me."

Teachings that had once seemed to be just repetitive, heady philosophy came alive for me now. Over time there have been new depths to this Awareness. I sense there's an endless depth, where I fall deeper into emptiness, void of everything I cherish, where all that is left is the Heart. This Heart has always been with me, still and unchanged for as long as I can remember. It's so close to me that there's nothing closer, yet it's so vast and inclusive that it's infinite. So it was easy to miss it. The more I rested in this Awareness, the more intimate it became to me. I found that, in fact, I cannot be aware of anything that isn't contained within this vast Heart. There's nothing I can see, nothing I can feel, nothing I can know or experience, nothing I can ever be aware of that could exist outside of my Awareness. It's no different than in a dream, where things seem to be happening to me and there are other people in my dream, but in reality it's all happening within my own consciousness.

I learned to trust that if something happened outside of my awareness, then I wasn't meant to be aware of it yet. I could not and need not figure it out with my mind. With the realization that all experience is contained within the intimacy of this Awareness, I could now see how I'd objectified everything and everybody in my life. Even the activity of the mind, judging and categorizing, was within this Awareness. Yet I used this objectifying activity of the mind as a way to protect my sense of being a separate self. This was actually creating the illusory sense of being a separate individual. Within the deep intimacy of Awareness, I could feel the pain I was causing with these separative thoughts. Every judgment aimed at the object would instead cause a division within me, and a loss of felt intimacy with Awareness itself, isolating me while having no direct effect on the object I was trying to neutralize or separate from.

All my life I'd been looking for relationships to resolve this sense of separation, when, in fact, I'd been creating it in myself, in and from my own Awareness. I couldn't deny that I was as intimate with the Awareness of apparently external or separate objects as I was to the Awareness of my own personal experience. I related to all objects and all beings as other and separate, when in fact they are all me — arising within my own Awareness just as intimately as "I" am arising within my own Awareness. Because I couldn't separate myself from external objects or experience,

I realized that there's no "other." Both subject and object arose simultaneously within my own Awareness. I'd been trying to resolve this separation through relationships, when the separation was actually in me.

But also added to my human experience was the very real phenomenon labeled *autism spectrum*. I experienced this as too much stimulus coming continuously from too many different sources at once. My highly sensitive nervous system often automatically shut down, contracting to filter out unmanageable and disturbing stimuli and perception.

All humans operate within a certain spectrum, automatically filtering out unmanageable stimuli in order not to be overwhelmed by the continuous avalanche of stimuli that is life. Those on the autism spectrum are simply vulnerable to, and overwhelmed by, a range of stimuli most people can tolerate and manage. So they stand out and seem abnormal. This was my experience.

From infancy, in order to survive, I had to shut out a significant range of perceptions most people take for granted. I didn't consciously shut out each individual perception, though occasionally I might contract and dissociate to avoid some particularly disturbing stimuli. It was mostly an automatic response, like flinching from a blow. In time, as I became more self-aware, I became more conscious of the process by which stimuli overwhelmed me, and I dissociated to avoid it. As I matured, I learned to listen to my nervous system. And I gradually discovered, often under great stress, that I could consciously engage and to some degree manage some aspects of this process.

I learned to fragment and compartmentalize my awareness of stimuli, only allowing in what I was comfortable experiencing.

What I could not tolerate, I left in an undefined fog. Gradually I became able to handle more experience, more pressure and stress, more life. This is how I lived most of my life. And in doing this, I was simply doing, to an exaggerated degree, what everyone does to live on a daily basis.

Only when I fell into the heart was I able to trust my experience and live a full life without the rigorous filtering process that had always been my shield of protection.

After the dream, I no longer identified with my story and with getting in my own way. It was an unspeakable relief. It was as if the weight of the world had been lifted from my back, a weight that I didn't even know I was carrying until it was removed. Gratitude for the freedom to live as Awareness permeated my life.

Epilogue

*A*lthough I would never have chosen any of the difficulties I experienced, I found they were also a gift. In the end, seen from the larger perspective of the Awareness that is my true Self, the suffering I experienced as "me" was my own unwitting creation. I've found that I can reside in a clear, quiet place, profoundly aware and awake, with all my senses open, not holding back or shutting down. I can only find this Awareness when I make friends with the present moment, no matter what the worldly conditions are in this moment. For it is only in the present moment that the Awareness that is truly "me" ever exists. This meant nothing to me when the world was working for me — or as long as I hoped it could, or as long as I thought I had to do something, or had to be something I was not, or thought there was something missing from the present moment.

When I stand intimately in Awareness, I'm available to being informed by all my senses as needed. With the mind we're only capable of doing or considering a couple of variables at a time. That's a far more limited capacity than what our nervous system generates when connected to all our senses at the same time. No wonder premiere athletes talk about getting out of their heads and into the "zone." Our senses are intimately in touch with our surroundings and the world in ways we cannot be aware of with our mind. This gave me a different perspective on why people say "I came back to my senses" instead of saying "I came back to my mind."

I remember the schizophrenics at Jacqui Schiff's and how hard it was for them not to believe the ranting of their minds and the random things their minds seemed to be telling them. My thoughts weren't as delusional or overwhelming as those of the schizophrenics. Or were they? I had the constant ranting of stories in my mind that I believed to be true: *I will never have a family*, or *I'm not smart enough to make it in the world*. The mind was a distraction, a filter that isolated me from reality and the truth of who I am. As Awareness, I could use the mind as needed; but as the mind, I had no access to my true Self. I'd been identified with my mind when in fact it was Awareness that was always with me and never deserted me. It was the only thing in my life that had never deserted or failed me. It never judged me or separated from me. The source of my suffering was in the identification with my mind.

In the dream of my unawakened life, I'd been taking life personally, and identifying with all the things I had or did or thought I was. But I wasn't my job. I wasn't the role of a parent. I wasn't this story and all of my past. I wasn't this body, damaged and limited. I am Awareness. Awareness cannot be measured. It just is aware in this moment, living as this body, in this world —and that is enough. I am not who or what I thought I was. It's not personal. Nothing is personal. Human beings suffer in ways that other creatures don't—mostly because we tend to identify with some level of our limited form. But we can choose to begin to identify with our true Self as pure Awareness. Ultimately this leads to the natural dissolution of all identification. As it turns out, it's all a case of mistaken identity.

I used to be ashamed that my brother broke me, and that life itself broke my will. It made me feel weak. But I couldn't have been more wrong. As it turns out, my true happiness is proportional to my yielding to the brokenness, not to my refusal to accept it, or my struggle to overcome it. In that snow tunnel in my childhood, I found a calm spaciousness that results from giving up personal will. That spaciousness contains infinite potentiality and a quiet strength that is vastly more powerful than my personal will. It's what remains when I surrender to what is.

When I looked into my brother's face as he tormented me, he seemed to be looking not at me, his brother, but at an object in his way, denying him what he needed most. He saw me as something to be gotten rid of so that his life would work again. He was at war against the world, and I was the enemy. Looking in his eyes, I saw no empathy, no humanity, and it filled me with terror. And in the depths of that terror was an infinite silence.

I had sought safety in the world through empathy, but my pleading and pain inspired no empathy in him. And the world offered only silence. So I split from myself in order to save myself. And I made a sacred promise to my frightened self to stand in opposition to the world and fix it. To be safe, I would have to force empathy from an indifferent world. But to do this, I had to become a warrior.

And so I went to war against the world to save a boy the world had abandoned. And in doing so I abandoned myself. I went to war against a world where everyone seemed always to be pretending and hiding from the truth—denying or rationalizing as necessary the cruelty, suffering, and death all around them. And in this way, I lost my true Self and became like the world I was at war against.

In response to my childlike promise, my cries, my war, the world offered only an infinitely deep silence. To be free, I had to admit that I couldn't save the frightened little boy to whom I made that sacred promise. To be free, I had to break that sacred promise and let him go, unsaved, into the silence. I've since realized that in that infinitely deep silence lies the truth of who I am.

I found that I couldn't fix the world and make it have empathy. I couldn't defeat the world and make it right according to my understanding. The world doesn't listen to me, doesn't surrender to me, and it never will. I had to give up my attachment to empathy, and to the world being different than it is. And to do that, I had to forgive my brother, who is also the world, for his inability to have empathy with me. Only then could I let the world be. Only then could I be happy and free.

A Buddhist admonition says, "Put down your butcher knife and become a Buddha in that moment." To find myself, to have peace in the world, I had to surrender, to accept the world as it is, to become its compassionate witness. And in doing this, I've discovered that I'm able to act most effectively in the world when I let the world be. I can only experience the intimacy and deep silence of my Self and of the world when I put down my butcher knife. Then I'm able, by doing very little, to do the most. Then I find the Heart hiding behind the mask of a world I thought was the enemy.

But this only happened for me when I fell into a deep depression where everything seemed unimportant, meaningless, and empty, and the distractions and illusions of possibility in the rat race died, and all I was left with was the infinite depth and sorrow of a broken heart. It seemed my life always ended up here, in a place that was darker than dark, and the only meaning was this brokenheartedness. It was the worst feeling in the world. But when I accepted it, everything fell away, and all that was left was the heart, albeit a deeply broken one.

Somehow, seeing the heart as all there is — sometimes broken, sometimes ecstatic — was inspirational. The heart is the source of all that I am and do. Understanding this, I don't need to be or do anything that is not sourced from the heart. Because it is all the heart, I can allow all experience, regardless of the intensity. Good feelings or bad, it doesn't matter. This relieved me of a burden I had been carrying all my life, of what I think I am, or am supposed to be or do. For the first time I was free to experience the intensity of it all, including my old autism spectrum overwhelm. It was no longer necessary to fragment experience into good or bad, happy or sad. Everything was just something to experience, part of life.

This acceptance of brokenheartedness morphed into a quiet acceptance of all consequences, even death, in order to live from the heart. I began to relax my conditioned autism spectrum demands and controls on life. There was only one priority, one task — to look for the heart, and live from the heart, the best I could.

— 🤖 —

In my all-too-human life, I finally got the family I'd always wanted. It came in the form of my wife, Ria, who loves me in ways I didn't think anyone ever could. Having met me when I was doing well and had much to give, she stayed with me through times that were darker than dark, always finding some way of loving me. I have two wonderful kids who have great depth and are exceptionally smart. They have never withdrawn their hearts from me whatever my momentary misstep or loss of face in public due to my inability to read. They also saw strength in me when I did not.

My wife and I live just a few minutes' walk from one of the most beautiful beaches in the world. My life far surpasses even my most hopeful dreams. I live a very comfortable lifestyle with a freedom to live however life moves me. I will be forever grateful that I'm not in charge of the future.

I'm thankful that the fourteen-year-old kid I once was didn't succeed in his suicide attempt. If he'd succeeded, I wouldn't have been able to touch the lives of those I've loved since. It was my daughter who encouraged me to write this book. I remember how heartbreaking it was when she was a little girl, before she was able to read, and she wanted me to read her a bedtime story — but we only looked at the pictures because I couldn't read the story. Out of frustration, she would try to read it, and I was unable to help her. Then, as an early reader in her childhood, she became one of the main readers for me. Now, years later, she helped me to organize my ideas for this book and to find ways, with the help of others, that I could write it. She's also one of the funniest people I know.

My son is a rare and wonderful human being. He has had his own challenges with learning disabilities, and those challenges have given him an uncommon depth of humanity. He's the kind of person who meets everyone face-to-face, stands up for others, and is openhearted and emotionally present. He has inner and outer strength, and genuine confidence. My wife and children are the kind of people my father would have been deeply proud of.

I've heard it said that happiness can be defined as "I love you," and suffering can be defined as "Do you love me?" When my father died, I was desperate, wishing he could know how much I loved him. I wasn't thinking about whether he loved me; I was only wanting him to know how much I loved him. When I'm on my deathbed, I know I will care more about whether I have loved than whether I was loved.

I've been asked by editors and agents, "Who is your audience? Who are you writing this book for?" I told them I didn't know; I just had to write it. But now I think maybe I do know who I wrote it for. It's for those boys and girls in crisis who might be looking up at all those books on the shelves in their room. Maybe this is the book they're looking for, with some of the answers they hoped to find on those shelves.

If I had young David in front of me now, I would tell him this: "The fact that you can't read is not a comment about you in some personal way. It doesn't diminish or define who you are. It's just what it is. Yes, it's painful and it makes your life difficult. But you will only suffer by worrying about it and feeling bad about it, by believing it says something fundamental about who you are, and by turning such beliefs and ideas into sad scenarios about your future. If you listen to others, you might believe that you're defective—just a misfit who can't read. That isn't true. You're made of the same stuff as everyone else.

"You are, in truth, the observer of all that's arising—the Awareness of experience and not the content of your life. You don't need to be something you're not; you only need to be the Awareness you are, in the moment you find yourself in. Be that. Not because that's what you want, but because that's what *is*, and therefore what and who you truly are. You may try to control, manage, and shut off unwelcome experiences, believing it will bring you the best possible life. But I've found that we're here to experience all of it, good and bad, without judgment or resistance of any kind.

"It was often the world's apparent denial of the heart that you've suffered. This looked like truth to you in the 'successful' faces of sociopaths or some of the most powerful. What you didn't see was the desperation in their endless cravings, the suffering and hollowness of their lives and in their hearts, a suffering they couldn't escape, no matter the turmoil they caused or the temporary riches or power they accumulated.

"As you know, there's only one thing guaranteed in this life: You will not survive. If you insist on trying to be safe and survive by diminishing yourself and your world, instead of trusting the Infinite of which you are a part, then you'll suffer. If you think about it, what little you might have been able to control in your past is a tiny fraction of what has happened. You'll be the happiest when you release your stranglehold on life, stop trying to know and control your future, and cease identifying with the apparent successes and the failures. That's all you can do. Just be the Awareness you are in each moment, let the heart's kindness be your guide, and do the best you can without attachment to results. Let this free you to finally rest in the happiness that you are, and leave the future to what is greater than you. The rest is none of your business."

COLOPHON

This book was set in Aldus,
a text companion typeface to Palatino,
both of which were designed by
Hermann Zapf.

Made in the USA
Charleston, SC
26 March 2012